HEARTBREAK OF A
CIVIL WAR WIDOW

Life of Sarah Harper McWhirter
1825 - 1883

Including
Harper Family Ancestry Traced to
Oxfordshire, Noke, England in Early 1500's
and
Selected Information
on the
1st Alabama Cavalry, USV

Glenda McWhirter Todd

Author of *First Alabama Cavalry, USA: Homage to Patriotism*
and
McWhirter Memoirs: From Scotland to Tennessee

HERITAGE BOOKS
2010

OOKS

...AGE BOOKS, INC.

Books, CDs, and more—Worldwide

For our listing of thousands of titles see our website
at
www.HeritageBooks.com

Published 2010 by
HERITAGE BOOKS, INC.
Publishing Division
100 Railroad Ave. #104
Westminster, Maryland 21157

Other books by the author:

First Alabama Cavalry, USA: Homage to Patriotism

International Standard Book Numbers
Paperbound: 978-0-7884-5252-9
Clothbound: 978-0-7884-8484-1

Dedication

It is fitting that this book is dedicated to Sarah Harper McWhirter, my great, great grandmother. Her dedication to her family was immeasurable as she cared for and fed her younger children while her husband and three older sons were away fighting in the most abominable war ever fought on American soil. This war killed over 620,000 American men and boys, some barely fifteen-years old. Some Civil War historians estimate over 700,000 were killed or died during the war.

The 1st AL Cavalry, USV was a unique Union regiment from Alabama, which was made up of many Alabamians including Sarah Harper McWhirter's husband, three sons, three brothers and several uncles and cousins, most of whom did not live to return home. During their absence, Sarah was being abused and molested by not only the Confederate Home Guard but by some of the very men assigned to help protect the Union wives and widows and keep them in needed supplies.

This book has been bearing on my heart and mind for several years but I could not bring myself to begin writing about Grandma Sarah because of her sad, tragic life. It brought tears to my eyes each time I thought about her. It was only after so many Harper cousins, including Max and Lynda Harper and Quinnie Harper, began sending me their Harper information tracing the family back to Noke, England in the early 1500's, and wonderful old pictures that I was able to sit down and write about this wonderful, courageous lady. However, the tears continued to flow as I wrote about some of the tragedies and humiliation she endured during and after the war only because of her families' love for their country.

I learned a long time ago that when you say, "Here am I, send me Lord" you might find yourself traveling to many places. I feel God led me to write this book about my great, great grandmother so others might know what a wonderful, loving and caring lady she was and what a tragic life, not only she, but other Civil War wives and widows lived and how difficult times were in northwest Alabama during and after the Civil War.

It is also dedicated to my other ancestors. (See next page)

TO MY ANCESTORS

I see you toiling down the tedious years,
You bearded gaunt, and bent old Pioneers,
Sowing, and reaping, sowing once again,
In patience for an unborn race of men.

I see you struggling in the wilderness
Where failure meant starvation – and success,
A cabin in the wilderness, rough hewn, rude,
Garments of homespun and the humblest food.

Tradition scarcely tells me whence you came,
I only know a few of you by name.
I only know you lived and multiplied
Quite prolificate in progeny – and died.

Yet in my heart I know that most of you,
Were strong and steadfast and that one of two
At least had weakness that still may be
Traced in the trends of atavistic me.

One I am sure was blest with native wit –
I'm thankful he transmitted some of it!
That helped him dodge Dame Trouble's swiftest dart.
And meet misfortune with a merry heart.

One was rather a worthless wight I fear,
Who when the bluebird whispered Spring was near
Forsook his plow – a shiftless sluggard one
And roamed the woods alone with rod and gun.

And one a gentle dreamer was, I trow,
Who, lured by shadows, let the substance go
Twas he who dared the raging Western sea –
I'm glad he handed down his dreams to me!

By "Eclus" in the *Chicago Tribune*
(In free domain)

Table of Contents

Foreword

Why do I crave this true, but fragmentary history of my life and those who have gone on before me? For you, dear ones, who come along behind me, who look backward and also crave to know from where you came and the stories surrounding the lives of our ancestors, I have tried to record, in part, these facts, devoid of literary embellishments, for your record. Someone once said, "If you don't know where you came from then you can't know where you are going". We need only to look at the footprints our forefathers left in America to know that they loved and worshiped God.

We have had some extremely brave and gallant forebears who were builders of hopes while conquering fear, disappointment, the disadvantages of poverty, and the pain of heartache. They also stood up and fought for what they thought was right, even when it was politically wrong in the eyes of so many others. I not only salute my brave Harpers and McWhirters, who lived in Tennessee and Alabama but chose to fight for the 1st Alabama Cavalry, Union Army in an area filled with Confederates, but mostly, I salute my great, great grandmother, Sarah Harper McWhirter, a devout Christian, for the trials and tribulations she suffered before, during and after the Civil War, which left her a widow.

You came from strong stock and you're grandfather crossed the mountain barriers in their covered wagon with their family and friends. They helped push the line of civilization across the Appalachians from their known setting to the unknown wilderness, with your father being one of the younger members of the wagon train. Fusing the hardships of trails with the beauty of skies and the blossoming wild flowers. You grew up in a new land watching your father clear the virgin timber and plant crops in a fertile, new land.

You watched your husband, three sons, four brothers; a son-in-law and several nephews and cousins bravely go off to fight in the most horrendous, bloody war ever fought on American soil, brother against brother, and it would be the last time you would ever see most of them, including your husband, one son, and three brothers. You watched your father as he cried when he was informed his sons died bravely, some fighting for this country while others fought against it. You cried when you lost several grandchildren at an early age, some died in infancy while others succumbed to the tragic diseases of the times. You wove the beauty of the pine bloom into the fabric of your coverlets and pieced the loveliness of lilacs into your quilted Irish chains; stilled the small cry of your infant from the lurking showdown of the wildcat and the crouching form of the panther. Although you could tenderly caress your small babies, you could wield the hoe and plow a straight row after you were left alone with small children while your husband, sons and brothers were off fighting for their lives and families.

Your path to the mountain spring was one of beauty and danger. How often your quick sense caught the glint of light on the coils of a serpent in time to prevent a tragedy, or the glint in a wild animal's eyes as they rushed to attack.

You have bequeathed us, your descendants, your traditions, your love of God, your quest for life and a better life for your children.

You were tired that day when you lay down to sleep your long, sweet sleep in the mountains of northwest Alabama, and you lived a much better, easier life after you reached up to accept the outstretched arms God.

Very reverently and belatedly, I salute you, Grandma Sarah Harper McWhirter, and it is my desire I can one day express to you just how proud I am of you, how I honor you and how I love you.

Glenda McWhirter Todd

Preface

It seems fitting at this point to offer the reader some explanations about the conventions used in the book, given the many period sources incorporated into the text. Each of the excerpts from diaries, Southern Claims, Civil War Pension Applications, speeches, Official Records, wills etc. was left in its own unique style. In some instances, the people who wrote them were illiterate but the spelling was used exactly as it was found.

Please be forewarned that some occurrences and images disclosed in the book are horrific and will most likely be difficult for the reader to envision.

The story of Sarah Harper McWhirter and letters to her, from her husband, sons and brothers were written at the discretion of the author from Civil War diaries census records, documents obtained from the National Archives, history of the areas where they were at the time, stories from ancestors and other documents and events.

In recounting the personal history of Sarah, the author has detailed some ghoulish and particularly horrible behavior committed on the part of the Confederate Home Guard. These men were either too old or in some way not suited to become soldiers in the Civil War, so formed their own bands of guerrillas, in some instances, who reeked havoc on, not only the Union wives and widows, but other Unionists, burning their homes and crops and taking their meat, corn, horses, mules, etc.

In dealing with the Civil War, people still tend to take sides. Regardless of victories in individual battles, the average soldier on either side displayed equal bravery, forbearance, perseverance and devotion to their cause. All sacrificed and suffered greatly, some by disease, lack of rations, clothes, shoes and many other sacrifices where made all during the war.

Although history tells us of the atrocities committed by the Confederate Home Guard on the Southern Unionists, the Confederates did not have the monopoly on the burning, looting, murder, etc. As stated in the book, there was enough blame to go around. However there has been more written about the sufferings of the Unionists in northwest Alabama, it would appear the Unionists suffered the most of the tragedies. As you will read, two of Sarah's brothers had served their time in the Union Army, had been discharged at different times and were on their way home to there families when caught by the Confederate Home Guard, brutally tortured, murdered and left hanging. The military records state one died of measles but as you will see from the affidavits, that was not the case. The murders, burnings of homes, etc. became so numerous they began to be published in the *Nashville Union* newspaper in Nashville, Tennessee. The abuses and molestations committed on the Union widows and wives were not only undertaken by the Confederate Home Guard but by the actual Union men assigned to help protect them and furnish them with needed supplies, salt, etc.

The reader will find the author has skipped around in the book, which is intended to hold their interest without becoming bored by reading about one person or event over many long pages. Some of the Union Pension Records listed in one chapter may also be in another chapter about the soldier.

Each side developed derisive phraseology for their opponents and some of the less irreverent terms might be found through out the book. "Secesh," "Johnny Reb," "Rebels," "Billy Yank" and "Bluebelly" are a few of the noted terms used.

Acknowledgements

There are many people to thank for their contributions to this book, including my deceased husband, Carl Newton Todd, Sr., who was always willing to travel anywhere from California to Florida for me to research this and other books. All I had to do was mention I needed to go to North Carolina, or where ever, for research, and his golf clubs were the first item in the trunk of the car. He would play golf while I was in a library, archives, courthouse or other researching the necessary items.

Mary Louise Hanson in Mississippi, who spent years researching our Harper family and so graciously shared her information with me. She answered hundreds of my emails full of questions about our families throughout the writing of this book.

My dear friend, L. Kent Henson, whose guidance was immeasurable throughout the writing of this book. He also designed the beautiful creative cover, front and back.

Quinnie Harper and Max Harper, who shared their Harper family information and wonderful old Harper family pictures.

Mary Pattie, my long-time friend, who spent days proof-reading and editing this book, and who kept me on track urging me to keep writing so I would be able to meet the deadline.

Norman Peters in Washington, DC who immediately copied wills, military, pension and other records in the National Archives that I needed, and mailed them to me.

John and Retta Waggoner from Smith County, Tennessee for sharing their wonderful pictures of Smith County structures.

Randy Vaincourt for his permission to use the wonderful, fitting poem, "A Soldier Died Today," that was so appropriate. His father wrote the poem many years ago.

My friends I have ignored while writing this book.

Introduction to *Heartbreak of a Civil War Widow*

By Glenda McWhirter Todd

This book ranges from the factual to the fictionalized. The factual obviously being the facts dealing with families, dates of birth, marriage, death, and other historical events. Civil War documents and diaries were also used. The letters written to Sarah by her sons and brothers were based on Official Records, Thomas A. McWhirter's diary, and diaries written by other 1st Alabama Cavalry, USV members who were serving along side her sons and brothers when they wrote home.

Of course, it is obvious to the reader that, with the long passage of time, it was necessary to take a fictionalized approach in recounting Sarah's thoughts and actions not witnessed or recorded by anyone else. In so doing, I have made every attempt to match the fictionalized portions with the documented experiences and actions of the true Sarah Harper McWhirter. I beg her forgiveness in places where I may have failed to faithfully do so.

I am not suggesting that I had supernatural help in writing, but as I delved into the life of this remarkable woman, I sometimes felt her presence at my shoulder. The joys and the horrors of her life in this historic moment of our history, I felt her soar and rejoiced, I felt her pain and cried for this strong great, great grandmother of mine who bore so many sorrows. As a dear cousin stated, "Sarah was the wind beneath my wings" as I tried to tell her story as best I could.

I have placed Sarah Harper McWhirter telling the story of her life growing up as the oldest child in a family of fifteen children, her marriage, the wagon train trip from Smith County, Tennessee to Alabama, her children, and her experiences during and after the Civil War. Sarah's story is based on Civil War Pension Records and Southern Claims sworn to and signed by different friends and relatives. It also includes facts written in books, newspapers, stories told by other Union soldiers, and memories of her grandchildren as told by them. The fictionalized supplementary thoughts and actions I have added, I sincerely hope will make the story flow for the reader's benefit.

Why do we crave this true, but fragmentary history of our lives and those gone before us? Should you, my dear ones, who have and will come along after me, look backward and also crave to know from where you came and the places and stories surrounding your ancestors, maybe the knowledge I have gained through my research, will also help in the quest for your heritage. I have tried to record in part, these facts, devoid of literary embellishments, for your enjoyment and record.

Most of the days of one's life simply meld into the general memory forming good or bad impressions, but some days, for whatever reason stand out in memory as clearly as if they were yesterday. Since locating the documents and information on the life of my great, great grandmother, Sarah Harper McWhirter and her family, the story of her life, especially during the Civil War, is so vivid in my mind that it stands out like I was there with her.

It is a proven fact we have had some extremely brave and gallant forebears who stood up and fought for their beliefs, even when it was politically wrong in the eyes of so many others. I salute my brave ancestors for their courage, and this book is a tribute to Sarah Harper McWhirter, who endured tremendous heartbreaks before, during and after the Civil War.

To Andrew Ferrier McWhirter, Sarah's husband, I salute you in the highest regard. So many of your seeds have been nurtured that your earthly immortality flows in a mighty stream of humanity. A long strong file, linking you with the ancient boundaries of long ago, projecting you into the limitless expanse of the unknown future. The bright-dull threads of your lives are interwoven forever into the changing fabric of your country. You emigrated with your family from the border of Smith and Warren County, Tennessee to Walker and Marion Counties in Alabama in a covered wagon with your family and friends. You were put in the middle of something in which you wanted to remain neutral but were forced to make a decision you never dreamed you would have to make. You finally made you wishes clear and stated your Scots-Irish ancestors came to this country from Scotland and Ireland looking for a place to worship as they pleased and America embraced them and allowed them to do just that. You also stated some of your ancestors fought diligently for this country during the Revolutionary War and there was no way you could take up arms against the same country and you certainly would not fire on "Old Glory," the flag of your forefathers. You and your sons wanted to remain neutral rather than fight against your southern neighbors, but this type of thinking wasn't an accepted fact in northwest Alabama. You, along with three of your sons, joined the 1st Alabama Cavalry Union Army where you served gallantly in the most horrendous, bloodiest war ever fought on American soil.

To Andrew Jackson McWhirter, Sarah's son and the author's great grandfather, I salute you because along with your father and two brothers, you also joined the 1st Alabama Cavalry, USV but you were fortunate enough to survive. You were a God-fearing man, my great grandfather, and brought many others to know Him. Maybe it was all the blood and carnage you witnessed during the war that sealed your decision to become a Primitive Baptist minister and devote the rest of your life to God and bringing others to Him.

To all of you, the bright-dull threads of your lives are interwoven forever into the changing fabric of your country. I see you in a newly plowed field; I glimpse you with an old powder horn and flintlock rifle as you smile at me from the gloss of an old walnut cradle you made, as you reach a hand from the weathered logs of a crumbling cabin.

To Sarah Harper McWhirter, to whom this book is dedicated, I will begin to open the door just a little way toward your beginnings and the hardships and heartbreak you were forced to endure. Your path to the mountain spring was one of beauty and danger. You instilled in your children the love of sunlight on a hilltop, the delicate beauty in the colors of the flowers.

Reverently, although belated, I salute you for your strength, your abiding love, your perseverance, and your ability to accept the Grace of God and His strength, and continue with your life after you lost your husband, son, brothers, cousins, and uncles as they fought to preserve this great country. You were truly a most remarkable woman and my heart goes out to you. I love you, Grandma Sarah, and wanted to honor you with my feeble attempt to tell others of your difficult life. You are an inspiration to all of us!

Glenda McWhirter Todd
May 15, 2010

Growing Up In Smith County, Tennessee

...Between wordless sobs the soul cries out....

Life in rural Smith and Warren Counties in Tennessee in the 1820's and 1830's was a challenge, to say the least, but we farmed, planted a large garden, raised a few hogs, cattle, including a few milk cows, and chickens and had enough to eat, but if we came up short of fresh meat, wild game was available. Momma and I prepared vegetables, dried apples and we had a root cellar that would keep potatoes, turnips, onions, rutabagas and other root crops edible all winter. We also stored some of the apples in there to eat during the winter, or however long they lasted. Making do with what we had at hand was not a choice, but an absolute necessity. I will talk more later on foods we ate and the preparation and preservation. My father, Thomas Harper, worked hard to feed and care for his house-full of children, and his hands were callused to prove it. Unfortunately Momma died when I was young, but she taught me a lot about cooking, putting up vegetables, churning, sewing and everything she had do to. Papa was grieved when Momma died but he would live to marry the third time after losing his first two wives, including my Mother.

Being the oldest of fifteen children, I had to grow up in a hurry and had to help look out for my brothers and sisters. After Momma died, I had to stay home to help Papa care for them and wasn't able to attend school, so it was a long time before I learned to read and write as well as I wanted to, but I was determined to learn. Sometimes I resented not being able to go to school or go out and play because I had to stay in and watch them and if I did get to go out, I had to take most of them and watch after them. I loved my brothers and sisters but sometimes resented having to be so confined taking care of them and helping Momma with all of the chores. (I would live to regret having these thoughts about my siblings.)

No matter what else happened, there was one known standard in our lives, and that was God, and Momma and Papa's faith which was infallible.

I remember as a young girl on Sunday mornings Momma dressing me up in little dresses that she meticulously made for me. If she could find any lace at all, she would sew it on the dress to make it a little frilly and keep it from being so plain. She would put little rounded collars around the neck with lace between the seams in the collar. If we had extra eggs, Momma would have Papa take her into

1

town to the general merchandise store with a basket of eggs and she would barter with the owner for some lace to go on my dresses. Sometimes if she had more eggs than she thought we would need, she would trade them for a piece of Calico fabric to make me a dress, but this one was only worn to church. If she had enough eggs, she would get enough Calico to make us a bonnet, which we used mostly when we were outside working. Papa even carved some buttons out of wood that actually turned out pretty. As my two brothers just younger than me got older, she made them bright red hunting shirts and sewed some of the buttons Papa had made on them. You would have thought they came from a store in New York they were so proud of them.

Momma also made us hats out of fur from animals that Papa killed, but I never did like them, just because of knowing where they came from. They surely did keep my head and ears warm on the way to church in the wagon, though.

I'm sure you ladies remember as small children how difficult it was to sit still and pay very close attention to the preacher in church. My Momma talked about what a loving God we had and how He would always take care of us, but in my little girl mind I felt she had to be confused because this preacher we listened to talked about how God was going to burn the earth up and destroy all the people. But I really decided that Momma knew more about it than this preacher and she had just not had time to tell the preacher what a loving God we really did have. As the years rolled on, I began to pay more and more attention to several different preachers that visited our little country church but found it very difficult to understand just exactly how I was going to get my heart out of my body and give it to Jesus, because I really did want Jesus to love me. Finally at the age of nine Momma was able to explain to me in a much more simple method than my little mind could figure out, and I decided this was the real road to travel, and I needed to go with God.

I have never been and never will be a perfect Christian, but I consider it nothing but joy to serve a Lord that loves me just like I am, picks me up when things seem to fall completely apart, and forgives me when I fall short and fail Him. God loved me enough to let His own son die for my nasty old sins and this God will do exactly the same thing for you if you will also love my Jesus. This is what Momma told all of us and I'm thankful that I grew up in a Christian family.

We were taught from an early life about God, who He was and why He was so important in our lives. We were also taught the difference in right and wrong, and Papa dealt a hard blow with his paddle when we did something that didn't meet with his approval. We knew when we got up on Sunday morning that we would be going to church because that was what we did on Sundays and we were expected to get up and get ready without having to be told. Momma would cook a large breakfast but on Sundays, she would usually cook bacon or sausage from the smokehouse that Papa had put up and we would have that with her wonderful biscuits and gravy and maybe eggs if I could find enough in the hen house. I loved gathering eggs because it reminded me of Christmas when I pushed the hens off their nest and there were eggs under her. We also had a few ducks and geese that we ate, especially around Thanksgiving and Christmas, and their eggs were much larger. The only chickens we killed and ate were the ones that had quit laying because we needed the eggs for cooking and bartering. Some of the ducks and geese laid eggs, also and sometimes Momma would let them set on the eggs until they hatched, so we raised a lot of them.

We took turns washing dishes, however, since I was the oldest I had to wash most of them for years, until my siblings were old enough to help with them. After the breakfast dishes were washed, dried and put back in their proper place, we all got ready for church while Papa hitched up the horses or mules to the wagon. No matter the weather or season of the year, we climbed up in the wagon and went off to church. People who went to church first would build small fires along the side of the road, put large cobble or other stones in the hot coals and whoever came along next would take a hot stone, wrap it in a blanket and put it in the floorboard of the wagon to keep our feet warm until we got to church. Also, when we took a stone, we put another one in the coals to heat up for the next wagon that came along. When the stone became cold, we dropped it off at the next fire and picked up another hot one, all the way to and from church. If the fires were getting low when we got to them, Papa would stoke them and add a few sticks or dead branches to keep them going. Everyone else who came along did the same thing. The preacher usually got to church first and built a good fire in the old wood stove so the church was fairly warm when we got there, and of course everyone wanted to sit close to the stove.

When we arrived at church, we took our seats and didn't talk during the service lest we suffered the revenge of Papa's paddle when we returned home. Usually for Sunday lunch, Momma would kill, scald, pluck and fry a chicken, but after three or four more of my siblings were born, she had to kill and cook two or three chickens and it was easier, when we were in a hurry, to take a large piece of meat from the smoke house and cook it. Since I was the oldest child, I would have to help her with the chickens and nothing smelled much worse than a scalded chicken. I detested that job but dared not complain. If you have never prepared a chicken for a meal, you don't know what you have missed. We first had to catch one and then wring its neck until it was dead unless for some strange reason Papa wasn't busy and could chop off its head with the ax on the chopping block. Momma would actually do that sometimes but she didn't like to. Then we would build a fire under the cast iron pot, carry water from the creek, pour it in the pot over the fire and boil it. When it was hot enough, we dunked the chicken in it a few times and that made the feathers come out easier. It took me a long time to pluck all of the feathers out of a chicken but Momma had a lot of experience and she could yank those feathers out in the blink of an eye. Then we had to cut it up ready for frying. I never did like taking the innards out and wondered if I would ever get as fast as Momma was at getting the chickens ready to fry. Sometimes when she would wring their necks and turn them loose, they would continue flopping around on the ground for several minutes. I always hated to see that happen. Momma would roll the chicken pieces in flour mixed with salt and pepper, and then fry them in lard. She could fry the best chicken I believe I ever ate. Sometimes she would melt the lard in a large cast iron skillet, put the chicken pieces in it, cover and bake it in the oven. It was always so tender it would just fall off the bone. I liked it better that way than fried on top of the stove. I never thought my fried chicken was as good as hers but Andrew thought it was and he bragged on it all the time. (More about Andrew later.)

To preserve the eggs if we had more than we could use at one time and didn't need to take them in to the store and barter for something with them, we greased them and layered them in a sealed box covered with sand or ashes. We had to be sure to cover the box back when we took one out or they would spoil.

In order to preserve our root vegetables, we would harvest them in dry weather, stack them in rows on top of each other in the root cellar and cover them with sand. If a root cellar wasn't an option, people buried them in sand one or two inches deep between each layer. We had to keep them in a dry place away from dampness and frost. This is why a root cellar was a must for large families, and most families were indeed large back then. There were four outer

4

buildings that were essential for large families to have, a smoke house, out house, corn crib, and a root cellar, not listed in the order of importance, though. However, the root cellar was normally under the house but not all the time.

After the corn was gathered in the fall and placed in the corn crib, Momma would make hominy by shelling the hard, dry corn. First she filled up the large cast iron pot hanging from the tripod Papa Harper had made, added the lye, and then built a fire under the pot so the water would be boiling by the time she was through shelling the corn. After the water began to boil, she put the washed hard corn in the water and let it boil until the husks loosened to where it would be easy for her to remove them during the several times she rinsed them. Since the kernels swelled, she had to be careful and not put too much of the corn in the water. It took several wash pots full of clean water to rinse the corn to get all the husks off. This would mean carrying the water from the creek to where the wash was hanging. She had to rub the dark tips off the kernels and then put them back in the wash pot full of fresh lye water for about five minutes. She then put the finished hominy in jars, adding a teaspoon of salt per quart of hominy. I have seen her calloused hands bleed from shucking so much of that hard corn, and now mine do the same thing when I make hominy.

We gathered beans when they were the proper size, washed and scalded them a few minutes but we had to be careful to take them out of the water before they lost their color. We then drained them and laid them out on towels to dry and cool. When they had cooled enough, we put them in a two or three-quart jar but had to be careful layering them so as not to pack them so tight the liquid mixture wouldn't get to all of them. We mixed a handful of salt with enough water to cover them and let them sit overnight. Then we poured it off and covered it with a pickling type mixture which consisted of two parts water with one part vinegar and two or three hands full of salt. Then we covered it with melted butter in order to seal them and preserve their flavor and color. Of course Momma and I had churned the milk to make the butter. She had an old wooden churn with a paddle at the end of the handle and we had to sit there and just churn the paddle up and down until the butter formed on top of the milk. That wasn't my favorite chore and Momma would do it if she had time because she knew I didn't like to.

It took longer to pickle gherkins but they were so good the way Momma fixed them. I would help her pick the little cucumbers and then we would scrub them and cut the stems off. She had a large crock she would put them in, pour salt over them and stir them occasionally for a day or two. She had a large plate she kept on top of the crock. Then she would throw out what liquid and salt was in there, add more salt and vinegar until the next day when she poured that off and replaced it with vinegar, tarragon, small onions, garlic, allspice, cloves and whole peppercorns. Sometimes she would do this once and a week later she would pour that mixture off and add another one like it, put them in jars and seal them tightly. They were really better if that was done the second time but it surely did waste a lot of vinegar. We had to be careful to seal them very tight because if air got to them it would ruin the flavor and color.

We preserved a lot of different fruits. The more firm and hard the fruits were, the better they would preserve. Apples, peaches, pears, apricots and other fruits had to be dried and in order to dry them, they had to be peeled, seeded, cut up and spread out on boards or planks. It was supposed to be kept in a closed room where it was dark, but Momma thought putting it in the sun to dry was better. She had to be careful that they didn't get wet. She also had to be careful the pieces didn't touch because it could ruin them if they did. Momma and Papa saved everything, and Papa had a piece of tin left over from the roof so Momma would spread the fruit out on it and put it out in the sun but it had to be covered or brought in at night to keep the dew or rain from getting on it.

Momma used to make raspberry vinegar by picking a couple pounds of raspberries and letting them steep four or five days in strong vinegar. She would strain it off, add two pounds of sugar and let it simmer in a slow, gentle fire stirring it to mix the sugar well with the vinegar mixture. Then she would boil it in an old black kettle, strain and cool it and then put it in bottles. She used to make cough syrups for us, also, and she made other "remedies" for us that couldn't be purchased anywhere at the time. Certain remedies were meant to prevent illnesses. Some of the pioneers believed that eating large amounts of onion prevented colds. We all drank a syrup made from molasses, sulfur and cream of tartar. Pioneers believed this mixture prevented many diseases. Most colds and other illnesses were treated with a variety of herbal teas. Momma would sometimes add a few drops of kerosene to a teaspoon of sugar to quiet a cough. When we complained of the taste, she would try to conceal the taste by dissolving it in coffee or wrapping it in a piece of fruit. Some of our neighbors used a mixture of goose grease and snake oil over cuts and bruises but Momma didn't believe in that mixture. Some would also spread a lotion of sweet cream on sun burn or poison oak to sooth it but Momma didn't think that worked very well either. Each spring she would give us all a dose of kerosene mixed with sugar to "clean us out after winter", and it tasted terrible.

Papa always raised a turnip green patch for Momma in the fall so we would have lots of turnips and greens. We were able to keep the turnips in the root cellar for a few months. My brother hated turnip greens with a passion and absolutely refused to eat them. He and Momma had an argument every time she served them. One time when he was a teenager, she served turnip greens and told him to clean his plate. As soon as she got up from the table to get more cow peas, he stuffed the turnip greens in his pants pocket and asked to be excused. He went out on the front porch and was dumping them from his pocket over the side of the porch on to the ground. Momma went to see what he was doing and couldn't believe her eyes. She was appalled that he put the turnip greens in his pocket but she thought it was too funny to punish him. She went outside, after she quit laughing, and told him to come on back in. She hugged him and told him that if he despised turnip greens that much, she would never force him to eat them again, and he never ate anymore. He didn't like to smell them cooking even after he was grown.

We ate a lot of peas because Papa planted a large field of cow peas and they were plentiful. One of my brothers told his friend that peas saved his life on numerous occasions, especially during the Civil War.

Corn cribs were the most common outbuildings around as almost every family had one. The corn was hauled in the wagon from the field and stored in the crib, still on the cob and in the shuck. Some corn cribs had a large drive-through center where the wagons could drive up into the crib, unload the corn on one side or the other and keep on going. It was made out of logs about 2 or more inches apart to let the air flow through and dry the corn so it would not mildew and ruin.

The corn in the corn crib would air-dry sufficiently to be ground into meal, made into hominy, or fed to livestock. Papa had a grist mill so he didn't have to pay to get his corn ground. The very early settlers didn't have any way to grind their corn so they pounded it into meal with a mortar. Papa sawed a block about three feet long from a large tree and set it up on one end. He mortised a hole in the upper end in the shape of a funnel, which would hold about a half gallon of corn. The pestle was hung at the end of a long limber pole, which would spring up and down. The corn was then soaked in water until it became soft and was then put back in the mortar, and using the pestle, it was pounded into meal. In 1818, corn sold for about $1.00 per bushel.

Smokehouses were also common as the settlers had to be able to preserve the meat they killed and butchered and they needed a smokehouse in order to do this.

Back then, the smokehouses were rather elaborate since they were used not only as meat smokers but as storage facilities for the meat afterwards. Not all families could afford to build a smokehouse so Papa let a few other families use ours. It wasn't that we were rich, not by any means, but with the money Papa took in from his grist mill, he was able to build one.

The smokehouses were built away from the main house and barn, and preserved the meat so it would last for a long time. Preservation was achieved by curing it with salt which took about two weeks or more to cure with cold smoke. The meat continued to hang in another area of the smokehouse for up to two years, and during that time, it lost more moisture and acquired more smoke, although at smaller rates.

The smokehouses were small, usually square structures, however a few were round. They would have a steep chimney in the shape of a pyramid. They didn't have any windows, just a door and they normally had screened openings just below the roof to keep the insects out and provide ventilation. It also helped the smoke to escape. Just below the roof Papa had beams with hooks where he hung the meat.

This might be a good time to tell you about hog-killing time. If I thought killing chickens was bad, I didn't know what bad was until I started having to help Papa kill hogs. Every winter when it was cold enough, Papa would kill a hog, later on when the family started growing, he would kill two. That was the nastiest thing I ever saw in my young life and I certainly did not like watching or helping him! However, everyone in our family would learn how to butcher a hog. Not only that, but they had to learn how to hitch a mule and skin a

8

rabbit. The weather had to be cold enough for the meat not to spoil in order to kill hogs but not cold enough for it to freeze.

Papa let our hogs free-range but he kept up with where they were and what kind of condition they were in. He would round up one or two of the biggest, fattest hogs and herd them into a pen he had built for about a month or so before he was planning on killing them. He would then fatten them up on corn. He didn't want them to get into any acorns and eat them because they tended to make the meat taste bitter. Also, we HAD to make lard from the hogs and if they had eaten a lot of acorns the lard wouldn't be a clear white like it was supposed to be.

The hog had to be hoisted to a tree limb with a block and tackle or hung from a tri-pod where it could be lowered into a barrel full of boiling water. The water had to be just the right temperature for them to scrape the hog and get all of the hair off of it. I think he also put something like ash in the water to help with this process.

I couldn't stand to watch Papa kill the hogs so I stayed in the house. While he was killing and bleeding the hog (it had to be bled within two minutes of killing it) my brother next to me would build a fire under an old cast iron wash pot and had it boiling so it could wash off the grime that the pigs had gotten into from wallowing in the mud and dirt in the pig pen. However, the boiling water also softened the hog's bristles and made them easier to scrape off.

Papa was so particular with his work space and it and his tools had to be meticulously clean. I will skip the grossest details but after he took the innards out he gave them to Momma and I to clean and there were yards and yards of intestines that had to be washed over and over. After the pig was scraped, he would start trimming the fat which he cut in chunks for Momma to render and make our lard. The lard required careful attention to detail and was about the most important chore of the day. It could be very rancid before winter was over if it wasn't done right, and of course the lard was all we had to fry chickens, make cornbread, biscuits, and a number of other things. We cleaned and scrubbed Momma's other black iron wash kettle to cook the lard in. We also used the same kettle to make hominy when the corn was ready. Please keep in mind that all of this water had to be brought from the creek or spring in buckets, and that took a lot of trips. I thought I had developed the art of looking busy and hiding but I didn't fool Papa, he knew exactly where I was and what I was doing although he let me get away with it if he had enough help from neighbors. Neighbors would get together and help each other at hog-killing time.

All of our neighbors had their own recipe for making sausage but Papa thought his was the best, and it WAS good. We used his same recipe year after year and the sausage was stuffed into the intestines that we had washed so many times, and then we tied them at each end. He would cure some of it by leaving it in a dark room but most of it he would hang in the smoke house. He made fifteen pound batches at a time and was careful about how much of the spices he added because he said he could always add more but couldn't take it out. He would make mild AND spicy sausage because Momma and I liked it mild and he liked it spicy. For the spices, he would add ground cloves, dry mustard, sage, ground red pepper, salt and black pepper to the ground pork and we washed our hands good and mixed it all up. I sort of enjoyed helping with that. Sometimes he would just add salt, pepper, thyme and sage to the mild sausage.

Not much of the hog was wasted. He even ground up the head, mixed it with salt, black pepper, red pepper, onion powder, garlic powder, a little savory and marjoram to make souse meat. Papa loved that but I couldn't eat it, probably because I knew how it is made and what it was made from. A lot of salt was used to preserve fresh meat in the smokehouse, and preserving it was the reason people built smokehouses when they settled into a new area.

A fire pit was built somewhere in the smoke house, normally away from the meat that was hanging but sometimes it was built in the center of the dirt floor. A fire would be built each morning and the meat actually needed a break from the smoke so when the fire went out, the meat would 'rest" until the fire was started again the next morning. Most of the smoke houses would have small screens at the top of the walls for ventilation, but not all of them went to the trouble of doing that. It didn't have to have a certain temperature or draft to cure so they didn't have to keep checking on it all the time. The meat would be hung from the boards in the roof and were mostly hung with leather straps, and was hung at least five feet from the fire. (See picture in back of book.) After it had been smoking for the proper length of time, it would be rearranged away from the fire where it could be left hanging for up to two years.

After the meat was moved out of the direct smoke from the fire, it would still receive smoke but with a different intensity and the smoke house would just be used to store that meat until it was eaten.

Papa had a good heart and didn't like to kill the hogs. Some of the neighbors would slit their throat but he thought it was more humane to shoot them, which is what he did. He said he wanted to make sure the animals' deaths were as painless as possible. I questioned having to kill them at all when I was younger but he explained that we had to do that to have the meat to eat, just like we had to have the vegetables from the garden. Still, I hated to see cold weather come around because I knew what we would be doing.

Butchering a cow was actually done before killing hogs because while it needed to be done in the fall when the flies weren't so bad, it didn't have to be as cold as it did to kill hogs. Papa said the meat was most tender when he killed a calf that was 12 to 15 months old but it had to have been born at the right time to be large enough to kill at the proper time in the fall of the year. However, he had several so that wasn't often the problem. We didn't kill our milk cows because they were too important. Milking cows was normally women's work but it was seasonal work as they ceased giving milk in the winter months and didn't resume giving milk until after calving. A large quantity of milk was required in making cheese. In the early years cows were allowed to graze wherever they could so they didn't give as much milk as they did later when they were kept in pastures. Most of our neighbors kept at least one milk cow expressly for milking and most of them kept two or three.

The quality of cream, the fat from milk, depended a great deal on the richness of the milk, which in turn depended both on the breed of cow and on the richness of the pasture. Cream floated to the top of milk left in a cool place in a large, shallow bowl, called a milk pan, whereupon it could be skimmed off and set aside for use as cream or to be churned into butter. Momma used the cream occasionally as a surprise desert for us. She would sweeten it slightly with sugar, or even molasses, and put a dollop of it on top of fruits, berries, or cake, if she happened to have time to make one.

Butter was sometimes salted to promote its preservation and was used probably more than cheese on bread for breakfast or supper. There was nothing much better than good home-churned butter on one of Momma's good ole biscuits and then molasses poured over that. We had a large crock and a paddle on a stick and had to sit for long periods at a time moving that paddle up and down in the crock, churning the butter. It was also an indispensable ingredient in pastry, cakes, and puddings, and was sometimes melted as a sauce

11

for vegetables. It was also used at times for frying or possibly mixed with lard in frying some items. Melted butter was also used to seal the tops of potted meats to keep the air out and keep the meat fresher.

The first butter churn we had was a smaller one, but as the family grew, Papa had to find a larger crock. Later on we had even a smaller glass one you just sat in your lap and churned and it was much easier than holding the paddle handle and churning up and down, although all of them were hard on my shoulder and elbow.

As I said, it wasn't easy making butter and it took a lot of milk. It took 21 pounds of fresh, wholesome cow's milk to make just one pound of butter! It also took a lot of time and energy. After the cows were milked, the milk was poured in a pancheon or other like containers to let the cream rise to the top. After four or five hours, the cream was skimmed off and was ready for the churn. However due to the effort involved in churning, we would do this each day after milking and then churn several days' worth of cream at one time providing it was not in the hot summer time when we had to churn it nearly every day.
(The pancheons were earthen bowls used to hold milk while the cream was separating, making cheese, dough, and other uses. They were quiet essential to the homemaker.)

After the cream was all in the churn, the top was put on and the churn dash was moved up and down with the hand at a fairly fast speed, and that essentially separated the yellow fat, or butter, from the buttermilk.

I can remember Momma singing a little song sometimes while she was churning, and if I remember it correctly, it went something like this:

"Come butter come,
Come butter come,
Peter stands at the gate
'Waiting for a Buttered Cake,
Come butter come"

She would also sing Amazing Grace and other Spiritual songs while churning.

Butter has been used for centuries; it was even mentioned in the Bible: Judges 5:25 "He asked water, and she gave him milk; she brought forth butter in a lordly dish."

That may have been more information about butter than you wanted but not much of the cow was wasted, either, since the ears and tails could season a pot of beans, Papa could make gelatin out of the hooves, the stomachs could be cleaned and used to hold the sausage. I won't go into detail about the process of all this but it was dreadful. Most people preferred to eat beef fresh but the fattier portions were corned or salted and some were subsequently smoked. In some areas, meat was simply "jerked" by drying. The suet in beef could also be used to make beef sausage. In most cases, the beef hearts, liver, tripe, and kidneys were all commonly used fresh, while the tongues were salted and smoked.

Well, so much for the explicit details of killing hogs and cows, but one grows up fast being the oldest child in a family of fifteen children, and having to help with all of this work.

Sometimes we visited neighbors on Sunday afternoons and when we did, we sat quietly with our arms on the arms of the chairs rather than in our laps to keep our dresses from getting wrinkled. We were taught that children were to be seen and not heard and we knew to behave anytime we went anywhere, as well as at home. We were taught manners and we all knew to say "Yes Ma'am, no Ma'am, yes Sir, no Sir", and we never called our elders by their given name. We were even taught to call some of our close elderly family friends "Uncle" and "Aunt", even though we were not related to them. At the time we were growing up, we thought Momma and Papa were too strict on us but the older we got, we realized they were just trying to teach us to be good citizens, do what was right and grow up responsible like they were. They also wanted us to be sure to know what we needed to know in order to survive when we had families of our own.

I really don't know why Grandpa Josiah had wanted to leave Virginia and settle in Smith County, Tennessee, but I suppose he, as well as several other families, heard there was land opening up in Smith County, and wanted to follow the wagon train and settle here for a while.

Smith County, Tennessee was organized in accordance with an act of the General Assembly of the State, passed October 26, 1799,

13

providing "That a new county be established by the name of Smith, to be contained within the following described bounds: Beginning on the south bank of Cumberland River, at the south end of the eastern boundary of Sumner County; thence north with the said eastern boundary to the northern boundary of the State, and with the said boundary east to where it is intersected by the Cherokee boundary, run and marked agreeably to the treaty of Holston; thence with that boundary to the Caney Fork of Cumberland River; thence with said fork, according to its meanders, to the mouth thereof; thence down the south bank of Cumberland River, according to its meanders, to the beginning." According to this description Smith County originally contained a portion of what is now Trousdale, DeKalb, Putnam, Jackson, Clay and the greater part of Macon Counties. By an act passed November 6, 1801, the county was changed in size by attaching to it a large portion of Wilson County, lying south of the Cumberland River and west of Caney Fork, and by cutting off a portion on the east side to constitute the county of Jackson. And by a subsequent act of the same session of the Legislature Smith County was extended southward to the line between Tennessee and Alabama—thus causing the county to embrace a strip of territory extending from the northern to the southern boundary of the State. In 1805 an act was passed to reduce the county to its constitutional limits of 625 square miles, still allowing its northern boundary to reach the Kentucky line. And by an act passed January 18, 1842, the northern portion of Smith County became a part of Macon County in its formation. And in 1870 a tract in the northwestern part of the county was cut off to form a part of Trousdale County. And thus by these and other acts of the Legislature, Smith County has been reduced to its present limits, embracing about 360 square miles.

The reason I am telling you all of this is because of how the county lines changed from time to time. As a matter of fact, some people were enumerated in one county on one census and enumerated in another county on the next one without having moved because the county lines changed.

Papa was the son of Josiah Harper, Sr., who was born in 1762 in Franklin County, Virginia and was a soldier in the Revolutionary War. (See Josiah's parents and the Harper ancestry traced to the early 1500's in the Appendix of this book.) He moved his family to Smith County, Tennessee about 1820 in a Conestoga wagon in a wagon train with many other families. Grandpa Josiah said it was extremely difficult getting the large Conestoga wagons across the Allegheny Mountains but that is what his father came in to Virginia.

Since that was what they had, they made do after revising the wagons somewhat to be able to maneuver the narrow rough roads through the mountainous area. The Conestoga wagons were made in Conestoga, Pennsylvania, and were most likely started out as farm wagons that were adapted for use on the rough, hilly ground in Lancaster County. A large cover was added to protect the goods inside the wagon from the rain. The bottom was bowed in the middle to make it less likely that the material inside the wagon might slide as the wagon went up and down hills, and the wheels were large so the wagon could pass over streams without getting the products inside wet. Also, large wheels meant the wagon could pass over stumps in the roads or large rocks. In those days roads were rough to say the least and the Conestoga wagon is a perfect example of how a farm wagon was modified to make it better able to move over the rolling hills, the many streams and the poor roads of Lancaster County.

Originally the Conestoga wagon was six feet long, four feet wide and four feet deep.

The wagon driver didn't sit inside the wagon on a seat but rather walked along side the wagon, at times, rode one of the horses, or pulled-down the "lazy" board, which was built on the outer left side of the wagon. The driver had a long leather "jerk" line that ran usually to the front horse on the left and he would use this to send directions to his horse.

Papa said he found it interesting that on the trip from Virginia to Tennessee, there were signs that had pictures of a Conestoga wagon which would advertise taverns, and he said they did this because back then, a lot of people traveling couldn't read but they could look at the picture on the sign and know it was a place to stop and rest, eat, water the horses or spend the night. An example of one of these signs can be found in the back of the book.

My grandfather had married Sarah "Sally" Parrott December 27, 1787 in Franklin County, Virginia. Grandma "Sally" was born about 1764 in Virginia. Grandpa Josiah died September 9, 1838 in Smith County, Tennessee and Grandma Sally was devastated, as well as the rest of the family. She didn't even last a year before she went to be with her beloved husband in 1839. Grandpa Josiah's last will and testament typed and spelled as it was in the will, can be found in the Appendix with the rest of the Harper family history

Before Grandpa Josiah's death, he had passed along a lot of his knowledge he thought his children needed in order to survive. Making Sorghum molasses was one of the things he taught Papa and it involved everyone in the family old enough to help. As a matter of fact, some of the neighbors would bring food and the men would help Papa while their wives set up a table with the food they brought. Momma would be busy in the house also cooking but as soon as she finished, she helped, too.

Every year Papa would dig out a bag of sugar cane seed he had saved from the previous year. I suppose Grandpa Josiah had given him his first start of them. He would plant them around the middle of May in order for the sugar cane to be ready to harvest by September and make into Sorghum. Molasses is what some people called them, but most of the country folk simply called them "lasses".

There was nothing better than molasses on biscuits in the morning, and I think that is why Papa went to all the trouble of making them.

The sugar cane grew to look sort of like corn, but it had larger leaves and the seeds were on the top rather than tassels, like corn. He always looked forward to and making the sorghum, although it was a long drawn-out process. He had a long-bladed knife that he cut the sugar cane off with, about five or six inches from the ground. He would then cut, what he called "fathers", but I called them "leaves", off the stalk and then stand several "stalks" up and tie a piece of twine around them about two feet from the top because he said it was better if it stood in the field like that for a week. Then he would cut the seeds off the top and save them for next year. The men did this work because the fathers/leaves were so sharp, so they had to wear long-sleeve shirts and gloves to keep from getting cuts.

After he hauled the sugar cane to the mill, he had to hitch up his mule and tie it to the long pole where it would walk around and around the mill squeezing the juice from the sugar cane into large buckets as he fed the sugar cane into the mill. He would have a piece of cloth in the top to strain it as it went in the bucket.

Since there was little money, people had to grow and make what they could to have enough to eat. Sorghum was used in a lot of recipes and we used it quite a bit in cakes and cookies. It was also used to sweeten some things when sugar was in short supply. Momma not only traded extra eggs to the owner of the general merchandise store for things she needed, but she also traded some sorghum to the proprietor for needed items. He in turn, would sell the sorghum to other customers who did not make it themselves.

Making sorghum was a long drawn out process. It took a long time for the mule to walk around in circles enough times to squeeze the juice, better known as squeezings, out of all the sugar cane. The old mule would keep a constant slow pace with the pole attached to his harness while the juice dripped into buckets below the mill. It took about all day just to get this done. Then, early the next morning, they would strain the juice into a large metal vat about seven and a half to eight feet long, four feet wide and about seven or eight inches deep. The vat would be propped up on large stones to where a fire could be built under it. It took several people to stand there and stir it constantly all day with large wooden paddles until it had cooked to the right consistency. Some of the neighbors would come to help and Papa would give them a jar of sorghum for helping. It was very important for the fire to be the right temperature, and it needed to just burn slow. Someone had to be watching the vat all the time it was cooking. There was a green scum that floated to the top when the juice started boiling. It had to be kept skimmed off, and then the juice would get darker and thicker. The sweet aroma of the juice cooking could be smelled for a long way.

Papa could always tell when the molasses were ready and then it would be poured into containers using a dipper and funnel. This also took a long time. Would you believe that 100 gallons of juice would boil down to fourteen or fifteen gallons of molasses? After working all day for two days, we had to start all over the next morning to use up the rest of the sugar cane. Sometimes it took all week, even with several neighbors helping.

Wagon Train Trip to Alabama

Only an open heart can break....

Papa began to get restless after Grandpa Josiah died, and he wanted to move but Grandma "Sally", as we called her, wasn't up to a long trip and Papa wouldn't go off and leave her. However, after Grandma Sally died in 1839, he was determined to move on to northwest Alabama. Papa was close to his parents, especially his father, and took their deaths very hard. He really hated to go off and leave the graves of his beloved father and mother, not only because he would not be able to stand at their graves any longer, but he felt like he never would get to visit their grave sites again. However, at the same time, he didn't want to remain there without them, there were just too many memories and he felt like he needed to move on and begin a new life. My step-mother was skeptical of the move because she did not want to give up her comfortable home for the unknown. Plus, she dreaded the wagon ride all the way to Alabama. Papa promised her that everything would work out for the best and she finally gave in, just as she did anytime he wanted to do something. . After she agreed, things changed hurriedly because I had just met the love of my life and I didn't want to move off and leave him. I thought he was the most wonderful man I had ever met, other than Papa, and Papa approved of him, for which I was grateful because I believe we would have run off and married had he not given us his blessings.

Talks continued about some fertile land opening up in the Chickasaw Nation in northwest Alabama so Papa met with several of his friends, neighbors and family on several different occasions to make plans to move to northwest Alabama.

Papa and his friends had actually been talking about moving to northwest Alabama for a long time, even before his parents died and the friends and neighbors who were also interested in going, had been meeting periodically to discuss the move. I actually met and fell in love with one of the men one day when they met at our house. I knew he was also interested in me by the way he looked at me and talked. After the meeting, he stayed behind even after everyone else had gone but fortunately he had ridden his horse rather than riding with someone else so he had a way home. He came back to call on me several times and Papa really liked him.

18

The man soon to be my husband was Andrew Ferrier McWhirter and he was of Scots-Irish heritage. His grandfather, George Marlin McWhirter, established the first high school in Wilson County, Tennessee about 1810 and he taught the boys while his wife, Martha McCandless Balch McWhirter, taught the girls. George Marlin McWhirter taught Greek and Latin and was called the "First Teacher of the Classics in Tennessee". His school was known far and wide and many of his friends and family migrated from Mecklenburg, North Carolina to Wilson County just to attend his school. The school was finally merged in the Preparatory Department of Cumberland University which still operates in Lebanon, Tennessee. Martha McCandless McWhirter had previously been married to the famed Hezekiah James Balch, one of the authors and signers of the Mecklenburg Declaration of Independence. He was a noted teacher at Nassau Hall, now Princeton University where George Marlin McWhirter attended and had classes under Balch. Balch was also licensed by the Presbytery of Donegal on April 20, 1768, and was ordained to the full work of the ministry in 1769. He was called to Poplar Tent and Rocky River Presbyterian Churches in Mecklenburg Co., NC (now Cabarrus Co.) on June 22, 1769, but met an untimely death in 1776 at only 30 years of age. George Marlin McWhirter had known Martha through his association with Hezekiah Balch, and after Balch's untimely death, George Marlin married her on August 29, 1782 in Mecklenburg, North Carolina.

Papa had mentioned moving to a place called Alabama where there was rich land and new territory opening for settlement and I was concerned about us moving off and leaving Andrew but when Andrew heard Papa and the other neighbors might move, he asked me to marry him. Although I wanted to marry right then, we waited but we definitely wanted to get married before we left on the trip to Alabama. Andrew was a tall, handsome, stately frontiersman, a genial and pleasant gentleman of splendid physique. He had black hair and hazel eyes which expressed a kind and benignant nature, with courtly, winning manners that invariably converted strangers into friends immediately upon meeting him.

I had no doubt that Andrew loved me and had the greatest of admiration for me. As soon as he heard about the fertile land and plentiful waterways in northwest Alabama, he decided that would be the best place for us to begin our awesome life and raise our family. We waited until June 7, 1842, when we were married in Papa's house by William Newby, a Justice of the Peace, who was related to the McWhirter family. After the marriage, Papa was happy that my new husband and I would be moving to Alabama with them and things couldn't have been any better, we were so very happy. Right after we married we started packing and making plans for the move. We not only had to decide what clothing, furniture and other belongings we had to take but we had to make a list of the things we would need to eat and to cook with along the way. Andrew said it would be a long trip because a wagon train only moved about two miles per hour which meant we would only travel about ten or twelve miles a day.

All of the families who planned to join the wagon train to Alabama met several different times to discuss the route, what to take, how much food we would need, etc. Most of the families would be tying their cows to the backs of the wagons and we would have milk daily for the children. Some were even pulling a cart behind their wagons carrying their chickens in a cage.

We used horses, oxen and mules to pull our wagons but the most popular animal to pull wagons was the oxen. They were cheaper, stronger and easier to work than horses or mules. They were also less likely to be stolen by Native Americans on the journey and would be more useful as a farm animal when we reached our destination. Oxen were able to exist on sparse native vegetation while the horses and mules had to be fed grain, therefore we didn't have to use precious space in the wagons to carry feed. The oxen were also less likely to stray from camp, although they were slower than the mules and horses but they had better traction in sand and mud. The main argument against oxen was that they could become reckless when hot and thirsty and were known to cause stampedes in a rush to reach water. Also, in the 1840's, oxen cost $25 whereas mules were $75.

It took much longer to plan for the trip than I thought it would because the people didn't have the necessary wagons in which to travel. We didn't have the Conestoga type wagons that Grandpa Josiah and friends had used crossing the Allegheny Mountains so most of us used our farm wagons by stretching a canvas, which had been waterproofed with linseed or other oil, across 5 or 6 bows of hickory. Inside our "covered wagon" was an enclosed space about five feet high from bed to peak which provided storage space and shelter. Because these simple wagons had no brakes (and, of course, no springs) the teamsters learned how to tie chains around the rear wheels to lock them, and thus provide a drag when the teams started down a steep slope. The bed of the wagon was about nine or ten feet long and four feet wide, with sides and ends about two or three feet high. Since we had to pack the wagons with water kegs, food supplies, cooking equipment and other necessities, we had to sleep on the ground most of the time, therefore we had to have another waterproofed canvas to put on the ground before making our bed out of quilts.

The time finally came about 1842, when we were to prepare for the journey to Alabama. We loaded the wagons with our essentials, a few pieces of furniture, clothes, cookware and some things our friends had given us when we married. Our clothes were simple and made from homespun fabrics and most of mine were made from feed sacks. On the trip, our clothes were normally worn several days before washing because we didn't have room for many clothes. We were advised not to take much furniture for fear of having to leave it along the way in case we got bogged down in a swollen stream. Papa's father had told him it was so rough crossing the Allegheny Mountains in the wagons that several families had to leave furniture along the way to make the loads lighter. I couldn't bear the thought of leaving what little we had along the side of the trail.

The day finally came when everyone was ready, the wagons were loaded and the oxen and horses were hitched up to the wagons. Our mule, two cows and a goat were tied to the back of the wagon, and everyone was ready to begin the exciting, long awaited adventure.

We were in search of our own property which sounded exciting, our first land, our first home in which we would raise our children. On the way to Alabama I planned what our house would look like and thought about the children we would have to fill up the house, and how we would take them to church and teach them about God just like our parents had taught us.

Andrew's parents, Alexander Hamilton McCandless McWhirter and Elizabeth "Betsy" Robinson, were disturbed by the fact their son was leaving with his new wife because they were afraid they would never see him again. We tried to get them to go with us but they stated they didn't want to make that type of change in their lives at their ages. I didn't look at them as being old because Pa Alexander was born August 27, 1785 in Mecklenburg, North Carolina and Ma Betsy was born September 10, 1798 in either Tennessee or Kentucky.

It was a difficult trip but Andrew and I were so happy we didn't pay much attention to the hardships. It was exciting to think of starting out our married life in a newly established area of Alabama. The so-called trail we took was not a trail at all but in some places it had been defined with only narrow ruts in the earth. It was actually an old Indian trail. Most of the days were similar, we would stop and camp by a creek or river along the way so we would have plenty of water, be able to take a bath or wash clothes and the larger children would be able to go swimming. I would help cook while Andrew was working on the wagon or hunting. It was fun being newly married and cooking at our campsites, although the older women would get together and help. We cooked a lot of Johnnycakes and Corn Fritters. The pioneer women didn't let the wagon train pass a berry patch or nut tree. We would stop along the way to pick whatever was in season, black berries, blue berries, huckleberries and gooseberries, hickory nuts, chestnuts, etc. We picked wild crab apples to make jam. We couldn't afford to waste anything or pass up anything to eat in case we had trouble on the trail and didn't make our destination within the scheduled time frame.

If there was time when the children finished their chores, in the evening before bedtime, they would keep busy jumping rope, playing marbles, checkers or tic-tac-toe, and entertaining themselves. Sometimes we would sing and dance around the campfire at night while some of the men who brought their musical instruments would play, and then the men would tell stories that interested the children. They thought that was fun, but we had to get up early in the mornings before sunrise to get the morning chores done and get ready for the long day of travel. We would have to start a fire first thing to make coffee and cook breakfast. Then we used the fire to warm the water to wash the breakfast dishes and utensils. I would fold up our bed and pack it away while the bacon was cooking and some of the other women were making coffee and preparing biscuits. While we were doing that, the men would be hitching up the oxen and mules to the wagons. Many of the men and older children would walk until about lunchtime when we would stop for about an hour to eat lunch and then start moving again. We normally stopped about six o'clock at night.

A few nights into the trek I was looking up at the stars, reminiscing and remembering things as they were back home before we left. There were some necessities we had to have to survive the trip but mostly we had a dream of moving westward to a promising future, and settling a community that would always be defined by its hardworking, unyielding spirit. All I knew about the area in which we would settle is, it was supposed to be good fertile land, was blessed with waterways and was previously inhabited and hunted by Native American tribes, mostly Cherokee and Chickasaw but just a little ways west had been land owned by the Choctaw Indians.

It had taken a long time to save up enough money for the trip because we had to have at least one good wagon and enough supplies to last us until we reached our Alabama destination. During the meetings about the trip to Alabama held before we left Tennessee, one of our older friends who had traveled to Warren County, Tennessee from Virginia and knew what provisions we would need, made a list for all of us or we wouldn't have known what all to take. I packed flour, sugar, salt, yeast (for bread), bacon (packed for the climate), coffee beans, coffee grinder, lard, spices, dried fruit, rice, honey, sorghum molasses, hard tack, and parched, ground corn plus some sassafras Andrew had dug for tea. We also had kegs of water. With all of this, the trunks, the cast iron pots and pans and kettles, we didn't have a lot of space left in the wagon. I also took a few small pumpkins because it was easy to make Pumpkin Cake along the trail. I had imagined cooking creamed corn, dried cornmeal mush, corn on the cob and cornbread. Some of the large families had no choice but to take two wagons. Andrew wanted to take some of his tools such as, an axe, hatchet, augurs, chisels, drawing knife, handsaw, spade, froe, mall, and a rope. He believed in being prepared for anything that might happen. I had Papa's old trunk so I packed 2 pillows, sheets, 2 quilts, a comforter and the other waterproofed canvas cloth to put under our bedding at night. We brought along our own cow for milk. We would need matches to light the campfires so we carried them in tightly sealed jars to keep the moisture out. We also took along some quinine, opium, a little blue mass and some cathartic medicine for emergencies along the trail. One of my favorite cooking utensils was Momma's and Papa's old Dutch Oven and I just had to take it.

We were immensely happy to be starting our married life in a newly opened area of Alabama. Our blissful lives loomed ahead of us and we were ecstatic! Andrew was such a handsome young man, tall and stately. The trip took longer than I imagined and was rougher than I had thought it would be but was fairly uneventful. A couple of wagons had to stop and put new wagon wheels on, because one broke crossing a deep, wide creek and the other one hit a large rock and broke. Extra wagon wheels also had to be carried on the trip for emergencies such as this, but they were strapped to the outside of the wagons like the water barrels were and didn't take up any space inside. One lady was expecting a baby the next month but went into labor as we were approaching McMinnville. She was in labor and writhing in agony all night long and the baby was born about noon the next day. We had camped around what was called "the birthing tree". One of the other women said the baby probably came early because of the way the expectant mother was bounced up and down in the wagon. I can certainly see how that could induce labor. That held us up over a day, but it couldn't be helped. We were all there for her and one of the ladies with the wagon train was a midwife and was able to help deliver the precious baby without any complications. However, it was very difficult on the new mother traveling in a wagon, especially one with no springs, but she never complained. The baby was extremely good and didn't cry much at all unless it was hungry. The new mother and her husband already had two older daughters and they were able to help with the baby.

Some stragglers came up to the wagon train one night and Papa had been keeping an eye on them for several minutes. He was afraid they might start trouble, so he notified several of the other men. When they got close enough, Papa greeted them, talked with them a few minutes and determined they were just hungry so he invited them to sit down and eat with us. As they were leaving, Papa gave them some of his bacon and they acted very appreciative. Then one night a couple of Indians sneaked up on the campsite without anyone hearing them until they were right at our wagon. Papa couldn't understand what they were saying but he knew from the signs they made with their hands that they were hungry. He knew they meant no harm or they could have already done something drastic. Papa dug out some beef and a little coffee to give them and Mr. Gann gave them a little bag of something and they left. We were afraid when we saw them but they didn't mean us any harm. I don't know if Papa was afraid of them or if he felt sorry for them, but anyway, Papa wasn't afraid of much. We didn't see them anymore.

The children had their assigned chores to do. It was up to them to milk the cows, if their family had one, and they had to be milked every morning and night. They helped watch out for the younger children, carry water from the creek for cooking, and laundry and then help with all of that. They helped pack and unpack the cooking supplies and bedding from the wagon, gather the wood for the camp fires and cooking. If they went through rugged territory, the children would walk ahead with some older men and throw rocks and clear brush out of the way and put it and tree limbs over muddy spots so the wagon wheels would not get stuck. The older boys would go out hunting for small game with their fathers. They killed such animals as deer, wild turkeys, rabbits and squirrels.

If it was still daylight after the chores were done at night the older ladies would bring out their quilt pieces and stitch a few of them together. That thrilled me because I hadn't been quilting long and I could learn by watching them. However, there wasn't too much time to quilt before dark and the campfire wasn't light enough to sew those small stitches, but it was fun and I couldn't wait to get our house built in Alabama so I could make Andrew and I a quilt to snuggle under.

After climbing over the hills and wandering through the gorges, we finally arrived in Walker County, Alabama. After carefully searching, Andrew picked out some fertile land for us to build our new house.

Building Our First New House

Let perpetual light shine on them…

Andrew settled our wagon close to where the house would be but before he started on the house, he first built a lean-to of boughs and a canvas next to our wagon and we were able to live there and keep our possessions stored in the wagon while Andrew was felling the trees and building our first house. We didn't mind living there temporarily because we were blissfully happy and I could have lived anywhere as long as I was with him. It didn't take as long as I had originally thought it would because he had friends and relatives who helped him fell the trees on occasion. He hand-peeled and hand-hewn the logs. Andrew was good with his hands and he used his froe and maul to make the wooden shingles and shakes, although he said it was quite pains taking. He used his draw-knife to remove the bark from the trees. I enjoyed watching him work.

Andrew first selected trees with straight smooth trunks of approximately the same diameters. He felled the trees, cut them into logs of the desired length and pulled them with our mule to the site we selected for the cabin. He had first dug out a flat area and split logs in half lengthwise and laid them close together with the flat sides up for the floor. He dug a pit about three feet deep for the base of the fireplace, filled it with cobblestones and other rocks and then finished filling it in with mud. He then started on the walls but was only able to lift six or eight tiers of logs by himself. A neighbor came over to help when he got that far and they built a skid consisting of two logs, leaned it against a wall at an angle to slide the logs up and then put them in place. I continued to be amazed at how much Andrew knew about building, and he wanted everything done right. He built the front door from heavy wooden slabs and wooden pegs and even made the hinges to hang it by and the latches to keep the doors closed. I had assumed it would open inside but instead he opened it toward the outside to save space inside. He hung a latchstring on the outside of the door which had become a symbol of pioneer hospitality as an open invitation for the friendly stranger to enter and share the family's table and the warmth of their fireside.

Although Andrew started on our house right away, it was important that he first build an outhouse, some called it a "privy". He had searched very carefully for the perfect spot to build it so we wouldn't smell the odor from it in the hot summertime. He had to dig a deep

26

hole, for the same reason, and it was difficult because while the new soil was fertile, it was extremely rocky in places. He finally got the hole deep enough to start building and it didn't take him but a day after he fell the trees and cut the wood. Since he was in a hurry to start building the house, he only built the outhouse with one hole, which we called a "one-holer" but later on as our family grew he built another one with two holes, taking the dirt he dug for the new one and filling in the hole in the old one. They were not only used as a privy but we threw old glass bottles and other things that wouldn't burn, into the holes. Most all outhouses had a half-moon cut into the door. During the summer months, it wasn't so bad going back and forth to the outhouse but during the winter when it was extremely cold, it was uncomfortable, to say the least, walking out to the outhouse and sitting on the cold seat. We kept a chamber-pot under the bed to use at night rather than going all the way to the outhouse in the middle of the night, and then we would carry it out there, empty it, wash it out, bring it back in and put it back under the bed the next morning. Andrew called it a "thunder-mug". He had a very good sense of humor and was always saying something comical. Some of these were kept under or by the side of the bed to be used at night and emptied the next morning in the outhouse.

After the logs were in place for the house, the spaces between the logs forming the walls were chinked by filling them with smaller pieces of wood or tightly wedged stones and caulked with moss or wet clay mixed with straw. He used his froe and maul to make the wooden shakes for the roof. The chinking was something I could do while he was busy with the other walls. I enjoyed helping and thought it was great that we were building our first log cabin together. I gathered up the small rocks and pieces of wood lying around and carefully placed it between the logs where they wouldn't fall out until I could mix up some mud and straw to place between the cracks inside and out. It was more tedious than I anticipated and took much longer than I planned, but it was something I could do while Andrew was doing the heavy work. Before we were finished with the chinking, I started having sick spells in the morning and wondered why my stomach was staying upset, especially when I would start cooking breakfast. I tried to keep my illness from Andrew because I wanted to keep chinking the logs so we could get in our house sooner. I continued being sick nearly every morning but would go out to the woods hoping Andrew would not see or hear me, and before I returned I would pick up some small rocks and twigs in my apron and bring them back and Andrew would just think I was out looking for chinking material. Finally I didn't make it to the

27

woods in time one morning and Andrew heard me and came running. He knew immediately what was wrong and when I looked up at him to explain it was just an upset stomach, but he had a big smile all across his face which shocked me because I had thought he would be upset. His pet name for me was "Sallie" and he picked me up, kissed me on the cheek, slung me around and said, "Sallie, girl, we are going to have a baby!" I had been so wrapped up in our new house that it hadn't even dawned on me I was pregnant. All I had on my mind was chinking as many of the logs as fast as I could so we could hurry and move in, and I just thought I had caught some type of stomach illness. After that, Andrew didn't want me picking up rock, chips, etc. for fear it might hurt me, but I assured him I would be alright, and kept helping. He was stacking the logs faster than I could chink them.

Andrew worked even harder and faster trying to get the house finished and he wanted to get the roof on before he built the chimney. It was a fortnight before he could find all the rocks he needed for the chimney and get it up and finished. I tried to get him to let me pick up some rocks and bring back to the house while he was working on the roof but he wouldn't hear of it. He didn't want me doing anything that might hurt me or the baby.

At first the cabin was only one large room so it didn't take a really long time to finish it and we were so very happy to be able to move all of our stuff out of the wagon into the house. Andrew had made us a bed and a table for the kitchen area. I could see why he needed all of the tools he brought with him.

Immediately after Andrew finished the house, he dug and built a root cellar, which was an absolute necessity back then to keep apples and root vegetables through the winter. We also kept jars of vegetables and fruits that I had canned during the summer months, in the root cellar.

I didn't realize how much pains had to be taken building a root cellar, but Andrew knew all about it and how they should be built to retain the correct temperature and humidity in order to preserve the fruits & vegetables during the winter. The root cellar was supposed to retain a temperature of around 55 degrees and a humidity of 80-90 percent in order to keep the fresh vegetables from losing their moisture and shriveling up. The damp earthen floor helped keep the temperature and humidity where it was supposed to be, especially if the floor was kept damp.

There was a little knoll immediately behind the house, so that is where Andrew decided to dig the root cellar and the roof would be covered with dirt. It took a long time to dig a hole large enough for a root cellar and he made ours about eight feet square. Then he had to build a door for the opening and a couple of steps going down to it, and the door had to be away from the sun and the hot summer breeze. After he was through with that, he even built some shelves for me to sit my canning jars full of fruits and vegetables, and he put the shelves about three feet out from the earthen wall to keep the jars of food from freezing. The door had to fit extremely tight in order to keep the rodents out of the fresh fruits and vegetables. We were able to store beets, carrots, turnips, rutabagas, potatoes, apples, pears, & pumpkins, and with that plus the dried beans and canned vegetables and fruits I put up, we were able to eat well all winter.

On July 10' 1843, I started having labor pains early in the morning so Andrew rode off to get the midwife, who was one of our neighbors. She had made the trip from Tennessee to Alabama with us and had helped many of the women bring their babies into the world, so Andrew wanted her to help me. After he left, I was afraid I might have the baby while he was gone but it didn't take him long to bring her back. She had been there a few hours when our first baby, Thomas Andrew McWhirter, was born. Andrew thought he was the most beautiful baby he had ever seen and he couldn't wait to take him around to show him off to all of his friends. He was deliriously happy he had a baby boy. I was still nursing Thomas when I realized I was pregnant again. I wasn't very happy about it but when I told Andrew, he was thrilled and it lightened my spirits somewhat, mostly because Andrew wanted a large family.

Andrew decided he better get busy and build a loft for the children to sleep in when they were a little older so he worked from early morning until late night getting that finished. He made a nice ladder to get up to the bedroom loft, out of strong tree limbs because he was in a hurry to get it finished, but later he made another one out of boards that one of the neighbors had left over from his house. We also used this loft for company if they were staying overnight.

Since Thomas Andrew was born in the middle of the summer, it made it difficult for me to work in the garden, but I did what Andrew would let me do and he kept the weeds out and gathered the cucumbers, tomatoes, squash, and other vegetables for me and I was able to put it up and keep it from spoiling. Of course we ate some of it, also. By the time the dried beans and peas were ready to shell, I was able to pick them, sit on the porch and shell them and then put them up. They had to be kept in tightly sealed jars in the root cellar to keep insects out of them. I still had to pick and can the green beans just a couple of weeks after Thomas was born. I was actually able to do more than I did but Andrew was afraid I would do too much in my condition.

We needed the vegetables to last as long into the winter as possible so we would plant a garden soon after the last frost, gather and put up those vegetables and then plant another crop as soon as the first one was harvested and hope it matured before the first frost of the winter. Of course the potatoes and other root crops could stay in the ground past the last few frosts thus lasting longer in the root cellar after harvesting late. Another reason for harvesting late is if it is cold when the vegetables are harvested, they are prone to store more sugars and starches and less water. Most of the root vegetables had to be stored in the root cellar immediately after harvesting but the garlic and onions had to be dried out before storing. We didn't wash the vegetables or cut off the tips of them because they stayed fresh longer that way.

I was amazed that Andrew knew so much about gardening and harvesting, and glad that he taught me because I would come to need this information in a few years. He had really paid attention while helping his father, Alexander, plant and harvest crops for their family. Of course I had to help Momma harvest and preserve the fruits and vegetables for so long that I knew how to do all of that.

Thomas Andrew was less than two years old when I gave birth to our second son, George Washington McWhirter. We waited until the boys were a little older to let them sleep in the loft and when we finally put them up there they were happy and thought they were so big and grown-up, to have a bedroom all their own.

Our wonderful family was growing and it was unbelievable how happy we were, and then on June 23, 1847, our third son, Andrew "Jackson" McWhirter was born.

We had settled in a new community in a new state along with my father, step-mother and several neighbors, and then had these sons. After Jackson was born, Andrew decided the loft was too small for three children so he started building again. He built a nice sized bedroom onto the house with another bedroom over it. It took quite a while to finish and it wasn't very large, but it was a mansion to us and we loved it. Andrew loved working with his hands. How could life be any better? In 1848, our fourth son, Robert McWhirter was born but he was sick off and on all of his short life. I tried everything I knew to do, to nurse him back to health but it seemed nothing would work. We had a goat and fed him goat's milk, but it didn't seem to help. For the next few years we watched him wither away right in front of our eyes and nothing we or the doctor did helped him. We knew it wouldn't be long before he finally succumbed to his illness and we were crushed. I cried so much I couldn't cry anymore; thinking about my son, who wasn't even going to reach his tenth birthday, much less live long enough to be a young man. It's hard losing any close family member, but losing a child you have carried for nine months, given birth to, nursed and care for, for several years, is completely different, and the people who haven't experienced this, have no idea how it hurts. Parents shouldn't outlive their children but that is God's business and we know He is still in control, and Robert had served his purpose that God put him here to do. We couldn't understand why our son had been taken from us but we knew at the same time that God had a reason and we had to trust in that. Everyone has a purpose in life and Robert's purpose didn't take long to fulfill. I think the day we buried Robert was the saddest day of our lives, but it was only the first of several sad times I would experience.

It was nice having Papa and his second wife, Mary E., who was only eight years older than me, living next door to us but she died in 1890, and then Papa married Mary Jane Griggs, who was only four years older than me and she was more like a sister. She was the widow of William Miles who died about 1869.

Papa and his family attended Hopewell Baptist Church which he represented as a delegate to the North River Baptist Association from 1855 to 1860. During this same time period, he acquired several more federal land patents to the north and south of the church.

After Robert's untimely death, Andrew became restless and he had to find something to keep him busy constantly. The church had been built and all of the people on our wagon train were settled into their new homes. Some new settlers came to the area and he started helping them fell trees to build their houses. Then July 19, 1852, William Hamilton, our fifth son, was born and Andrew was happy

31

again. He didn't go out as much to work on the other houses and things got back to normal.

On May 17, 1855, God blessed us with our first daughter, Mary Caroline McWhirter and she was a beautiful baby. Andrew was the happiest man on the earth and thought there was nothing like Mary Caroline. She was the apple of his eye and he showed her off everywhere he went. He stated he was hoping for a girl when he built the other bedroom and loft. Things seemed to be back to the wedded bliss we first experienced when we married. God had really been good to us and blessed us with these beautiful children. What more could we ask, we had the perfect family and were sublimely happy.

Mary Caroline was a beautiful child, and spoiled being the only girl in a house full of boys, but she never acted spoiled. If she had asked for the moon, and Andrew had thought he could get it for her, he certainly would have tried. She grew up to marry George Washington Harbin, born February 22, 1846 in Cherokee County, Georgia and who had served in the Confederate Army, Company K of the 2nd Georgia Cavalry in Cherokee Co., GA. I liked George and knew Mary Caroline loved him so I gave them my blessing and they were married November 29, 1873. I was really distraught when they decided to move to Texas because I had already lost my dear husband, father, two sons, four brothers and two sisters, and felt like if they moved out there, I would never see them again. She was a pretty lady even in her older years.

Then on February 15, 1858, God blessed us with another son, John Madison McWhirter. Andrew loved to go to town and show the children off to anyone who would look at them and listen to him. He loved his family so and we loved him, he was the perfect father and husband.

Before continuing with this story, let me first give you a brief history of the area up to the time of the Civil War. The scenic beauty of northwest Alabama is probably what drew the pioneer settlers to the area. On March 3, 1817, the Alabama Territory was by law formed from the approximate eastern one-half of the long existed Mississippi Territory. It was in 1817, that Mississippi became a State of the Union as Alabama began to function as a Territory. Marion County was created by the Alabama Territorial Legislature on February 13, 1818, drawing its name from the great Southern Revolutionary War General, Francis Marion.^{i} Initially the county encompassed land along the Tombigbee River that now makes up parts of Monroe and

Lowndes counties in the state of Mississippi. In fact, before 1821, the first two county seats were located on the Tombigbee in what is now Mississippi. All lands east of the Tombigbee and Southeast of Gaines' Trace had been considered Alabama Territory until the state line was officially determined in 1820-21. Thus, when first formed in 1818, greater Marion County stretched half the North-South length of the Alabama Territory along the Tombigbee to its convergence with the Warrior River. In the initial description of the county drawn up by the Alabama Territorial Legislature in 1818, Marion was the largest territorial county. Then, by 1819-1820 the county was reduced in size by the Legislature and the establishment of the Mississippi state line. However, the county remained extensively large into 1824, retaining most of present day Walker, Winston, Fayette and Lamar Counties within its boundaries.

All the lands that were at one time encompassed in Marion County initially served as "hunting grounds" of the Chickasaw Indian Domain before the vast Indian Cessions across the Alabama region in 1816. The Chickasaws were one of the three "civilized tribes" of the South and played a key role in the pioneer settlement of the county; providing corn to establish new immigrants, and trade goods for early county seats.

A key Indian location is marked by three large mounds on the Buttahatchee River just south of Hamilton, Alabama, at the so-called "Military Ford", where Andrew Jackson's Military Road crossed that river. Indian arrowheads, grinding stones, and pottery are found throughout the county.

By the winter of 1817-18, just prior to county creation, approximately 1000 pioneer settlers had arrived in what would become "greater Marion County". This sparse settlement was thus scattered throughout what became Marion, Fayette, Lamar, Walker and Winston Counties Alabama; and most of Monroe and Lowndes Counties Mississippi. Most early settlers came from Tennessee, but sizable numbers came from Kentucky, Georgia and the Carolinas. By the mid 1850's an extensive number of settlers came especially from Georgia. The earliest initial settlement in what was considered Marion County was along the Tombigbee River, but the hill country received numerous pioneers in the 1820's. Indeed, in the early ante-bellum years, Alabama was considered a part of the Western frontier where Federal lands could be obtained by grant and reasonable purchase prices, thus settlement came fast.

33

It was this original county that provided as many troops for the Union army as for the Confederacy.

Marion County's second seat of justice was located just north of present-day Columbus, Mississippi which was on the lower Buttahatchee River near where it empties into the Tombigbee. Thus, in 1819-20, the community of Columbus (now Mississippi) became the first real town in Marion County, Alabama and basically served as the Marion Court Town. However, before Marion's first official Post Office could be established there in 1820 the Federal Government determined the town was located on the Mississippi side of the Alabama state line, and designated Marion's first projected official Post Office as Columbus, Mississippi.[ii] The establishment of the present day Alabama/Mississippi state line in 1820-21, deprived Marion County of all its "Tombigbee bottoms", making most of the county "hills and valleys" of Northwest Alabama.

The next chosen site for the county seat was Pikeville which was surveyed in 1821. Pikeville was destined to become the historical focus of the county in the Ante-bellum period. However, being located on a rather narrow and isolated ridge along the Military Road among rather poor lands, it would not attract many settlers or many nearby farming ventures. By 1860, it contained no more than 15 business establishments and 20-30 homes. The primary businesses from the 1820's through the 1880's were tan yards or leather tanning and products such as shoes and saddles. Pikeville was also noted for beaver hat production and several good hotels/taverns and saloons. Pikeville's society was led by Judge John Dabney Terrell, Jr.

After Pikeville's village status led to rapid community dissipation, its viable central location and usefulness as a County Seat was diminished. The formation of Lamar County from Marion and Fayette Counties in 1867-68 left no choice, but to choose a more centrally located county town.

Hamilton was eventually selected as the county seat of Marion County and the Court House was built in 1882-83, however, it burned in 1887, destroying valuable records collected in the county since the 1820's.

34

Winds of War blow Through NW Alabama

Grant them eternal rest, O Lord....

Not long after our son, John Madison, was born, Andrew and I had been going about our daily chores, enjoying our lives and talking about how fortunate and thankful we were for our incredible family, and everything God had blessed us with, when the winds of war started blowing through northwest Alabama and sent everyone into turmoil. Bedlam swept through the area and everyone was overwrought. I had always thought that the unknown was worse than the known and although that applied in this case, no one could have ever imagined how horrifying the "unknown", in this case, was going to be.

Although this story is about my life, rather than that of the 1st Alabama Cavalry Union Army, it effected every member of our family, each friend and neighbor, and was such a large part of our lives that I have to also explain that story in order for you to understand the abomination of the war and the enormity of the savageness across northwest Alabama. It left no life untouched in the area.

Andrew and I had discussed the upcoming war at length with our neighbors, along with the possibilities that might happen, however, we kept hearing the word "secession" and I had to ask Andrew what they were talking about. It seemed that some of the southern people wanted to secede from the Union and form their own government, and I didn't understand. Andrew was also confused and upset by it all. We would later learn secession would pit us not only against our friends and neighbors, but our very own family, including some of my brothers who fought on opposing sides. Each day brought with it such terrible and shocking events. The letters I received from Thomas and Andrew Jackson telling of their skirmishes and battles were unbelievably cruel and it was difficult to imagine human beings doing things like that to other human beings, especially when some of them could have been their brothers, fathers or sons.

The reason I'm going into detail about this is, it is a story that is largely unknown. It is a story of courage, conviction, patriotism, persecution, retribution, and murder. It is a story about love in the face of dishonor. Above all, it is a great American History story worth telling and preserving, even as brutal as it was.

35

The Civil War split what remained of my family after the war. My loyalties were torn between my sympathy with my husband, three sons, three brothers and Unionists friends, and my love for my other brothers who enlisted in the Confederate Army.

When the gathering dark clouds of war were all encompassing in the South and in northwest Alabama in particular in the spring of 1861, the voices of dissent were loud and clear. While some were eager to fight for a newly created secessionist government, many others, like the Harpers and McWhirters, considered an impeding war as a wicked, treasonous undertaking and wanted no part of it.

Indeed, a majority in the mountains and hills of Northwest Alabama, mostly yeomen farmers, saw little value or reason in taking up arms against the federal government. They recognized quite early that this was not their fight, but that it was the landed gentry. It was obvious to all of us, the Unionists, that the plantation owners and their political spokesmen were fanning the war flames and talked the loudest about separation. With their money and property and political power, it was the planters who felt most threatened by the election of Abraham Lincoln as president. They thought he would destroy everything they built as a finer civilization. Southern women would not be safe from roving gangs of black thieves if Lincoln freed the slaves. The only thing to do, the planters contended, was to fight to protect their very way of life, to secede and create a government that would protect their interests, protect their property rights, and protect that "peculiar institution."

Of course, the peculiar institution was slavery! However, in the rugged landscape of northern Alabama, slaves were few and far between.

Few slaves were owned in the upland south, simply because the land would not support a plantation economy. Those of us who did work the land in the mountain South were a fiercely independent breed, not rich but proud, and of no mind to lend support to plantation owners who looked down upon us as inferior.

The Harpers and McWhirters did not believe in slavery!!

The Loyalty to "Old Hickory"

Bless the pain, as proof it was real....

If the inhabitants of the upland South were willing to give a new president the benefit of the doubt, they revered a former president. This was a man who led their fathers and grandfathers against wild Indians and who tamed the land. He made their very existence here possible. President Andrew Jackson, "Old Hickory" was seen as a man of the people. He was also a staunch unionist who warned the Southern aristocracy years before that any talk of busting up the union was madness and any actions to do so would be punished severely.

General Andrew Jackson did indeed warn South Carolina on December 10, 1832, that he was prepared to do just that. "Are you really ready to incur its guilt? If you are, on the heads of the instigators of the act be the dreadful consequences; on their heads be the dishonor, but on yours may fall the punishment. On your unhappy State will inevitably fall the evils of the conflict you force upon the Government of your country. It can not accede to the mad project of disunion, of which you would be the first victims."

At a time when the country was about to go to war, many Alabama Unionists spoke about how President Jackson would have dealt with secession by hanging the ringleaders and crushing the rebellion before it got started. According to "Prominent Tennesseans", George Ferrier McWhirter, son of George Marlin McWhirter and brother to Andrew Ferrier McWhirter's father, Alexander Hamilton McCandless McWhirter, fought with General Andrew Jackson during his Indian Campaigns, and participated in the battles of Talladega, Emuckfaw and the Horseshoe. He was a man of strong sense and thorough education.

Many Alabama unionists would remember the parting words of their fathers and grandfathers who served with Jackson, and who sensed years before that a war over secession could erupt. The old veterans would warn on their deathbeds to be loyal to the "Old Flag". And their words were ringing true and remembered and taken to heart.

One of Thomas' and Jackson's friends, David C. Spears, was captured at Faison's Station, North Carolina on the way back from the march to the sea, and he died in the hands of the enemy. David's parents, Joshua and Nancy Spears told their four sons to never fight against the United States.

Let me interject a point at this time about how history would portray the Alabama Unionists as "poor, uneducated, dirt farmers", the McWhirters were actually educated people and my husband, Andrew Ferrier McWhirter's grandfather, George Marlin McWhirter, studied at Princeton University, when it was called the College of New Jersey and was located in Newark, New Jersey. It was also called "Nassau Hall" before it was changed to "Princeton". After completing his studies at Princeton, he taught there before moving on to Nashville, Tennessee about 1800 and opening a school in Wilson County where he taught Greek and Latin. One of his grandchildren described him as follows: "He was a man of commanding presence and courtly manners, a typical gentleman of the old school, over six feet in height, with unusually fine features, and was strikingly handsome, even in old age. His life was devoted more to literary pursuits than money-getting, but he was always prominent in the community and exerted a decided influence on those around him." Other McWhirters were preachers, teachers, lawyers, court clerks, post masters, commissioners, and in short, leaders in their communities, not to mention frontiersmen and pioneers of their times. So don't believe those who try to portray all of the Unionists in northwest Alabama as illiterate and uneducated!

The people in Marion, Fayette, Winston and surrounding counties were of modest means and were typical of southern unionists and only about 2% of them were slave-owning families. Most of the southern unionists who would go on to join the Union Army were descendants of grandparents who fought for this country during the American Revolution and many died for their country. Little did I realize at the time, how many of my family, including my husband, son, brothers, cousins, nephews and a son-in-law, would also die for the same country that we all loved.

The Unionists were largely an isolated mountain people who knew full well that the aristocracy viewed them as socially inferior and saw the impending conflict as "A rich man's war and a poor man's fight."

It would eventually come to that but only after the southern unionists proclaimed their neutrality. For the most part, they wanted to be left alone, to sit the war out, but that was not to be. Governor

John Gill Shorter warned that if requisitions made upon the state for volunteers were not duly met by the "hill people", then a draft would be ordered on the delinquent counties.

In response to Governor Shorter's statement, the leaders of Winston County, Alabama responded by calling a meeting at Looney's Tavern in the eastern portion of the county. An estimated 2,500 people attended from Winston, Walker, Lawrence, Blount, Marshall, Marion, Franklin and Fayette Counties. Several resolutions were passed as a result of that meeting. One of the resolutions passed stated, "We agree with Jackson that no state can legally get out of the Union; but if we are mistaken in this, and a state can lawfully and legally secede or withdraw, being only a part of the Union, then a county, any county, being a part of the state, by the same process of reasoning, could cease to be a part of the state." This is what created the legend of "The Free State of Winston".

Another resolution passed was a plea for neutrality stating, "We think that our neighbors in the South made a mistake when they bolted, resulting in the election of Mr. Lincoln, and that they made a great mistake when they attempted to secede and set up a new government. However, we do not desire to see our neighbors in the South mistreated, and therefore, we are not going to take up arms against them; but on the other hand, we are not going to shoot at the "flag of our fathers, "Old Glory," The Flag of Washington, Jefferson and Jackson. Therefore, we ask that the Confederacy on the one hand and the Union on the other, leave us alone, unmolested, that we may work out our political and financial destiny here in the hills and mountains of northwest Alabama."

Had the authorities in Montgomery been wise, they would have treated these Alabama Unionists with kid gloves. Instead, they were branded as traitors or Tories and a systematic campaign of persecution was launched by the Confederate Home Guard. Ironically, it was that harsh treatment that pushed many Alabama Unionists into the federal camp to take up arms against the Confederacy.

Conscription and Consequences

...to bear the shock, to question why
in God's great plan they had to die....

When the Confederate Congress passed the Conscription Act on April 16, 1862, requiring every able-bodied man between the ages of 18 and 25 to be subject to military service, the hill people found themselves in a quandary. Unwilling to fight for the Confederacy and unable to remain neutral, the Harpers, McWhirters, and many others took to the mountains, caves and caverns to hide from conscription patrols who would force them to join the Confederacy.

The following is what they said about wanting to be left alone and remain neutral:
"But the question is, what are we to do? We did not, nor do we now, want to take up arms against our neighbors in our own state. We desire to be let alone that we may remain neutral. If the Confederacy continues to treat our county as a part of it, and attempts to force our citizens to serve in the Confederate Army, as we hear threats that indicate it will, then in that case, neutrality will cease in Winston County. The people in Winston County rather than be forced to fight for the perpetuation of slavery in the Confederate Army will abandon neutrality, join the Union Army and fight for the Union. It looks, now, like that is what is going to take place. Again, in closing, what are we to do? And thank you." This was not just in Winston County, but in Marion and other counties.

Murder or political assassination was a constant threat for Alabama unionists who chose to remain at home. Three sons of Solomon Curtis were all killed in Winston County. Joel Jackson Curtis was killed in 1862 for refusing to join the Confederate Army. George Washington Curtis, home on leave from the Union Army, was murdered by the Home Guard in his yard while his wife and three children watched. Thomas Pink Curtis, the Probate Judge of Winston County, was arrested near Houston by Confederate authorities in 1864 and taken to a bluff on Clear Creek where he was summarily executed with two shots to his right eye.

Henry Tucker, a private in Company B, of the 1st Alabama Cavalry, USV, was arrested by the Home Guard at his home in Marion County and tortured to death. He was tied to a tree, castrated, his eyes removed and his tongue cut out before he was literally skinned

40

alive. He is buried at Hopewell Cemetery, south of Glen Allen, Alabama. (See story later)

But Tucker's vicious death was avenged. Home Guard leader Stoke Roberts, who personally directed the torture of Tucker, was eventually caught by a group of Unionists near Winfield, Alabama, in Marion County. By this time, the Unionists were fighting mad so when Roberts was caught, some of them took a long iron spike and drove it through his mouth and out the back of his head and nailed him to the root of a big oak tree.

Northwest Alabama would soon be torn apart by the worst sort of warfare witnessed by man. There was a vicious guerrilla struggle between former friends and neighbors with atrocities committed by both sides. It was similar to the Southern frontier during the Revolutionary War, and it was a fight which nobody wins and everyone loses.

After the Confederates passed the Conscription Act in 1862, saying all healthy white men between the ages of 18 and 35, were liable for a three-year term of service in the Confederate Army. Quite unlike Arkansas who required all males between the ages of 16 and 60 to join the Confederacy. The males younger and older than this or the ones unfit for military service joined what they called the Home Guard. This drove my husband, Andrew Ferrier, our sons Jackson, George Washington and Thomas Andrew McWhirter, three of my brothers, and many of their friends to the mountains in Winston County, Alabama where they lived in a cave known as "The Rock House". Because of this, they were called "Mossbacks". Many other Unionists hid out there as well, trying to escape the wrath of the fire-breathing Confederates and being forced to join the Confederacy. However, the Confederate Home Guard found them and ordered them to join the Confederacy or be shot. Many of them got away before the Confederates arrived on the scene but many were still around. Several of them made their way to Huntsville, Alabama, a town the Union had captured, so they were able to join the Union Army. Others were caught and forced to join the Confederacy but soon found a way to escape and made their way to the Union lines and immediately joined up with them. If they were going to be forced to fight, it certainly wasn't going to be for the Confederacy because they loved their country and flag too much.

When Huntsville fell to the Union Army in 1863, there were still groups of Confederates there who decided to fight to keep the Union

41

from taking over another town, but they were outnumbered. Anytime the Union soldiers found a Confederate soldier inside their lines, they labeled them "bushwhackers", so all of the Confederates within Huntsville after the Union had taken over, were subject to that appellation. They actually didn't have to be in a town captured by the Union to have a label attached to them because as much terror as they had already inflicted on the Union families, the Union had names worse than that for them.

Leroy Pope Walker, a forty-three year old lawyer from Huntsville, was selected as the Confederate Secretary of War and he insisted there would be no more conflict between the North and the South. He recklessly went a step further to say "I will wipe up all the blood that might be shed with my own handkerchief." Of course it wasn't long before those words came back to bite him. Little did he know.

Many of the Unionists first tried to hide their political views in order not to draw attention to themselves. It only worked to a point.

A Marion County resident, John R. Phillips, spoke for many when he said, "It was firmly in my mind that I would never go back on "Old Glory," I had heard too much from my old grandparents about the sufferings and privations they had to endure during the Revolutionary War to ever engage against the Stars and Stripes. However, I went slow and talked but little and thought by not talking either for or against it and giving them all they asked for and treating them kindly, they would let me alone."

Trouble Brewing in Northwest Alabama

Oh shed a tear or two, if you must, for our time now ended....

The day was gloomy and the rain beat down on the windows which prevented me from washing clothes. My chores were done and I needed something to do to try and get my mind on something other than the war situation. Working in the garden was out of the question, so I decided to get the quilt pieces out that I had already cut out from the flour and feed sacks Mamma had left, and I wanted to make the quilt all by myself because I knew Andrew would be proud of me when I was finished with it. It had been a while since I had worked on it so I sat the basket next to the rocking chair, lit the candle on the table next to the chair and was sitting there sewing the little pieces together when Ellen Head, one of our neighbors, came in and invited me to her quilting bee. This was to help Sally Hallmark finish quilting her quilt she had been working on for several months. We had these quilting bees in different neighbors' homes where several of the women pitched in and helped with quilts as each one had their quilts "sandwiched" together and ready to be quilted. It was fun talking as we were sitting there sewing and helping others. Not everyone had a quilting frame so it was necessary to use someone else's. They had to be hung from the ceiling which took up almost all of the room in which they were hanging so it was important to finish quilting one as quickly as possible. Some of the frames were hung so at the end of the day they could be raised up to where they were out of the way and there was room to walk under them. With several women working on the quilt at one time, it didn't take long to finish one. Besides using feed and flour sacks as fabric for our quilts, we cut up and used our worn-out dresses, blouses, men's shirts, suit coats, etc. that I kept in the rag bag after they were beyond use. I could most always find a few pieces of an old dress or suit jacket of pants.

Quilts were the only thing we had to keep us warm at night and I loved snuggling up to Andrew under a warm quilt. I had two of Momma's and Papa's old quilts that Momma meticulously made, but each of the children needed one or more on their beds so I had to work hard to get them all made. I definitely wanted to have, at least one finished before Andrew got back home and I could hardly wait to be able to show him my finished quilt, knowing how proud he would be of me. I could just visualize the smile of approval on his face. I enjoyed making them, when I had time, but they were

43

difficult to wash outside. It was almost impossible to wash them in the wash pot. I had brought Andrew's mother's large wash pot with us from Tennessee, but it was still cumbersome to handle in the hot water, especially if there was a good fire going beneath the pot and the water had to be carried from the creek, which took several buckets full. If the weather was nice and warm I would just carry them to the creek where there was more room and I could scrub them on the large rocks if they had difficult stains on them. The children always went to the creek with me to wash but they did more playing in the water than they did helping with the wash.

The quilts were very hard to handle when they were wet, and especially difficult to wring the water out. As a rule, they did not get washed as much during the winter time. I would hang them over the fence to dry but it would take a long time for them to get completely dry. I had to be careful when wringing the water out so as not to break any of the stitches because when one broke, it just kept raveling, and it took too much time and hard work to make them.

While I was at Mrs. Head's house helping her quilt, Andrew, William Head, George Hallmark and some of the other husband's came in from a meeting they had attended about the Civil War and we were frightened at what we heard.

Andrew said trouble was brewing and if things didn't change or they couldn't figure out anything else, they were going to have to ride up the mountain and hide out in the "Rock House" to keep from being forced to join the Confederacy, which many of them did, and they remained there for several weeks until the Confederate Home Guard found them and ordered them to join the Confederacy or be shot.

Andrew and I had moved into this volatile region of southerners in northwest Alabama, but there were many of our relatives and friends whose heritage would not allow them to fight against the very country for which their grandfathers fought so diligently during the Revolutionary War, and they had no intentions of fighting against the same country. They stated their Scots-Irish ancestors came to this country looking for a place to worship as they pleased and America embraced them and allowed them to do just that, so they were going to remain faithful to the country of their forefather's choice and there was no way they would fire on "Old Glory", the Flag of their forefathers. I think we can all understand this.

When the McWhirters lived in Scotland, they were persecuted for their protestant belief and their only option was to submit to persecution or flee abroad. Some of the Scottish families escaped to Germany and Switzerland while others escaped to America.

In all of the British Isles in the 16th Century, everyone was expected to define themselves as a Christian and was required to attend the services of the established church. The practice of any other religion was punishable by fines, imprisonment and sometimes, even death. This was not acceptable to the McWhirter family, so they, along with many others of their belief, escaped to America.

The Civil War Breaks Out

When we, defeated by the truth, surrender to death's other face, robbed
of innocence and youth....

Can we not picture this? Our patriotic Scots-Irish Ancestors, who did not want to fight against their southern neighbors but absolutely refused to fight against the country they loved and the country that embraced their ancestors who were only looking for a place to worship as they pleased? A group of patriotic men who refused to fire on "Old Glory", the Flag of their forefathers? One of them told his wife he had to go try to help save the Union that his ancestors helped to form. They were SO determined that they hid out in a cave for months, wanting to be left alone to their own fate. How can loving America this much cause so many people so much pain and suffering? But it did! Just think about this a few moments, put yourself in the place of these Unionists....they had no slaves, they had no reason to secede from the Union, they loved their country that embraced their ancestors and allowed them to worship as they pleased, they had absolutely no qualms with America but they were about to be forced to fight for something in which they didn't believe!! So what did they do? They rebelled, they remained patriotic to the country they loved, they stood up for what they thought was right, and they fought for their convictions, many to their deaths!

Due to the involvement of his ancestors in the Revolutionary War, John R. Phillips believed in a strong Union. He would have been content to remain neutral in the Civil War and tried to avoid Confederate conscription. He was finally caught and forced to join Patterson's Fifth Alabama Cavalry, CSA. He deserted from the Confederate army and then helped Sanford Trammel in his recruiting efforts for Company L, First Alabama Cavalry, USV. For his help in recruiting, John was made a sergeant.

Eventually, John R. Phillips would be found out and the Home Guard would come calling! He stated, "They commenced robbing my family of the support I had left for them, they drove off my cattle and took my horses and mules, also my corn. They even went so far as to pour what meal my family had out in the floor and fill the sacks with meat. They even took our cups, saucers and plates, not leaving anything for their sustenance."

The severe treatment to his family by the Home Guard is what pushed John Phillips to making his way to federal lines and joining the 1st Alabama Cavalry, United States Volunteers.

In Alabama, of 52 counties, 23 voted to remain within the Union. These counties lay mostly within the Appalachian Highlands of northern Alabama, and this division was one that was repeated everywhere within the South. The people of the uplands were pro-Union and the people of the plantation areas represented the Confederacy.

On the night of July 14, 1862, after all the destruction and murders by the Confederate Home Guard, Streight, who was intent on organizing the Alabamians into a fighting force, spoke to a gathering of unionists before introducing Charles Christopher "Chris" Sheats.

Sheats gave a touching and fiery speech, telling his fellow Alabamians that the time had come to join the army of the United States and fight the Confederacy "to hell and back again." He urged them to fight side-by-side for a cause they believed in and put down the rebellion. He stated that the time had come to either fight in an army for which they had no sympathy and in a cause for which they hated, or join the army of the United States for a cause they loved and put down the rebellion so peace would again prevail. His closing statement was, "Tomorrow morning I am going to the Union Army, I am going to expose this fiendish villainy before the world. They shall hear from me. I have slept in mountains, in caves and caverns, till I am become musty, my health and manhood are failing me, and I will stay here no longer till I am enabled to dwell in quiet at home." (The "Rock House" is the cave where Sheats hid for several months, along with many other Unionists. See picture of the "Rock House" in back of book.)

Typically of the Southern Unionists, one-by-one took a stand and risked their lives traveling, in some cases, hundreds of miles to join the Union Army. Within three days of the urging of C.C. Sheats, one-hundred and fifty men joined the Union Army. On July 24, 1862, Andrew Ferrier McWhirter along with sons, Thomas A., George W. and Andrew J. McWhirter, and many neighbors joined the Union army in Huntsville, Alabama. Some of our closest neighbors who joined were: William Head, James Killensworth, Franklin Morton, Drury Whitehead, and four Hallmark brothers, John Madison, George W., James Washington, and Thomas Frank Hallmark. This would take all of men in our neighborhood leaving the wives and children vulnerable to the marauders and Confederate Home Guard. To give you an idea of how bad things were, I will go ahead and tell you what was said after the war. "Consider the loyal men in the South, especially as far south as Alabama, what they had to endure for their country. They were exposed and in danger every minute of their lives. They were shot sitting by their firesides or walking on the road; they had to leave their families to the abuse of the enemy; had to keep themselves closely concealed like the vermin in the woods until they could make escape through the lines, and then had to share the same hardships of soldiers life that the comrades of the North bore."

They had managed to escape the Confederate soldiers still scouring the woods for these Southern Unionists.

The following was their exact words: "But the question is, what are we to do? We did not, nor do we now, want to take up arms against our neighbors in our own state. We desire to be let alone that we may remain neutral. If the Confederacy continues to treat our county as a part of it, and attempts to force our citizens to serve in the Confederate Army, as we hear threats that indicate it will, then in that case, neutrality will cease in Winston County. The people in Winston County rather than be forced to fight for the perpetuation of slavery in the Confederate Army will abandon neutrality, join the Union Army and fight for the Union. It looks, now, like that is what is going to take place. "

Understandably, many of those hiding in the hills looked forward to a Federal invasion. In July 1862, Unionists began arriving in small groups into the camp of the 51st Indiana Regiment in Decatur, Alabama. The regiment's commander, Col. Abel D. Streight was moved by these "brave mountaineers" who requested protection and a chance to fight the Confederacy. He had the following to say about them.

"I wish to say a word in relation to the condition of these people. They are mostly poor, though many of them are, or rather were, in comfortable circumstances. They outnumber nearly 3 to 1 the secessionists in portions of Morgan, Blount, Winston, Marion, Walker, Fayette, and Jefferson Counties; but situated as they are, surrounded by a most relentless foe, mostly unarmed and destitute of ammunition, they are persecuted in every conceivable way, yet up to this time most of them have kept out of the way sufficiently to avoid being dragged off by the gangs that infest the country for the purpose of plunder and enforcing the provisions of the rebel conscription act. Their horses and cattle are driven off in vast numbers. Every public road is patrolled by guerrilla bands, and the Union men have been compelled to seek protection in the fastnesses of the mountainous wilderness. They cannot hold out much longer. This state of things has so disturbed them that but very little attention has been paid to farming; consequently many of them are not destitute of food of their own and are living off their more fortunate neighbors. Such examples of patriotism as these people have set are worthy of being followed. One old lady, Mrs. Anna Campbell, volunteered to ride 35 miles and return, making 70 miles, with about 30 recruits, within 36 hours. When it is taken into consideration that these people were all hid to avoid being taken by the rebels and that the country is but sparsely settled, this case is without a parallel in American history.

Surrounded by a most relentless foe, mostly unarmed and destitute of ammunition, they are persecuted in every conceivable way yet up to this time most of them have kept out of the way sufficiently to avoid being dragged off by the gangs that infest the country for the purpose of plunder and enforcing the provisions of the rebel conscription act. Their horses and cattle are driven off in vast numbers. Every public road is patrolled by guerilla bands, and the Union men have been compelled to seek protection in the fastnesses of the mountainous wilderness...When it is taken into consideration that these people were all hid to avoid being taken by the rebels...this case is without a parallel in American history - I have never witnessed such an outpouring of devoted and determined patriotism among any other people....Never did people stand in greater need of protection. They have battled manfully against the most unscrupulous foe that civilized warfare has ever witnessed. They have been shut off from all communication with anybody but their enemies for a year and a half, and yet THEY STAND FIRM AND TRUE. If such is not to be rewarded, if such citizens are not to receive protection, then their case is deplorable indeed."

In a letter dated July 16, 1862, from Col. James B. Fry in camp near Mooresville, Alabama, he stated: "SIR: While in command at Decatur there were several small parties of loyal Alabamians who came into our lines begging me to give them protection and a chance to defend the flag of our country. The tale of suffering and misery as told by each as they arrived was in itself a lamentable history of the deplorable condition of the Union people of the South. Notwithstanding the oft-repeated assertion that there was a strong Union sentiment in portions of the cotton States, I had long since given up all hopes of finding the people entertaining it; hence I was at first incredulous as to what they said and even suspicious that they were spies belonging to the enemy, but as their numbers increased, each corroborating the story of the other, I at last became convinced that the matter was worthy of notice.

About this time (10th instant) I was informed by a courier that there was a party of about 40 men some 5 or 6 miles toward the mountain trying to come to us and about the same number of the enemy's cavalry were between them and Decatur trying to intercept and capture them. As my orders were to defend the town only I did not feel at liberty to send out assistance to the Union men without further orders, and there being no telegraphic communication with you I at once informed General Buell by telegraph of the circumstances, whereupon I received the following reply:

"Send out what force you deem sufficient to assist the Union men in and drive off the rebel cavalry, and see that they are not playing a trick to draw you out by these reports."

Col. Streight wrote the following letter: "SIR: I have the honor to report to you that the party of Alabama volunteers has just arrived and 40 of them have been mustered into the service of the United States. Their accounts of the hardships endured are sufficient to enlist the sympathies of the hardest heart. They report that there are several hundred who would come but for the danger of passing from the foot of the mountains here, some 25 miles distant......"

These men truly embodied everything that loyalty and patriotism were all about!

Not only were these loyal Americans driven from their homes, forced to hide in the deep gorges, coves and caves of the mountains, being pursued by their angry neighbors who were determined to force them to enlist in the Confederate army or shoot them to keep them from joining the Union army, they were now, not being taken seriously by the very people they wanted to serve! Col. Streight was finally given permission to go after them but the mission was not without incident.

Sarah Talks About the War

In memory of me, live to the fullest....

I live close to the O'Mary Cemetery and intend to be buried there. I worried constantly about my children, brothers, uncles and cousins fighting in this war. The following are stories of my husband and children in the war.

When talk of the Civil War broke out in northwest Alabama, approximately 2500 men in the area had one thing in common - they were totally against secession. While they did not want to fight against their southern neighbors, they certainly did not intend to fire on the "Old Flag" of their country.

Many of the anti-secessionists hid out in the hills and caves of north Alabama, wishing to remain neutral. The caves and deep gorges of Winston County provided a natural sanctuary for these men. When this attempt failed, these men chose to remain loyal to their country and the result of their choice was the First Alabama Cavalry, USA, which was formed in 1862. One of these men stated: "I have slept in mountains, in caves and caverns till I am become musty; my health and manhood are failing me, I will stay here no longer till I am enabled to dwell in quiet at home, I am going tomorrow to the Union army."

Brigadier General, Gideon J. Pillow reported in September, 1862, that at least ten thousand, including some who had deserted from the Confederate Army, were hiding out in the hills.

To make matters even worse on these brave, patriotic men, who were begging for protection and a chance to defend their flag and their country, Colonel Streight was skeptical when he first heard of them wanting to join the Union, he was afraid it was some kind of ploy by the Confederacy to infiltrate the Union. He sent out about fifty men to bring them in so he could question them and see what was really going on.

In talking about the men from northwest Alabama who wanted to fight for their country, Colonel Streight, calling them "Alabama Yankees", praised them most highly, stating: "The tale of suffering and misery as told by each as they arrived was in itself a lamentable history of the deplorable position of the Union people of the South."

51

He went on to say: "When it is taken into consideration that these people were all hid away to avoid being taken by the rebels, and that the country is but sparsely settled, this case is without a parallel in American History.....I have never witnessed such an outpouring of devoted and determined patriotism among any other people; and I am now of the opinion that, if there could be a sufficient force in that portion of the country to protect these people, there could be at least two full regiments raised of as good and true men as ever defended the American Flag....Never did people stand in greater need of protection. They have battled manfully against the most unscrupulous foe that civilized warfare has ever witnessed. They have been shut out from all communication with anything but their enemies for a year and a half, and yet they stand firm and true. If such merit is not to be rewarded, if such citizens are not to receive protection, then is their case a deplorable one indeed.

The tale of suffering and misery, as told by each as they arrived, was in itself a lamentable history of the deplorable position of the Union people of the South." He praised their courage in the face of the great odds, and wrote that their "examples of patriotism....are worthy of being followed."

The *New York Times* wrote, "Not for fifty-years has such a spectacle been seen, as the glorious uprising of American Loyalty which greeted the news that open war had been commenced upon the Constitution Government of the United States....millions of free men rally with exulting hearts, around our country's standard."

One Northerner wrote, "The Yankees self respect, their intelligence and conservative love, order, government and laws, all their instinctive love of liberty and their sense of responsibility for the safety of the blessings of freedom and popular government were stirred to their very depth."

General William Tecumseh Sherman, called "Uncle Billy" by his soldiers, knowing the value of his Alabama Troops as soldiers and symbols of the loyal South, honored the First Alabama by his selecting it to be his escort on the march from Atlanta to the sea. He remarked, "I do not believe a body of men ever existed who were inspired by nobler impulses or a holier cause than they who compose this army."

Four of the men in the 1st Alabama Cavalry USV included my husband, Andrew Ferrier McWhirter and three of our sons, Thomas Andrew, George Washington, and Andrew Jackson McWhirter;

three of my brothers; a son-in-law; and numerous other relatives. When their attempt to remain neutral was denied them, Andrew and his sons saddled their horses and rode over one hundred miles through the dense woods, dodging the Confederate Soldiers, to Huntsville, Alabama to enlist in the Union army on July 24, 1862. My brothers and other relatives enlisted in January, 1863.

On September 8, 1862, the 1st Alabama Cavalry, USA was ordered to report "without delay" to Nashville and was assigned to the Army of the Tennessee, Major General Ulysses S. Grant Commanding. After arriving in Nashville, there was an outbreak of measles and on October 8, 1862, our son, George Washington McWhirter died from this disease in Army Hospital #14. On October 23, 1862, just over two weeks later my husband Andrew Ferrier McWhirter also succumbed to this disease in the same hospital. Army Hospital #14 was in fact the Nashville Female Academy which was held by the Union Army from 1862 until 1865. It was also used as headquarters for the provost marshal and as a shelter for refugees.

My brother, Josiah Harper enlisted in Co. B, 1st Alabama Cavalry, USA January 20, 1863 in Glendale, MS and mustered in January 22, 1863 at Corinth, MS. He was serving as a scout February 8, 1863 and mustered out January 22, 1864. He was said to have been a "Home Guard" and made shoes for the army. On a return visit to his home, he was captured and killed by the Confederate Home Guard. He left a wife and four children. My brother, Thomas Wade Harper, enlisted in the 43rd Alabama Infantry, Co. H, CSA, and was killed in the Battle of Knoxville and is buried in Bethel Cemetery in Knoxville, Tennessee.

Andrew and our son, George, were buried in the Nashville City Cemetery, later being disinterred and reinterred in the Nashville National Cemetery.

Thomas Andrew McWhirter and his brother, Andrew Jackson McWhirter were forced to continue the war without their father and brother. They were involved in many battles and were with General William Tecumseh Sherman on his famous "March to the Sea". They survived the Civil War, although Thomas was captured three

53

times and held POW by the enemy but escaped twice and walked back to Alabama, and was paroled once or twice. He was mustered out in Nashville, Tennessee on July 19 1865. He returned to his home in Marion County, Alabama to face the hostilities of his southern neighbors, but he lived to marry and raise a large family.

My husband, Andrew Ferrier McWhirter stated his ancestors came to this country looking for a place to worship as they pleased and America embraced them and allowed them to do that. He also said his forefathers fought too long and suffered too much while fighting for this country during the American Revolution and there was no way he could turn his back on this same country and he absolutely refused to fire on "Old Glory", the Flag of his forefathers. On July 24, 1862, when Andrew and three of our sons, Thomas A., George W. and Andrew Jackson McWhirter enlisted in the 1st Alabama Cavalry, USV, my heart was broken. To me, Andrew Jackson was still a baby because he was barely 15 years old and it broke my heart to see him go off to war.

They firmly believed wholeheartedly in the cause for which they were about to fight, and possibly die, and were the embodiment of the words of Thomas Jefferson:
"When in the Course of human events it becomes necessary for one people to dissolve the political bands which have connected them with another and to assume among the powers of the earth, the separate and equal station to which the Laws of Nature and of Nature's God entitle them, a decent respect to the opinions of mankind requires that they should declare the causes which impel them to the separation."

Not only did my husband and three of our sons join the 1st Alabama Cavalry, USV, three of my brothers also joined the same Union Regiment, but for some reason, two of my brothers, James W. and Thomas Wade Harper, chose to fight for the Confederacy. James W. enlisted in Company G of the 1st Cavalry, CSA while Thomas W. served in Company H of the 43rd Alabama Infantry, CSA so I had brothers fighting against brothers and sons fighting against their uncles. Truly brother against brother. I couldn't believe my brothers were that divided.

It was cool and rainy one day and I knew I had to keep my mind occupied. I decided to build a fire in the fireplace to knock the chill off the house, and after it was going good I picked up my Bible and started to read. Then I said a prayer for my family and other families around me. After that, I felt a little better so I gathered my yarn and decided to work on the sweaters I had started knitting for the boys. I had been knitting about 30 minutes when my mind kept wondering back to the days I was told about my precious eighteen-year old son, George, dying and then just two weeks later, I was told about my dearly beloved husband, Andrew, dying. All this on top of losing my young son, Robert, when he was only in his teens was weighing heavy on my mind, and it was difficult to keep my mind on my knitting.

My heart was still broken and I cried until my apron was wet with tears and I couldn't cry anymore. After I dried my tears, I immediately began thinking of our wagon train journey from Tennessee and how happy we had been on the trip and while building our house. I remembered the day Andrew found out I was pregnant for the first time and how excited he was. Our past twenty-one years together flashed through my mind and the tears began again.

I thought I absolutely could not go on living without Andrew, but God's grace was with me and He gave me the inner strength to pick up the pieces and get on with my life, which is what Andrew would have wanted me to do. My inner voice keeps telling me to go on resisting the factions no matter how difficult things become, and deal with what comes. I was learning a little something about how strong people can really be when they have to. I had the other children to think about and wondered how I was going to raise and feed them alone, but knew God would provide. I longed for something better for my children, a meaning in a more humane existence.

I couldn't get Andrew out of my mind, every time I tried to think of something else, he would be right back in my mind thinking of the good, although some difficult, times during our married life. He had given me seven wonderful children and I knew I should consider myself fortunate and be thankful for what I had rather than crying about what I had lost.

I hate to go to bed at night because when I do, I have this lonesome feeling, longing to be next to Andrew and have his loving arms around me. Even up until he left, Andrew always slept with his arm around me and when he had to turn over, I turned over and put my arm around him. I really missed that, and it hurts to know I won't ever experience his arms around me again. There was too much time at night in that lonesome bed to dwell on my husband and the wonderful life we had. Also, it breaks my heart to think about my

55

brothers fighting against some of my other brothers and also fighting against my sons. I just don't think if they came up against each other in a battle, knowing it was them, they could really fire on their kin but as bitter as things were, I could not be sure.

Confederate Home Guard Molest Union Wives and Widows

Yet know the love and life we shared remain….

One day not long after Andrew and the three oldest boys went to hide out in the "Rock House" from the Confederate Home Guard, I went out to the well to get a bucket of water and just as I heard the bucket hit the water I heard horses riding fast through the woods toward the house. Frightened, I quickly tied the rope the bucket was on, to the side of the well and started running toward the house where the children were but several men on horses rushed in between me and the door. It was Ham Carpenter, Al Gipson and their dreaded gang of Confederate Home Guard wanting to know where Andrew and the boys were. I told them they had gone to town, but they didn't believe me. They went rushing in the house looking for them and terrorizing the children. I heard the children screaming and ran around the horses and into the house so afraid they would do something to Mary Caroline. As I entered the door, they were unnecessarily slinging things around and turning furniture over. I had been knitting some socks for Andrew and the boys and had a pair almost finished in a basket by my chair. One of the men spotted it, picked it up and saw what I was knitting. He said, "I guess you are knitting these to keep the damned old Tories' feet warm while they try to fight in the Northern Army." Just then he grabbed the yarn, yanked the needles out and proceeded to unravel the sock. I was too angry to be frightened. Carpenter yelled at him to come on and they left, assuring me they would be back, and they would find them where ever they were and force them to join the Confederacy. As they left, they rode through the garden trampling a lot of the vegetables and demolishing some of my tomato plants.

The Confederate Home Guard was a group of men too old to fight in the war, or exempt for other reasons, and roamed the country side terrorizing families of Union soldiers. There were also bands of vigilantes calling themselves "home guard" and they were as bad, if not worse then the Confederate Home Guard. The atrocities they committed on the Unionist were unbelievable. I gave them time to get out of sight and told Hamp to go to the well and get the water while I tried to salvage what I could in the garden. As I was trying to straighten up some tomato plants, I heard screams coming through the woods from the Head's house and I knew they were doing the same thing to Ellen as they did to us because her husband, William, had gone with Andrew and the boys and she was there alone with

57

her two boys. The gang ransacked her house and garden, just as they did mine. She had actually hid her oldest son, James, because he was 19 and she knew they would force him to join up with them. Fortunately they didn't find him. She told them the children had gone to town with their father.

This gang went from house to house terrorizing all of the women and children because they knew most of the men were all hiding from them. George and Sarah Hallmark lived four houses from us and although George was almost sixty years old and not able to fight in this war, he had four boys who were old enough and were anxious to fight for the Union. Ham and his bunch knew that and were determined the Hallmarks would join the Confederacy and fight for the South. All four Hallmark boys were hiding in the cave where Andrew and the boys were. When the Home Guard got to the Hallmark house, they really made a mess and one of them got into a scuffle with George. They would later come back on a killing spree and left a trail of blood all over northwest Alabama, but more on that later.

On July 24, 1862, ten days after Sheats made his speech, the men who refused to take up arms against the country they loved, packed a few items, mounted their horses and made their way through the woods filled with Confederate soldiers, to the Union Lines in Huntsville to join in a war that should never have happened. This included my husband, Andrew Ferrier McWhirter, our sons, Thomas Andrew, George Washington, and Jackson McWhirter. It also included many of the other Union sympathizers who were able to escape the Confederates at the Rock House. After traveling many miles from Marion County, Alabama to Huntsville, in Madison County, Alabama, they joined Company K of the 1st AL Cavalry, USV. My brother, Tennessee Polk Harper had already joined this regiment after he and his brothers had a disagreement over which side they were going to join. He rode off to Limestone County, Alabama where he enlisted in Company K of the 1st Alabama Cavalry, USV on June 26th 1862. I kept thinking about my son, Jackson McWhirter, just barely 15 years old going off to war and it just broke my heart to think about him being in battle and about the vindictive neighbors coming up against him and firing on him. I knew Thomas would try to protect him as long as he could, but I also had sense enough to know Thomas wouldn't be right there by him all through the war. Andrew and I pleaded with him not to go but he was dead-set on going to fight for his country, and said if he couldn't go with them, he would follow alone. We both knew he would, and we did not want him traveling all that way by himself for fear he would get caught by the Confederate Home Guard and we knew what they would do to him. Andrew gave in and told him come on and go with them, hoping they would not take him because of his age. I was devastated and cried the rest of the day and all night. About 4 AM, the sweet peace of slumber overtook my sobs and racked my body, but then I was awakened at 6:00 AM by my baby girl, Mary Caroline, tugging at my nightgown. I sat up, looked in her eyes, and she was also tugging at my heart-strings. She had a smile and face like an angel, and I thought about how proud Andrew was to have a daughter when she was born and how he would carry her all over town to show her off to everyone. Just the thought of her father and brothers not coming home made me sick at my stomach. I wanted to cry again but not in front of her as she was only seven years old and did not understand what all was going on. Besides my precious little girl, I had two other sons, William Hamilton "Hamp", age 10, and John Madison, age 4.

While I was preparing breakfast for the children, I decided I had to turn all this madness about the war over to God and try to quit worrying about it so I could focus on the young children still at home and what all I had to do to protect and feed them. However, while I was cooking and trying to pray, they kept asking questions about their father and brothers; where had they gone, when would they be back, what were they doing, why could they not come home, and many other questions. I really did not have the answers to give children that age to where they would understand what was going on, but I did the best I could. I talked to Hamp separately, about the war and what all was going on, because he was older and I thought he might understand, and he did seem to.

After we ate breakfast I started to wash the dishes but decided I would read a passage from the Bible to the children. I remembered Matthew 24 where Jesus said, "Take heed that no man deceive you. For many shall come in my name saying I am Christ and shall deceive many. And you will hear of wars and rumors of wars: see that ye be not troubled for all of these things must come to pass, but the end is not yet." I went ahead and tried to explain this to them the best I could, that God tells us not to be troubled by wars and rumors of wars, but down deep in my heart, I just could not help but worry about my husband, sons and brothers fighting in this agonizing war, especially some of my brothers on different sides, fighting each other.

59

I would never have dreamed of anything as dreadful as what was going on about this war. It had thousands of families torn apart and fighting against their own sons, brothers, and other relatives. I was fortunate in that most all of my neighbors felt the same way my people did and the ones who were able, fought for the Union.

I kept hoping and praying someone would stop Carpenter and Gipson and their gang because they didn't think a thing about raping and molesting the Union wives and especially widows, and I know this from first hand knowledge but don't want to think or talk about it right now, may not talk about it any further. Several of my friends and neighbors also had first hand knowledge of this. They were absolutely ruthless! They knew John D. Mitchell was a Union sympathizer and in the Union army so they terrorized his wife, drove her out of the house in the snow with no coat or any protection and she died from exposure. I would hear much later that John Mitchell heard what happened, came home from the Union Army, hunted Carpenter down like a dog, captured him, hung him upside down from a tree and built a fire under him. Not only did they kill Carpenter, but they found Al Gipson and killed him, too. This is just a sample of how bad things were in our area during the Civil War, and don't think the women who had been left alone with small children, weren't frightened, they were terrified.

I tried to keep busy with the other children to keep my mind off of the war but it was all around me, and that was all anyone talked about. I was glad it was warm weather so I could keep busy during the day with the garden, canning, cooking, caring for the children, and at night after they went to bed, I would work on a quilt but it was difficult sewing those little stitches at night by candlelight, so I mostly knitted or read my Bible. For some reason, unknown to us, my brothers, Thomas Wade Harper and James W. Harper, had disavowed the Union and joined the Confederate Army. This had Papa so upset I thought he was going to be sick. They were much too old for Papa to take his paddle to like he normally would, but he certainly gave them a good talking to. However, it did not help because Thomas went off and joined the 43rd Alabama Infantry in the CSA, while James joined the 1st Alabama Cavalry, CSA, (There was a 1st AL Regiment in both the Union and CSA) which was confusing to a lot of people. We were truly a family of "divided allegiance", and it made things so much more tragic and worrisome.

Papa and Momma had gotten word that my brother, Thomas Wade Harper, the one who ventured off to join Company H of the 43rd

Alabama Infantry, CSA, had been killed. Papa was distraught, and of course so was I, but felt as though I had to console him as much as possible and I tried not to let him see how upset I was. Thomas had first been shipped to Mobile and then to Knoxville, where he was killed about five months after he had enlisted. Actually the government wasn't clear as to how he died, just that he was dead. Several months later we heard he was killed during the Battle of Knoxville, but that didn't take place until November 29, 1863, and we had word he was killed or died September 15, 1862. He had just married a lovely young lady, Mary Elizabeth Lane, but they didn't have any children. Thomas Wade Harper is buried at Bethel Cemetery in Knoxville, Tennessee. His widow and her family left for Texas about 1869 where she remarried John Boren in 1871. She was the daughter of John Madison Lane and Phoebe Ann Walden.

There is a monument at Bethel Cemetery in Knoxville, Tennessee dedicated to Union and Confederate Soldiers who were killed or died in Knoxville during the Civil War. Names of deceased Union soldiers were engraved on one side while names of Confederate soldiers were engraved on the other. (See picture in back of book.)

The following is the only letter I received from Thomas Wade after he joined up with the 43rd Alabama, CSA:

Dear Sis,
We are camped in Cleveland, Tennessee and are on the way to Knoxville. Don't have any idea how long we will be here but hopefully not long because the war is bad up here and we have been skirmishing with the Yankees all the way. Besides all the killing, it has rained for a week and we had a terrible thunderstorm this afternoon. Someone said John Taylor was killed by lightening while he was sitting by the fireplace. I thought that was mighty fearful, a feller sitting by his fireplace minding his own business, out of the weather when he was struck and killed by lightening. However, I guess when God wants us He will take us no matter where we are or what we are doing.

Sis, I know I haven't been the best brother in the world and you aren't happy with me choosing the opposite side as your family, but I was conscripted into service early on and have had to stick with it. I have wondered what I would do if we started firing on the Yankees and I saw my brothers or one of your sons on the other side firing at us. It surely would pain me terribly if I happened to kill one of them, and I never would get over it. So far I have been in the back when we

61

skirmished with the Yankees and didn't have to fire, and we wound up retreating. I want you to know if I make it through the war; I will try to be a better brother to you and a better son to Papa.

We don't have all the rations we need but we were able to get some buttermilk at a nearby house last night, and it was lip-smacking good. There are too many Yankees around here to suit me, and I heard there were a lot of them on the other side of the river from Chattanooga. We even saw the light from their camp fires, last night.

Word gets around pretty fast up here and someone said there was a hanging in town the other day. Apparently Neal Brown was hung for killing Andy Johnson but I never could get the particulars about what happened, why he killed him, or anything else about it. A lot of people skedaddled out of town after the hanging.

Several of us went to Cohutta Springs, a well-known watering hole a few miles southwest of Cleveland, to get water this morning. We also picked up some corn on the way back and one of the troops killed a wild hog. Four of the troops took one of its legs, each, and threw it over in the wagon. They probably plan on eating it tonight or tomorrow.

Several of the men in camp have typhoid fever and a few of them have whooping cough. There is also a lot of dysentery in camp, but so far I have been quite healthy and am thankful for that.

The rain finally stopped and we had a pretty moonshiney night, last night. The sun is out and some of the boys have mentioned going to Cohutta Springs to wash some things, and themselves. There is a good place up there to wash and it is secluded. I think I will go with them as there is not much going on around camp. Then we stopped at that same cornfield and split some corn shucks to fill some pillows because there weren't enough pillows to go around for all the soldiers. There is a well-known fortune teller in town, Mrs. Traynor, and some of the men went over to get their fortunes told. They tried to get me to go with them but I don't believe in them and even if I did, I wouldn't want to know what is ahead of me. Some of the others went for a canoe ride and asked me to go along but I have had a headache all day and decided to stay in camp.

While we were on the way back from Cohutta Springs, we saw some muscadines and stopped to pick them. They weren't good and ripe but they tasted pretty good. The whole time I was picking them, I thought about Momma's Muscadine jelly, it was so good and I always enjoyed buttering up her wonderful biscuits and slathering a lot of her muscadine jelly on them. While we were picking them, I noticed a Chestnut tree on back in the woods and we were able to pick up a lot of chestnuts.

Well, we packed up and headed for Knoxville but it has been a journey fraught with problems. The trains didn't get here on time and we started on foot. When the trains did get here, they didn't have enough engine-power to get us over the mountain grades under this load, forcing us to dismount and walk alongside the cars in the steeper sections. The engineers didn't even have enough wood for fuel, and the men had to stop and take down the fences in the way to continue. It took twice as long or more for us to get there and it's raining again, such a dark, lonesome, rainy night. I'm going to close before I start crying thinking about home. Please forgive me for our differences and pray for all of us. Love, Thomas

It was about the middle of September and my gardening chores were winding down. I still had to dig the potatoes and make sure they, along with the other root crops, were protected in the cellar for winter. Also, the apples hadn't been picked but the children could help with that. Andrew had planted a little apple orchard, which consisted of about seven or eight apple trees. I had gotten to the point I was afraid for the children to even go outside with Carpenter and his gang still roaming through the woods, pillaging, murdering and anything else they took a notion to do. I knew I couldn't keep them locked up in the house all the time because they needed to be outside in the fresh air, but the gang had been known to even rape children of the Union soldiers. That was a horrifying thought!

I was on my way to the house with some vegetables to cook for supper when I looked up and saw Papa riding across the yard. One look at his face and I could tell he had been crying. I dropped my basket of vegetables and ran to him as fast as I could. I asked what was wrong and he said my brother, Thomas Wade, had died September 15, 1862 in Knoxville, Tennessee while fighting for the 43rd Alabama Infantry Confederacy. I hadn't seen Papa cry in a long time and seeing him like that hurt me almost as much as the fact that my brother had been killed. I started asking Papa questions about Thomas Wade's death but he was too upset to talk about it, he just hung his head, said he just wanted to tell me and he would talk to me later. He turned, got back on his horse and rode off. In the midst of everything else that was happening, we had a letter from a relative in

Texas saying my brother, George W., who supposedly went to Texas to avoid all this mess, and shoed horses for the Union Army. We don't know if he joined ever joined the Union or Confederate Army but he came back to Alabama.

This was the first and only letter I received from Thomas Wade after he left home for the war, and I was actually surprised to get this one because he knew how I felt about the side he chose, but he was my brother and I still loved him, just didn't understand him.

Sunday came and I missed going to church. Our church suspended services during the Civil War because people were afraid to get out of their houses, and churches were a prime target of the Confederate Home Guard because they could find so many people in one place to harass and intimidate. I also hated for the children to be away from church so long but I kept reading the Bible to them and making sure they said their prayers at night. They prayed diligently for their brothers and uncles and I thought Andrew would be so very proud of them.

I will jump ahead and tell you about our wonderful neighbor, George Hallmark, who lived four houses through the woods from us. Anytime anyone needed anything, George was there to help them. Our son, Thomas Andrew McWhirter, was sweet on George's daughter, Mary Jane, and they married not long after the war was over. One day in 1863, I was outside washing clothes when I heard screaming coming from through the woods toward the Hallmark home. However, I couldn't tell if it was at their house or where, but where ever it was, I could tell something bad was happening and I had a feeling it was Ham Carpenter and his gang of thugs so I gathered the children, took them in the house and bolted the door, just waiting for them to show up. I knew the bolt on the door wouldn't keep them out if they really wanted to come in and I was really frightened, but I tried not to let on to the children. They kept asking what was happening, where the screams were coming from, and why they had to come inside. All I could think of to tell them was that it sounded like trouble and I didn't want them outside in case anyone came by. I told the boys to go up to their bedroom in the loft and take Mary Caroline with them.

The guerilla warfare in the area was so bad that people were afraid to be outside. Ham Carpenter and Al Gipson were in charge of raising an army of Confederate soldiers in Marion and Fayette Counties and they didn't mind killing anyone who refused to join or that he knew was a Unionist. They delighted in abusing, molesting and harassing the Union families, and especially the wives and widows of known Unionists. I worried about them constantly because I knew what they were capable of doing. I would not let the children go outside unless I was out there and then we tried to stay close to the house in case we heard them coming.

I picked up my knitting thinking that might occupy my troubled mind for a few minutes but I could not remember the stitches I was supposed to take, and my hands were shaking so I would not have been able to knit, anyway. Just as I put my knitting down I heard someone running through the woods screaming something I couldn't understand. I jumped up and looked out the window and it was George and Sallie Hallmark's daughter, Mary Jane, Thomas's girlfriend. I looked all around and didn't see anyone else so opened the door and she ran in crying so hard she couldn't talk. I pulled her to me, put my arms around her and tried to console her but it was a few minutes before she could even tell me what had happened. Finally she calmed down enough to tell me that Ham Carpenter and his gang came to the house demanding her father's money. Her sister, Annie, was upstairs and started down the steps to see what was going on. Just as she got half-way down, Carpenter shot and killed her, and her lifeless body tumbled to the bottom of the stairs to the floor. Then they beat George unmercifully. Mary Jane said she didn't know if he was still alive or not. I kept trying to console Mary Jane and made her stay at the house because I was afraid if she went back home, they might still be out there and do something to her. I wanted to get word to Papa, who lived on the opposite side of me, but did not want to leave Mary Jane and the children there alone. I wanted Papa to go see about George Hallmark but it was just too dangerous for any of us to get out. All of the people in that area were Unionists.

George survived but he was so bitter about them killing his daughter that he vowed revenge. He met up with Carpenter and his vigilantes several months later and they were involved in a gunfight. Although George Hallmark was killed, he was able to kill two or three of the thugs who had been causing so much trouble in northwest Alabama.

It's difficult for anyone, who did not live through the war, to even conceive just how brutal it was. Ham Carpenter and his gang of Confederate Home Guard delighted in killing men even if he just thought they were Union sympathizers. They even killed Tom Pink Curtis, the Probate Judge because they thought he was siding with the Union. Not only was all of the killing going on, the businesses that were owned by Confederate sympathizers wouldn't wait on or service anyone they thought had any ties to the Union. The people who sided with the Confederacy and owned grist mills wouldn't grind corn for the Union people. Of course Papa had a grist mill so that didn't affect us. The worst thing I thought they did, besides the killing and harassment, was forcing the Union people out of the homes they rented from people siding with the Confederacy. They would evict them and they could only rent from the Unionists who happened to have a house for rent. Most of the time, they would move in with other family members.

My husband and three sons rode to Huntsville to join the Union Army. July 24, 1862, had brought many of the Union sympathizers from northwest Alabama into Huntsville, where the Union had taken over, and they asked for permission to join the army. They were tired of being bullied by the Confederate Home Guard. When they got there, they found out there had not been enough provisions for that many enlistments from citizens of the area, but Union officers seeing the enthusiasm of so many of them asked for permission to enroll them. This was granted by Maj. Gen. Buell, Army of the Ohio. What Maj. Buell didn't know, or maybe he didn't care was, there were not enough horses to carry all of these new recruits, and not only that, there were not enough handguns, rifles or ammunition to equip the new soldiers. That presented the Union with a complete new problem, but they were able to work through it because they could tell these men were sincere, loved their country, and wanted to help fight for it.

They decided that due to the mountainous terrain they would be traversing, that mules might be better and there were more of them available than there were horses. The mules would be more sure-footed, they thought. However, this would turn out to be a very unfortunate decision. Not only were the mules that were furnished to the soldiers stubborn, they were cranky and many had not been shod. On top of all that, the majority of them had not been broken and they did not have enough of them to go around. Thomas said when they complained about this they were told they did not want to use sound animals in case they fell in the hands of the Confederates. I absolutely could not believe what I read. It sounded to me like the Union was more worried about losing their broken-down mules to the Confederates than they were having good horses that would outrun the enemy. Someone stated they had nine-hundred broken

66

down mules, which had previously been condemned and pronounced unfit for service. Colonel Streight himself reported later:

"I then for the first time discovered that the mules were nothing but poor, wild, and unbroken colts, many of them but two years old, and that a large number of them had the horse distemper, some 40 or 50 of the lot were too near dead to travel, and had to be left at the landing; 10 or 12 died before we started and such of them as could be rode at all were so wild and unmanageable that it took us all that day and a part of the next to catch and break them before we could move out across the country...."

I was glad we had three horses for Andrew, Thomas, and Jackson, but George Washington rode with Andrew and I suppose he took Andrew's horse after he died, but then George died about two weeks later and I don't know what happened to his horse. Andrew knew I would have to have a horse to plow the garden and go to town when we needed to so they left me one.

Most of the men who rode into Huntsville had taken their own personal guns for fear of confronting the enemy on the way, so they told them they would use their own horses and guns. Still this wasn't enough because some of the men rode double and not all had guns. It would take several days for the blacksmiths to get the mules shod and he estimated about one-third of them were worn out.

This just shows how surprised and unprepared the Union Army was, when they arrived in Alabama that so many of the southern men wanted to join the Union. They just assumed most of the men in the South would want to fight against them in the confederacy so they were totally unprepared to furnish enough rations, guns, ammunition and horses to all of these men.

Col. Abel D. Streight was the Commander of the 51st Indiana Infantry Regiment, which played a large roll in the war. He was greatly impressed by the volunteers who showed up and learned from them that there were many other Union sympathizers a ways south of there. I had a letter from Jackson, and he was talking about this raid:

"Dearest Mother, I never dreamed when I joined up with Papa and my brothers what all of us would be exposed to and be expected to do. Of course I knew things were bad but had no idea I would be involved in what we just went through with our regiment having to

67

fight Nathan Bedford Forrest and his gang of hoodlums. They chased us all over Alabama and we were so outnumbered we didn't have a chance from the beginning.

Most of us in the 1st Alabama Cavalry US Volunteers played a dual role in the raid that was conducted by Union Colonel Abel D. Streight in April 1863. Our mission was to cut the Confederate railroad that ran between Atlanta and Chattanooga, supplying General Braxton Bragg's army located in Tennessee.

The raid was a disaster from the very beginning. In Tennessee, Confederate cavalry legend Nathan Bedford Forrest discovered us shortly after Dodge left the scene, and with four veteran regiments of cavalry, began his pursuit on all of us while we were poorly mounted. You may or may not know the Northern Army commanders had no idea when they came down here that there would be so many Alabama men who would want to join the Union Army. They just supposed we would all want to fight for the Confederacy. They had no where near enough clothes, shoes, rations, guns, ammunitions, or anything else we needed. The lack of good, broken horses hindered us greatly in this battle with Forrest.

Our scouts, including your brother, Uncle Josiah Houston Harper, were used as the rearguard and were under almost constant pressure from Forrest, and in spite of gallant conduct by all of us, exhaustion and lack of rations forced Streight to surrender to Forrest on May 3, 1863 near Cedar Bluff, Alabama.

During the week of the raid, we lost sixteen men killed, wounded, or missing. Captain David Smith, who was the leader of the Alabama companies in Streight's raid, was captured and taken Prisoner of War. (Captain David D. Smith was kept in Confederate prisons until his death from pneumonia in the US Officers Hospital in Annapolis, Maryland on April 18, 1865.)

Mother, please pray for us as I'm concerned for all of us but especially Uncle Josiah because the Rebels found out he is a scout and they are most definitely out to get the scouts, as well as our soldiers assigned to the secret service. These detestable Rebels would do anything to be able to kill us all. They are so angry that we sided with the Union rather than them.

I worry about you constantly, Mother, for fear of what some of the guerrillas roaming the country side might do to you and possibly

Mary Caroline. I think surely they wouldn't do anything to hurt a little girl as young as she is, but I wouldn't put anything past these barbarians. Please stay safe and give my love to Hamp, Mary Caroline and John. I hope to see y'all soon but don't count on it. Yours truly, Jackson"

The Execution of Alex J. Johnson

...Yet for us, the living, who remain, to mourn the loss, to feel the pain....

In June or July 1863, I received the following disturbing letter from my brother, Josiah Houston Harper, who was in Corinth, Mississippi:

"Dear Sis, I hope you and the children are alright. I pray those guerrillas roaming the countryside will leave you, Papa, Nancy Jane, and the children alone. I hear something nearly every day about how, the Rebel Home Guard have molested some Union women or beaten and/or murdered some Union man or men, just because we don't think like they do or believe the same as they do. I just don't understand. I am so homesick for Nancy Jane and the children and miss all of y'all so much. I worry constantly about Nancy and the children, but I'm not sorry I joined, because I wouldn't be able to live with myself if I had done nothing.

While I am on this subject, Sis, you need to be aware that some supposedly Union sympathizers have formed a "bandito association" for the double purpose of opposition to the Government and resistance to the laws, and for harassing, robbing and sometimes murdering the good and loyal citizens. I also hear they are riding daily in Marion and Walker Counties and north Fayette County. They are confiscating horses, arms, money, provisions, clothing, bed clothing, and any other usable property possessed by the good citizens along their route. They say they have hanged men by the neck until they were almost lifeless to learn where his valuables were stored. I have not heard who these men were but they are not any Unionists that we know or have anything to do with. I also understand that in addition to the "bandito association", there are several organized companies of, at least 100 men of deserters, conscripts and Unionists, led by scouts and members of the 1st Alabama Cavalry, operating in the hills. I'm just telling you what I heard and to let you know that you just need to be aware of them and be extremely careful.

This war is causing so much brutality, however, all of the brutality isn't just done by the Rebels, and I want to tell you what we were forced to witness here in Corinth last week.

Alex Johnson and William Brown, two of our 1st AL boys, although they were in another company, were talking while they were on

70

picket duty and they decided to just desert the army. Johnson wound up joining a band of guerrillas, but two or three weeks later, the Union Army caught up with him and brought him back to camp. He was tried by the military commission and found guilty of deserting the service of the United States and joining her armed enemies. He was sentenced to be court-martialed and executed. General Dodge sent a letter stating the Brigade Commanders would report their commands on the parade grounds east of Corinth to witness the execution of Alex J. Johnson, 1st Alabama Cavalry, USV. He stated the Staff Officers would assign the brigades their positions on the parade grounds as they arrived. You won't believe what happened next.

We were all standing there in the intense heat with the sun bearing down when they brought Johnson in. The band was marching and playing the dead march while four men of Company D, Johnson's Company, brought out a casket for him and the prisoner was following the casket. Well, sis, it was all I could do to hold the tears back. I was wondering what was going through his mind, if he was married and if he had any children. I couldn't help but feel sorry for him. They sat the casket down, placed Johnson on top of it in a sitting position, and then a solemn and impressive prayer was given by the chaplain. Johnson was blindfolded while the executioners took their position and the order was given by the Provost Marshall to fire, launching the prisoner into eternity. Then the Provost Marshall stated the following: May his ignominious death prove a warning to all those who might be tempted to do likewise. I knew then they were making an example out of poor ole Johnson just in case anyone else might be tempted to desert the Union Army and go to the other side, or just go home.

Well, Sis, I had no choice but to be there, but I certainly didn't have to witness one of my former fellow soldiers being murdered by the same army I was fighting for, so I just pulled my Kepi down to shade my eyes and closed them. I thought that was extreme punishment for a deserter but I certainly don't know what all he did while running with the guerrillas. It is my opinion there are too many men being killed by the enemy without us killing our own. However, our officers probably felt like he WAS the enemy. I didn't know Johnson very well but like I said, I couldn't help but feel sorry for him. Can you believe they even took a picture of him lying beside his coffin after they killed him? (See picture, in back of book, of Alex Johnson placed beside his casket after the execution, with his hat on top of casket.)

This is a part of the military service I had not seen and hope I don't ever have to see it again. However, after I started thinking about it, he could have caused us a lot of grief and harm because he possessed a knowledge of this place, it's situation and where we were at different times, and then he deserted, joined the enemy and could have easily led them here and killed many of us. I hope I can continue to just think about this rather than dwell on what they did to him.

I was told that none of the eight men who fired at Johnson knew which one actually killed him because of the way their guns had been loaded when they were not looking. Only one of their guns was loaded with real ammunition.

I'm going to sign off and try to get some sleep. I miss being able to talk to you about things like we used to talk about, and will be so glad when this dreaded war is over.
Love, Josiah"

Sarah Talks About Her Siblings

...Yet for us, the living, who remain
To mourn the loss, to feel the pain....

I thought a lot about the dreaded war and how it had torn, not only
our family, but so many other families, apart. I continuously worried
about my husband, sons, brothers and others off fighting in a war we
had absolutely nothing to do with and had tried to avoid. We had no
slaves and didn't believe in slavery even if we could have afforded
any of them. Only about 5% of the people in Marion County,
Alabama had any slaves. These Union men didn't want to fight
against their southern neighbors but they certainly weren't going to
fight against a country they loved...a country that embraced their
ancestors when they came here from Ireland to escape religious
persecution......a country that embraced them and allowed them to
worship as they pleased....a country their forefathers fought so hard
to defend during the Revolutionary War. They had their reasons for
fighting for the Union, but there are people who don't agree with
them. Then the day of reckoning came when the Confederates found
them in the "Rock House" and gave them a choice of joining the
Confederacy or be shot. Some joined the Confederacy just long
enough to escape and make their way to the Union lines and enlist in
the Union Army. They were given no choice but to stand up and
fight for what they believed was right. I couldn't understand why my
brothers, Thomas Wade and James Warren, went against everything
the rest of the family believed, and joined the Confederacy. This
concerned all of us very much, and Papa was extremely upset with
them. "It isn't right for brothers to be fighting against their own
brothers", Papa said, but there were a lot of families doing this and
they felt as strongly about fighting for the Confederacy as Andrew
and the others felt about fighting for the Union.

Then one day I was outside boiling corn to making hominy when
Papa and a Union Captain rode up. I knew then that my worst fears
were about to be realized as I could see a look on Papa's face that I
didn't like. He and the captain got off their horses and Papa came
over and hugged me. The Captain ducked his head and said he was
sorry to tell me that my son, George Washington, had died of
measles October 8, 1862, in Hospital #14 in Nashville, Tennessee. I
was heart-broken and that caused me to worry more, and realize
how possible it was that the same thing could happen to my husband
and other sons and brothers in the war, but I knew I had to remain
strong for the other children. I was too stunned to cry right then and

tried to act like it was just a dream and that I had been standing over the fire stirring the hominy too long and the heat had gotten to me. The captain left but Papa stayed with me for some time.

I didn't tell the children right then and Papa asked if I wanted him to tell them but I told him not to, that I would tell them later. I didn't cry until after I put them to bed and they went to sleep that night. It actually wasn't too difficult to hold the tears back because I was so stunned. I knew I had to finish the hominy and put it up and I just kept stirring and stirring looking out in the woods wondering when someone else would ride up telling me someone else dear to me had died or been killed. I was picturing my brothers in the Confederacy coming up against their brothers in the Union and briefly wondered what they would do and if they really would fire on their own brothers, but quickly put that thought out of my mind. Papa tried to get me to go inside and said he would finish the hominy but I refused. Looking back, I think I was in shock and have no idea how I finished the hominy and put it up. Papa told me later that he hauled several buckets of water from the creek for me to wash the hominy in but I didn't even remember it. I guess it was a good thing he stayed behind to help and oversee what I was doing because there is no telling what I would have done to the hominy.

It seemed like the rest of the day was forty-eight hours long, and I thought it would never get bed time for the children so I could cry for my son.

I didn't even want to think about my son, George, being dead in Nashville with no one to claim his body or bring him home for burial but it did cross my mind. I wished I had been there to hold my son's hand as he lay there dying, and I wondered if there was a kind nurse with him who tried to comfort him. I hoped there was because I was certain he didn't have an easy death. I knew who ever was with him, if anyone, wouldn't have given him the attention I would have had I been with him. I, again, quickly put those thoughts away and finished the hominy, washed it several times and put it up.

That night, I got the children ready for bed a little early and told them about their older brother. William Hamilton and Mary Caroline took it pretty hard but John Madison was only four-years old and didn't understand what was going on, he just kept asking when his daddy would be back home. Mary Caroline was only seven-years old and was at the age to be confused about death, but she didn't ask many questions. William Hamilton was ten-years old and while he could grasp the meaning of death, I don't think he fully understood that his older brother was dead and wouldn't be coming home. They were still asking questions about the war and what it was all about but I decided the less we talked about it, the better off we would all be. I always tried to answer their questions about the war which seemed to satisfy them at the time but it wouldn't be long until they would start asking more questions. Their little minds just couldn't grasp the horror of it all and why their father and older brothers couldn't come home.

I had already lost my son, Robert, to illness and now George. Two of my baby boys I carried for nine-months, gave birth to, nursed and raised, were now gone to be with God, and I was having difficulty not wondering just why this had to happen. I decided the only way to get this war off my mind was to get back outside the next morning and work as hard as I could and just keep busy.

The children weren't really large enough to help a lot with the plowing but together, we got it done and kept the farm up as well as we could because we knew our livelihood depended on our crops. I kept busy during the summer working the farm, tending the garden, canning, making jelly and preserves. I knew as bad as things were I would have to preserve everything we grew. We had to keep as much of the food hidden as we possibly could because the Confederate Home Guard would come by the houses of Union families and take whatever they could find for their army. One of my neighbors had just finished shelling 30 bushels of corn when they came by and took every kernel of it. She still had scars on her fingers and hands where they had bled because she shelled so much of the hard dried corn from the cobs. They wouldn't even leave one bushel for them to use. A lot of times they would even burn the crops of Union families and had been known to burn their houses and barns.

Most all of our men neighbors living around us had joined the Union Army so it left all of the women and children in such a vulnerable situation and subject to being abused by the Confederate Home Guard.

I prepared supper for the children but I couldn't eat much. I put them to bed and knitted an hour or so but just couldn't keep my mind on what I was doing. I blew out the candles and went to bed, and that is when the tears started pouring. I cried and cried and asked God why this tragic war had to happen. I prayed he would

75

take care of my Andrew, sons, brothers and other family members who were out fighting for what they believed was the right thing to do. I cried almost all night.

It didn't really matter how busy I kept myself, I couldn't get the war off my mind. I wondered what my sons and brothers were doing and how they were.

One day around the middle of November or earlier, it was a pretty nice day and I decided to wash some clothes. I had carried a couple of buckets of water from the creek and poured it in the wash pot but decided to go ahead and build a fire under the pot to be heating the water before I went back for more. I heard a horse and looked up to see the mail carrier go by in his little horse-drawn buggy, further from the house than he usually rides, and he didn't even look or wave like he usually did. He was a friend of ours and I wondered what was wrong with him but just thought maybe he was in a hurry and didn't have any mail for me. He was a little later than he normally comes through. I went ahead and filled up the pot with water and had begun washing when Papa rode up with that look on his face again. I knew before he got off his horse something was wrong and I wanted to run hide. As soon as I saw his frown and his mouth drawn up, I burst into tears and was sobbing hysterically even before he got to me. I knew someone else near and dear to me had died or been killed but just didn't know who.

The mail carrier had gone by Papa's and told him I had a letter from the government like the ones they send out when a soldier dies and Papa told him he would bring it to me, so the mail carrier gave it to Papa to bring to me. I didn't know it at the time, but Papa had told the mail carrier if there was ever a letter to me from the government, to give it to him and let him bring it because he didn't want me being alone if something happened to one of my children or my husband. He had always tried to protect me, and he knew how I was hurting. I didn't even look at him when he got off his horse. He walked slowly over to me, took the stick out of my hand, put it on the ground and hugged me. I was afraid to ask what was wrong. I knew within reason it was my husband or one of my children by the look on his face, but before I could say anything he told me he was so sorry but God had called my husband, Andrew, home with Him, and he would also be with George. Tears trickled down my face as I knelt in a small heap by an ancient oak tree and reflected on the turmoil of sorrow that filled my life. Papa stood there watching with a broken heart as I cried uncontrollably at the news of losing my wonderful husband. He stood over me letting me sob out my grief, knowing there was nothing he could do to console me.

The children saw me on my knees, took fright and came rushing out to see what was wrong. Papa told them to go back in the house and he would talk to them in a little while. Papa was so upset, he seldom used any bad words in front of me but he raised his voice and said "Damn this fighting, damn this war and all of the killing, damn the enemy, all of them!" He said, "Here, baby girl", put his hard-thewed arm across my shoulder and kept trying to console me. He began to tell me what happened but I didn't even want to know, it didn't make any difference to me what happened because all I could think about was the love of my life was gone, I would never see him again and my poor children would grow up without their loving father. The thought of sleeping alone in that bed Andrew and I shared for all these years was almost more than I could bear. I buried my face in my apron weeping, and just could not quit crying, which upset Papa even more. He lifted my almost limp frame as he wiped the tears from my red eyes and face.

This was the man I couldn't wait to marry, the man who was the father of my precious children and was so proud of them, and Papa was telling me he was dead. The man who built our first house along with the outhouse, smokehouse, root cellar and barn. He had worked so hard to build us a life and see that we had what we needed. The picture of us packing and getting ready for the wagon train trip to Alabama, and of me helping Andrew chink the house, flashed through my mind, and I had a gnawing pain in the pit of my stomach.

My heart was becoming more and more hardened toward war and the enemy which included some of my friends AND family. It had become extremely difficult for me to offer solace to these people when they lost a loved one in this war when they were actually part of the cause of me losing my son, husband and others. Papa had said that war had a way of taking the innocence from the people and the land, and he was right. I felt as though my life was over and thought for a few moments that I didn't even want to live any longer. All of our dreams we hoped and worked for were gone and buried with him and I couldn't imagine how I was going to live without him. Papa kept telling me he was there for me and that I had the children to think about. He said I was going to have to be both mother and father to them, and that made me cry harder. The same thoughts went through my mind as they did after George died. I wondered if someone was there holding his hand and trying to comfort him as he was dying, but I knew as many as they were tending to, there was no way they could pay any individual attention to any of the soldiers.

Finally I calmed down enough to ask Papa what happened and he said Andrew, had also died of measles on October 23, 1862, in the same hospital as George, in Nashville, Tennessee. They had both been thrown in a grave in Nashville, probably in a mass grave with other soldiers. I had heard there were so many dying of illnesses they were digging a long narrow ditch and throwing the bodies in the same hole and covering them up. Papa helped me up and gently half leading and half carrying me to the chair on the porch. Easing did not come soon, and I was like an empty shell, drained of strength and senseless to grief. I spent the rest of the day in dismal grief with my tangled emotions. I sat there on the porch until the moon finally arched its way across the night sky and night fell across the mountain. The darkness didn't help the pain.

Dinner came and went that night, but I was unable to eat. I fumbled my way through the cooking but could not have told you the next morning what I prepared. Whatever it was, it was solely for the children because I certainly couldn't eat. Darkness came but I could not find the strength to crawl in the same bed that my dear husband and I slept in for the past twenty-one years and conceived seven wonderful children. Just the thought of him not ever being in that bed again seemed more than I could bear. After the children went to bed, I thought maybe if I knitted, it would occupy my mind but I was not able to remember what stitches to take so I put the knitting down, went out on the porch and sat in the rocking chair. The night was tersely quiet and the tree frogs were not making any noise, which was unusual. Rage and fury boiled within me. I thought about the hatred in my heart for the enemy and knew it would ruin my life, and probably my health, if I did not get control of my emotions. Advice comes easy but no one can tell you how to adopt this advice. I rocked and cried and rocked and cried, until I could cry no longer. The thoughts were running wildly through my mind and I knew sleep would be impossible for me that night. Dawn found me still rocking on the front porch, shivering from the chill of the night. I knew it was up to me to raise these children in a manner befitting Andrew McWhirter's children and I certainly did not want them growing up with hate in their hearts. I also knew in order to do this; I would have to pull myself together, not only for their sakes but for the sake of my sanity. I prayed for God to be with us and give me the strength to do what I needed to do in order to bring these children

78

up in a manner pleasing to Him. I felt a sense of peace in my heart and a feeling that things would be alright, lonely, but alright.

It was too early for the children to be up so I took a quilt to the sofa and stretched out until time to begin breakfast. Sleep did not come easy for me but when I did I fall asleep, it was a very troubled sleep although my bombarded mind was unable to accept the situation. I began dreaming dreams of pleasant things I had never experienced in real life. Andrew was an officer in an officer's uniform which made him look even more handsome than he was in real life. We were going to an officer's ball in this beautiful southern mansion with large columns across the front portico. I walked to my closet where I picked out the most elegant ball-gown I had, which Andrew had purchased for me in Atlanta. I donned the gorgeous gown with the full petticoats and combed my long black, shining hair which had long dangling curls. Andrew had sent a chariot to pick me up so I slipped on my elbow-length gloves and was helped in the chariot by the driver, who also helped me from the landau and escorted me inside the mansion for the ball.

The driver extended his elbow, helped me down from my seat and as I stepped from the carriage, the silvery moonlight illuminated my gorgeous gown. As we entered the large arched doorway, I noticed Andrew and his eyes were glowing with warmth and pride as he immediately saw me and rushed to the door. The golden buttons on his uniform glistened in the candlelight as he rushed toward me. He escorted me into the room where everyone was milling around and drinking Mint Juleps and punch. He took me around and introduced me proudly to all of his friends. He continued to boast of his beautiful bride and as he led me to the dance floor and whispered in my ear that he had the most beautiful wife in the room. Andrew and I were having a wonderful time and he was waltzing me all over the dance floor, completely oblivious to anything or anyone around. We waltzed for some time and I was lost in his arms, deliriously happy to be with him again, and then the music changed tunes to a faster beat and we began dancing the Virginia Reel. Everyone was looking at us and Andrew was smiling so proudly. As the music began another waltz, I was completely submissive in his arms thinking about how we would spend the night together and I would once again get to sleep in his arms, when all of a sudden something tugged at my arm awakening me and brought me back to reality. Poor little Mary Caroline was asking why I was sleeping on the couch. Even though my wonderful dream was interrupted and I quickly realized I would not be sleeping with Andrew that night, I could not blame her as she was curious and didn't understand. The dream somehow helped put me in a better frame of mind, and the picture of me in the gorgeous ball gown and Andrew and I dancing around the room, continued in my mind throughout the next few days and helped me to accept the fact that my Andrew was gone. I wondered if God had given me that dream in order for me to have that picture to hold onto and remember him by. Maybe that was the answer to my prayer the previous day. I actually think it was this wonderful dream that helped me survive the perils of the war.

Ironically, that very day, I received the first letter from Andrew since they had left Alabama and it was one of the sweetest letters I ever read. I could tell he was homesick and so very lonesome as he wrote:

"My Dearest Sarah, we have arrived in Nashville, Tennessee and no one knows where we will go from here as they are getting so cautious about our movements and keeping them so secret that no one knows anything until they hear orders to leave. You must not be surprised if you do not hear from me regularly as we are most likely going to be on the move and there not being any post roads or mails, it will be difficult to send or receive letters. However, the Post Office in Nashville will undoubtedly use the means available to them to forward letters to us wherever we are and I will eventually receive all you write to me.

My health has been well although I have felt a little slack since arriving here. However, let me assure you that by the love you know I bear you, I shall not neglect my health. I have too many hopes and fond memories of us and our glorious marriage and am looking forward to even more exquisite bliss when I return home to you.

Oh, Sarah, how often I do think of you and the children. This is the first time we have been separated and how I long to see you and be with you with all the deepest fervor of my heart. This is also the first time I have been separated from the children and I never knew the longing of a father for his family. I have dreams of you all but the ones I have of you would make you blush. How sad it is to have wonderful dreams of you and then awake to only the coolness of the night and darkness of a small tent. There have been nights I have actually awaken to reach over and feel for you and was solely disappointed to find you were not there by my side.

Give my love to the children and kiss them for me. Please write me tonight, my dearest Sarah, of your love for me. Words cannot adequately describe my burning love for you, even after all these years. Word is going around that the plan is for us to move out in about a month or so toward Chattanooga and Atlanta but nothing of any proof from the top.

The pack I carry on my back when marching weighs 35 to 40 pounds and carries my tin cup, plate, utensils, blanket, and other items. It also has my Bible, a picture of you, paper and an inkwell so I can write of my love for you. We also carry our haversacks with what salt pork we have been issued, hardtack, coffee, sugar and 3 days' rations. The bags have a tendency to clang while we are marching so we have to be careful and know our surroundings at all times. Our regiment is composed of volunteers from Alabama, Mississippi, Tennessee, and Georgia. There are also men from South Carolina but they had already moved to Alabama before the war. One thing we all have in common is that we intend to do our patriotic duty and fight for our country.

I must go for now, my love, as it is getting late and I need to get to sleep. I will expect a letter from you soon and will write again as time permits.
Your loving Andrew"

Two weeks later I received a nice letter from a Union doctor who worked in the hospital the Union Army had taken over, which had formerly been the Nashville Female Academy in Nashville, Tennessee. He said he was so sorry about my husband but he had done all he could for him but just could not save him. He said he was sitting on the side of his bed when he died. He also said Andrew had given him my name and address and asked him to write me and tell me he died peacefully and proudly and wasn't afraid of dying, but he was sorry to go off and leave me and the children. The doctor said Andrew's last words were, "Please tell my wife that I love her and to please not grieve for me". While I was happy to hear from the doctor and know Andrew was not alone when he died, it made me feel sad and lonely. I could not help weeping as I read his words and know Andrew was still concerned about me, even as he lay dying.

It was getting close to Christmas and I was concerned about what I could make for the children. Andrew always made little gifts for the them for Christmas and I knew I could not do that. He made little wooden toys for the boys and I made little dolls for Mary Caroline.

We would always take the children for a walk into the woods and let them pick out a Christmas tree. They usually wanted one that was too large to fit in the house, but it was difficult for them to tell by looking at one growing out in the open. We would also pick up any little nuts or berries that might be used for ornaments. We tried to make Christmas special for them. We would pop popcorn and string it to wrap all around the tree. I showed the children how to make little things out of paper and color them for ornaments. After they colored some sheets of paper, I helped them cut out strips and made glue from flour and water so they could glue little two inch or three inch rings together to make a chain for the tree. They thought that was amazing and wanted to know where I learned to do that. I also made little birds and an angel from flour or feed sacks and stuffed them with quilt batting. Andrew would hold one of the children up and let them put the little angel on top of the tree. We picked up pine cones in the woods and hung them on the tree. I knew Papa would cut a little tree for us but that wouldn't be the same as all of us going out together to pick out one for Andrew to cut. I was going to have to be imaginative to come up with some Christmas presents for the children.

I knew it would be a sad Christmas. Andrew and I always sat the children down in front of the fireplace on Christmas Eve and he would read the story from the Bible about Jesus being born and the three wise men. I had a little Christmas story book that Papa had given Thomas a long time ago and I would read to them out of it. We always tried to make Christmas happy for the children and we always made sure they knew Christmas was about the birth of Christ, not for just gift giving. Andrew would tell them the gifts and decorated tree were in celebration of the birth of Jesus Christ.

I really dreaded Christmas this year but knew I had to make it happy for the children and not let them know how sad I really was.

I always cringed when I heard the mail carrier or any horses or wagons coming through the woods because I was afraid it would be someone bringing me more bad news about my family. One day around the first of December, I heard hoof beats coming toward the house and I froze, wondering what had happened now. I managed a "Good Morning" to the mail carrier as I reached for the mail and the top letter was from my son, Jackson. I hurriedly opened it and was relieved he was safe, although I could tell he was so very lonely. He started.....

"My Dearest Mother, Thomas and I are fine but we are both lonely with it being our first Christmas away from home. While I was trying to go to sleep last night I was thinking about how just last Christmas we were so happy and all of us were sitting around the table while Papa said the blessing and eating a wonderful Christmas meal that you worked so hard to prepare. Papa would always take us out in the woods and cut a Christmas tree for us to decorate. I thought just how quickly time goes by because just a year ago today, I was enjoying the blessings of a loving family in a warm, comfortable home, singing Christmas songs and Papa reading to us from the Bible. Now I am out here in the middle of nowhere surrounded by the enemy firing their guns and cannons trying to kill us. All we can do is continue to pray that the good Lord will end this war and let us get back home safely.

I know I shouldn't complain, but you and Papa always made Christmas such a wonderful time for all of us, and while I ate my stale piece of hardtack soaked in water and fried in pork fat, and little piece of fat meat that was barely fried, I couldn't help think about your great Christmas meals with a turkey Papa had killed, and all the trimmings. Incidentally, we found out later that the hard tack was full of bugs and worms. You made the best sweet potato pies, eggnog, mince pies and plum pudding. You have always been such a good cook and I really miss your cooking. I probably always took your cooking for granted since that was all I knew, but have really come to appreciate it and realized just how good it really was, since eating the rations we have in the army. There is nothing to drink but coffee and water and you know Thomas and I don't drink coffee. Besides that, the water we have to drink is never really good. Some of the soldiers managed to get some whiskey and did they ever get drunk. One was making fun of me for not drinking and started a fight. I just turned and walked off and he finally passed out. This has been the bleakest day of my life, and now I have to go on picket duty. Please write as often as you can and I do hope y'all can have a nice Christmas. Yours truly, Jackson"

Nashville National Cemetery

…Grant them eternal rest, O Lord….

In 1867, the hollowed grounds of the Nashville National Cemetery were established and the Union soldiers were removed from the old Nashville City Cemetery to the new cemetery and government headstones were ordered and erected for them. Roll of Honor, No, XXII, dated July 31, 1869, submitted to the Quartermaster General's Office, USA, Washington, DC, recorded the graves of 16,485 Union soldiers interred in the Nashville National Cemetery, Tennessee and remains as a part of the cemetery's historical records. A very large proportion of the dead in the cemetery, however, were transferred from the hospital burial grounds in and around the city of Nashville and from temporary burial grounds around general hospitals in Nashville and nearby battlefields of Franklin and Gallatin, Tennessee. Reinterments were also made there from Bowling Green and Cave City, Kentucky.

During the Civil War, if marked at all, wooden headboards or crosses with the names and identifying data painted thereon marked graves of those who died in general hospitals, on the battlefields, or as prisoners of war. Many of these headboards deteriorated through exposure to the elements. The result was that when the remains were later removed for burial to a national cemetery, in some cases, identifications could not be established, and the gravesites were marked as unknown.

In the Corinth, Mississippi National Cemetery, and probably many others, they have mass graves of unknown soldiers.

(See pictures of Cemetery in back of book.)

Thomas Harper Family

...robbed of innocence and youth,
no power on earth can e'er replace....

Let me digress a bit and tell you about my Harper Family and their role in the Civil War. This will prove what you have probably always heard about the Civil War being a battle, not only of the North against the South but brother against brother. One would think in a family of several young men, they would be of like mindset and all want to fight for the same side, but they all had their own thoughts and strong minds and could not agree, so they chose sides and while some did fight for the Country, others chose to fight against it and joined the Confederacy, which upset Papa almost to the point of tears. Papa could be hard on the boys when they didn't do what he thought they should do, or what he told them to do, but he loved his family and had a heart of gold.

I was born June 24, 1825 in Smith County, Tennessee to Thomas and unknown Harper and was the oldest of fifteen (15) children.

Robert Harper was born 1826 in Smith County, Tennessee, and married Nancy Jane Lane November 31, 1851 in Walker County, Alabama. They were married by John Gamble, Minister of the Gospel. Nancy Lane was born about 1828 in Alabama and was the daughter of Alfred G. and Mariah Pate Lane. Not long after Robert and Nancy were married they moved to Lampasas County, Texas with her parents and lived next door to them. About 1862, although Robert and Nancy already had five children, Robert decided to return to Alabama and defend his country in the Civil War so he packed them up and moved them back. He had become restless after reading about all the turmoil and hostility going on back home, and I had written him telling him about how his brothers were fighting between themselves over which side to choose. After he returned, he tried to talk and reason with them but they, too, had their reasons for fighting with the Confederacy even though they knew the possibility was great they would one day meet their brothers on the battlefield and one of them would possibly have to kill the other one. Robert was only five feet and four inches tall. He had yellow eyes, a fair complexion and his hair was black.

On January 20, 1863, Robert enlisted in the 1st Alabama Cavalry, USV, commanded by Captain Phillip Sternberg, in Glendale, Mississippi at age 38. He rode over seventy miles to Camp Glendale,

Mississippi to enlist. On February 8, 1863, Robert was on detached service working in Secret Service, which was a very dangerous job in the military and not a job well liked by the enemy since while they were out performing their job, they were also spying trying to find out where the enemy was located and which men were still hiding out who needed to be in the army.

Robert was sent to Corinth, Mississippi, which was only about ten or twelve miles from Glendale, and he came down with measles, which killed him on March 8, 1863, less than two months after he enlisted. Someone else stated he was killed in action but we never did find out for sure.

Robert wrote me not long after he got to Corinth to tell me what had happened and he didn't sound very happy.

"Dear Sis, I arrived at Camp Glendale, Mississippi and after I enlisted and got my supplies, a group of us had to go on to Camp Davies in Corinth, which was about eight or ten miles away. We have been on half-rations since I have been here because the leaders of the Union Army from the North had no idea when they came down here there would be any where near this many southern men who would want to enlist in the Union Army. They assumed we would mostly want to fight them rather than with them. Consequently, they were not prepared with enough horses, uniforms, shoes, guns, ammunition, food or anything else we might need. Most of us are using our own horses, mules, and guns, so it's a good thing I brought my own. In camp last night we were talking about the war and wondering how long it would last. Someone said they figured it would last a year or longer and I told them I came here and enlisted for the purpose of quelling this infernal rebellion and with God's help and enough good ammunition I intended to carry this out to the end, even if it takes us twenty years of toil and suffering!

Scouting and foraging parties go out from here almost daily but forage is pretty scarce in this part of Dixie. Sometimes we find a little corn which allows us to have a little extra boiled corn and cornbread, but for the most part, we have mostly coffee and hardtack until the supply train comes in.

We heard cannonading for a long time night before last and yesterday several of us rode over in the direction of the noise. I was sick to my stomach when we happened up on a field with dead horses and soldiers lying all around; it was the most gruesome sight I have ever seen. Some double-dyed traitors in our native states bushwhacked some Union soldiers and several were killed from both sides. The Copperheads, as we call them, are massing their foul hearts and deceitful minds in unison with the Rebels, and with their cowardly deeds, and their acts of desperation, they are trying to destroy our great form of Government. This is why I am fighting to try to keep this from happening. We discussed this for a bit but dismounted and commenced burying all of the dead soldiers, no matter what uniform they were wearing. Some still had their eyes opened and looked like they were alive. The sight was very disturbing and it will be a long time before I get that picture out of my mind. Wish, now, that we hadn't been so inquisitive.

Sis, you would not believe the number of refugees from north Alabama who are flocking into camp daily. Capt. Cameron is forming the men into a cavalry regiment while the women and children are cared for by the proper authorities. They are sending most of them to Glendale. They talk about how they were dogged-down and made to suffer by Jeff Davis' men. They said several loyal men were shot and brutally murdered just for expressing their loyal sentiments. Hundreds of loyal Alabamians are still hiding out in the hills from their heinous and unprincipled persecutors.

Several of us are going to go into town and see if we can find something good to eat, cheap. I'll write in a few days. Please give my love to Papa and everyone.
Your loving brother, Robert"

Not long after I received Robert's letter, we got word that he had died. We heard at first that he was killed but heard later he died from measles. Papa tried to hide his tears but the war and loss of his family was just about more than he could take. Robert was only about 5' 4" tall. He actually had yellow eyes, dark hair and had a light complexion.

When Robert died, he left Nancy pregnant, and she had the baby three weeks later on March 28, 1863. Now in addition to my son and husband, I had lost a brother in the war, leaving his wife with six young children, all under ten years of age. Anyone with grandchildren knows when they are hurt, you also hurt, and I hurt so badly for them and their mother, not to mention Papa for loosing a son. Nancy was fortunate to have her parents, Alfred G. and Mariah Pate Lane, living close by to help her with the children, but even at that, there were difficult times with her trying to get back on her feet after learning about her husband's death and then having a baby almost three weeks later.

There is a memorial marker for Robert Harper in the Jackson Cemetery in Wayne County, Alabama, but a family member states he is not buried there. In all probability, he is buried in the Corinth National Cemetery in a mass or unknown grave, with other soldiers. (It is possible Thomas Harper claimed his son's body and took him home to bury him in a family cemetery or Hopewell Cemetery where so many other family members are buried.)

Pension papers for Robert state the following: Pension #152.244, filed January 26, 1866, in Marion Co., Alabama by John Gamble, M.G. state he was killed in Action 7th or 8th of March, 1863 in Corinth, Mississippi.

Children of Robert and Nancy Lane Harper were:
Rubin G., born January 24 1853;
William A., September 26 1854;
Sarah E., August 29 1856;
Robert H., April 7, 1858;
Mary J., January 11 1860;
Martha S., March 29, 1863.

Affidavits: Thaddeus Walker & James R. Tucker, January 26, 1866, certified marriage (courthouse burned during war); Certificate from Probate Judge John Brown of Walker County Alabama; Martha Taylor & Nelson Walker, October 1868, certifying marriage; Sarah McWhirter, Delila Tucker & Matilda Tidwell, June 8, 1871, Winston County, Alabama. Robert and his family lived in Eldridge, Walker County, Alabama in 1866. Nancy, Robert's wife, died November 4, 1906, in Wayne County, Tennessee.

James Warren Harper was born about 1829 in Smith County, Tennessee, and was married July 15, 1846 in Alabama to Sarah Drucilla Byars. Sarah Drucilla was the daughter of James Joseph Byars and Elizabeth Walker. Drucilla was born in June 1828 in Jefferson County, Alabama. James enlisted in Company G of the 1st Alabama Cavalry, <u>CSA</u>. He was wounded in battle and "sent home to Galilee, Marion County, Alabama to die," which he did October 3, 1868, just three years after the war ended and six months after their youngest child was born. James and Drucilla had several children during the twenty-two years they were married:
Mary E, born September 01, 1848, died November 08, 1933;

Martha Emoline, born June 24, 1850, died August 3, 1937;
Sarah Elizabeth, born Jul 30, 1853, died May 20, 1926;
Nancy Jane, born Mar 24, 1855, died Jan 20, 1927; Thaddius Nelson "Ned", born about 1856, died after 1900;
Susannah Frances "Fanny", born Jan 11, 1858, died August 6, 1943;
Sissy, born 1864, died before 1880; Ann, born 1865, died before 1880;
Thomas H., born Apr 30, 1868, died September 22, 1940. They may have had another son, Enis Wood Harper. Sarah Drucilla Byars was the daughter of James Joseph Byars and Elizabeth Walker.

Mary Emaline Harper was born about 1831 in Smith County, Tennessee. She was married about 1851 to James R. Tucker, born May 26, 1826 in Alabama. Children of James and Mary were: Mary, born 1853, Henry, 1854, Josiah Newton, 1857, and Millie Alice Harper, born about 1865.

Mary Emaline died an untimely death around 1867, in Marion County, Alabama about 2 years after their youngest child, Millie, was born, leaving James to raise these four young children. James and Mary Emaline had already been through much torment during the Civil War. Here she was in a Union family and a hotbed of Unionists while her husband chose to join Co. K, of the 4th Alabama Confederate Army. However, she also had brothers in the Confederacy, along with those who served in the Union Army. It was definitely a family of divided allegiance, and a prime example of the "Brother against Brother War". This also caused me much concern to have turmoil such as this in her family as well as that of my brother's. Mary Emaline worked hard during the war to care for the children only to die two years after the war ended, leaving her four precious children motherless. We were all devastated....again, it just kept getting worse and worse and my family kept dying one by one.

After Mary Emaline died, James married Didena Webb and she raised these four young children born by Emaline Harper Tucker.

(The below information contained in the CSA Pension records filed by Didena Tucker for her husband's service in the Confederacy, took place after Sarah Harper McWhirter died.) (Sic)
"Member of Co. K, 4th AL Cav., CSA. My husband had his parole and was careful with it. I have seen it many times but could not read it, but he and kin read it. The Parole was burnt up when our house burned 35 years ago."

She submits this on her answers to said citation and if the same is not full and sufficient will try to furnish such other evidence as may be required.

Many of the Harpers, McWhirters, Tuckers and others suffered the same fate during the war. The husbands were killed or died during the war leaving large families, or the wife died leaving the husband to raise large families, and in some cases, both parents died.

Her husband lived in Marion Co. Ala. when he enlisted and it would be necessary for her to go there to get up any further evidence. Respectfully submitted Didena (her X mark) Tucker
Sworn to & subscribed before me this the 12th day of November, 1914. J.C. Shunpe, Judge of Prob.

Didena's given name differed in spelling on some documents, "D.M., Didena, Didema," but according to the census records, she could not read or write, which could also account for the differing birth dates she gave for herself. (Birth dates didn't appear to have been of great importance to illiterate people".) She also gave differing death dates for her husband as she got older. Note that she was described in 1914 as being "very old and feeble." However, to be eligible for the widow's pension, her husband's death had to have been before April, 1898, the date of her first application. The most reasonable date was the date she listed in 1899 of November 15, 1895. His tombstone shows November 28, 1894. Even then (in 1899) his death date could have been approximated by her with the help of the reviewer. If there is not a family Bible with the birth and death dates listed, the people were often unsure about exact family dates when called upon to give such data from memory.

In 1921 Didena said that J.R. Tucker was in the Chickamauga battle and not wounded, then in 1923 she said he was wounded in the Selma battle, captured and imprisoned. She signed her name with "X" until 1923 when she wrote her signature in what apparently is her own hand writing.
November 17, 1914, Lawrence County, Alabama: Mrs. Tucker appeared November 11, 1914, to restate her affidavit. She gave her husband's name as James Richard Tucker.
July 29, 1915, Lawrence County, Alabama, Pension #36444; Didena Tucker states that she was born at or near Winfield, Marion County, Alabama on September 4, 1836, being 88 years of age.
July 14, 1921, Lawrence County, Alabama, Widows Blank for Reclassification (condensed in this analysis):

Didena Tucker of Moulton, Alabama living with son, H.H. Tucker. She was born September 15, 1832, in Winfield, Marion County, Alabama. Her father was Thomas Webb. She married James R. Tucker in 1866 in Marion County, Alabama and died in 1898, in Franklin County, Alabama. He enlisted in Walker County, Alabama as a private in the Infantry & enlisted at beginning of war. He was wounded in the Battle of Chickamauga in leg and in neck.

Josiah Houston Harper was born March 12, 1833 in Smith County, Tennessee, and married Nancy Jane Berryhill, December 25, 1856 in Marion County, Alabama. Nancy was the daughter of James "Dominicker" Berryhill and his wife, Patience "Passie" C. McMinn. On January 20, 1863, Josiah enlisted as Private in Co. B, 1st Alabama Cavalry, USV in Glendale, Mississippi at age 28 and mustered in on January 22, 1863 at Corinth, Mississippi. On February 8, 1863, he was working as a Scout in the northwest Alabama and Mississippi areas. A Civil War Scout operated on the fringes of an army with the purpose of obtaining information about enemy locations, movements, and strength. Individual soldiers or small groups acted as scouts, often operating behind enemy lines, and was a dangerous job. On January 22, 1864, Josiah was mustered out of the 1st Alabama Cavalry and had returned home when the Confederate Home Guard began harassing him. The Confederate Home Guard came to Nancy Jane Harper's house and cursed and abused her and her children because of the roll her husband and their father played in the 1st Alabama Cavalry Union Army during the war. They stated they would take Josiah Houston Harper out and put him where the dogs wouldn't find him, and called him "a damned old Tory traitor", and everything else that was mean. Josiah Harper was at John Lyon's house when the Confederates caught him and took him out where they brutally tortured and murdered him and left him hanging. John Lyons and his family went out looking for him and finally found him still hanging in that shape. Lyons then went back home, hooked up his steers to his wagon, went back, cut Josiah down, put him in the wagon and hauled him to the grave yard and helped bury him. John Lyons swore to this in a Southern Claim affidavit.

Harvey Brown also testified that Josiah Harper was hanged by the Confederate Home Guard. He stated Josiah even cut wood and hauled it to his wife while he was in the Union Army. He went on to say: (Sic) "Those who could testify to his public reputation are, "George S. Tucker, William Tucker and Joseph Roberts. Prominent Union men in the area were, T.P. Harper, A.J. McWhirter, George

91

M.D., and Josiah Harper, James Mills and Peyton Burnett. I know the Confederate cavalry threatened him heavy and talked about killing him, said he was carrying news to the Union people. His property was taken as was said by the Confederate calvary."

Josiah Harper's Civil War Pension papers state he died from measles but sometimes the desperate people trying to recover from the ravages of the war did desperate things in order to obtain pensions from the Federal Government. It is possible Josiah's widow thought if she said he was hanged by Confederate Home Guard after the war ended, she might not be able to draw a pension, so she stated he died from measles contracted while in the military service.

The Civil War "Home Guard" was formed for protection from Guerilla attacks of neighboring cities. However, due to the fact the hostility between the Union and CSA in the South was so great the Confederate Home Guard in Marion and surrounding Counties in Alabama was more of a guerilla outfit than "guards". Josiah had already served his time in army, been honorably discharged, was enjoying time with his wife and children, working his farm and not bothering anyone when he went to visit John Lyons and was kidnapped by the Confederate Home Guard, brutally murdered and left hanging, as previously explained. This is the type of brutality these people were subjected to before, during and after the Civil War, just because their families loved their country, wanted to protect it and refused to fire on "Old Glory".

Rebecca Jane Harper was born about 1836 in Smith County, Tennessee and married Daniel Webster Tucker about 1854. She died February 1, 1902 in Union Parish, Louisiana and is buried in Zion Hill Cemetery in an unmarked grave. Daniel Webster Tucker was born May 26, 1825 in Alabama and died December 15, 1901, in Union Parish, Louisiana. Rebecca Jane Harper's husband, Daniel Webster Tucker served in the Confederacy while her brothers fought in the Union Army. Rebecca Jane and Daniel Webster had the following children:
Sarah "Sallie" Ann, born March 6, 1856, died January 4, 1931
Francis Marion, born April 15, 1855 and died as an infant
Mary Frances, born November 10, 1867, died November 10, 1939
Nancy "Nannie" A., born about 1874
Estella, born May 11, 1876, died February 16, 1944
William Riley, born November 10, 1867, died 10 Nov 1939
Martha W. Tucker, born about 1873.

Daniel and Rebecca Harper Tucker left Alabama for Louisiana in the 1860's. Daniel's parents, Thomas and Amy Beard Tucker, and his brother, Francis Marion Tucker and wife Evoline and two of their children went with Daniel and his family.

Rebecca Jane Harper's husband, "Kimber" Tucker, was a brother to the Henry Tucker who was so brutally murdered by the CSA Home Guard during the Civil War. There is a story about Tucker's agonizing death in the next chapter.

<u>Thomas Wade Harper</u> was born about 1839 in Warren County, Tennessee and died or was killed in action September 15, 1862, in Knoxville, Tennessee after enlisting in Company H of the 43rd Alabama Infantry, CSA. Just before he enlisted, he married Mary Elizabeth Lane, daughter of John Madison Lane, born February 22, 1805 in Jackson County, Georgia and died January 29, 1879, in Nolanville, Bell County, Texas, and his wife, Phebe Ann or Alice Walden, born July 12, 1817, in Blount County, Alabama and died December 29, 1906 in Nolanville, Bell County, Texas. Mary Elizabeth was born October 3, 1841, in Alabama. After Thomas' death, she requested and obtained bounty pay that was due Thomas due to joining the Confederate Army. Mary remarried in 1871 to John Boren from Texas and died in 1922 in Bell County, Texas. John Boren was born December 27, 1828 in Carroll County, Arkansas and died December 6, 1900 in Bell County, Texas. He was the son of Isaac and Elizabeth Standlee Boren. John and Mary had four children: Roxanna, born January 1873; John I., born March 30, 1874; Phoebe Elizabeth, born February 16, 1876, died November 14, 1951; and Judy Melvina, born December 8, 1876, died in September 1953.

"State of Alabama – Walker County
On this the 7th day of January 1863, personally appeared before me J.C. Myers, a Justice of the Peace in and for the County aforesaid. Mary E. Harper, who after being duly sworn according to law, states that she is the widow of Thomas W. Harper deceased who was a Private of Captain W. H. Lawrence's Company H, 43 Regiment of Alabama Volunteers, CSA. Thomas Harper entered the service at Tuscaloosa in Tuscaloosa County, Alabama on or about the 7th day of May 1862 and was killed or died Knoxville Tennessee the 15th Day of Sept. 1862 leaving her a widow with no children. She makes this deposition for the purpose of obtaining from the Government of the Confederate States whatever may have been due the said Thomas W.

Harper at the time of his death, for Bounty on or after allowances for his services as Volunteer aforesaid.

Sworn to and Subscribed before me the 7th Day of January 1863

J. C. Myers, Justice of the Peace.

Signed Mary E. Harper"

(There was a little "x" between the E. and Harper so she most likely was unable to sign her name)

Elisha Denton Harper was born about 1841 in Alabama. He was married in the early 1860's to Lucinda A. Lyle, daughter of John P. Lyle, born 1814 in Georgia, died November 15, 1895, and his wife, Elizabeth Noland, born 1813 in South Carolina. Everyone called Elisha by his nickname which was "Dent". Elisha and Lucinda had two children: Mary E. Harper, born about 1863 and died between 1900 and 1910, and John Thomas Harper, born about 1865 and died in 1930. Mary E. Harper married James J. Dutton in 1879 Walker County, Alabama, and her mother, Lucinda, signed a handwritten note giving permission for her under-aged daughter to marry. John T. Harper married Frances Evoline Welch. Lucinda A. Lyle Harper was still living with her father, John P. Lyle, and family in 1880. It was always thought the Confederate Home Guard also murdered Elisha, "Dent" about 1868, because of the roll his brothers played in the 1st Alabama Cavalry Union Army during the Civil War. The truth may never be known as to what actually happened to him. He was buried in the Hopewell Cemetery in Fayette County, Alabama where so many other Harpers are buried.

Tennessee Polk Harper was born about 1844 in Walker County, Alabama. On June 26, 1862 he enlisted in Company K of the 1st Alabama Cavalry, USV in Limestone, County, Alabama at age 18. Company K was immediately sent to Nashville, Tennessee where they were merged with the 1st Middle Tennessee Cavalry, and he died December 9, 1863 in Hospital #9 in Nashville. He is buried in Grave #C-7159 in the Nashville National Cemetery in Nashville, Davidson County, Tennessee. He was still living at home with Papa when he enlisted.

George W. Harper was born in July 1847 in Marion County, Alabama, and married Martha E. Morton in 1865. Martha was the daughter of James F. and Mary E. Morton, both born in Alabama. Children of George and Martha were Mary, born about 1868; Rosa E., born 1870; Nancy, born 1872; Thomas, born November 1877; Martin Emmett, born December 25, 1885, and died October 15, 1966; and Charley E. Harper, born May 1888. George was listed on a couple of census records and G.W. on the 1870 Sanford County, Alabama Census. The 1900 Lamar County, Alabama Census was the last census on which George was found, indicating he must have died between 1900 and 1910. (I have seen his name as George M.D. but have been told it was most likely George W. Harper, which is how it was enumerated on some of the census records.)

Jasper Green Harper was born in June 1850 in Marion County, Alabama. He was law clerk for a Federal Marshal in Birmingham, Jefferson County, Alabama. Jasper, called "Green", married Mary Elizabeth Hyder on December 17, 1874, and built the school house at Hubbertville, Alabama where Mary taught. Mary was born in 1855 and died in 1898. Green also owned the land where Hyder Cemetery was located and where his family is buried. The Harper family still owns the land where the cemetery is located. Jasper Green and Mary Elizabeth Hyder had seven children: Haley Preston, born about 1876; Sarah Sallie, born 1879; Willie/Willis R., born December 04 1882 and died July 24, 1906; Blanche, born August 26, 1886, died July 7, 1907, Charles "Charley", born April 12, 1890, died June 16, 1891; Walter Green, born February 1, 1892, died in 1980, and Annie Mae, born 1893 and died 1972. After Green's first wife, Mary, died, he married Martha M. "Mattie" Gilreath, April 11, 1899. Mattie was born November 1874 in Alabama but unfortunately she died in 1903, in Alabama leaving Green with some young children to care for. The 1900 Fayette Co., AL Census listed her as Mattie P.E. Harper. Jasper and Mattie had one daughter, Lena Harper, born July 26, 1900. Jasper Green Harper left with his oldest son, Willis, around 1917, and went to Oklahoma where more of the Harper and Tucker families had gone. In the 1920 McClain Co., Census, Muncrief Township, Green's son, Walter, his wife, Bessie Mae and two of their children, Stella, age 5, born in Alabama and George, age 2, born in Oklahoma, were living in the household with Green. Walter later wanted to go back to Alabama so he borrowed the money and they all went back home to Alabama. Jasper and Mattie had one daughter, Lena Harper born July 26, 1900.

Martha Ann Harper was born September 14, 1854, in Alabama and married Kimbrel "Kimber" Foster Tucker July 1, 1869, in Fayette County, Alabama. Martha and Kimber had ten children: Mary Silvaner, born March 19, 1870, and died about 1901 in Quitman, Wood County, Texas; Nancy Ann, born 1872; William Thomas "Bill", born 1873; Joel "Joe", born 1875; Rachael Elizabeth, born May 1876; Adaline M., born May 1880; Jessie, born 1881; Florentine, born 1885; George, born 1889; and Belle Harper, born

1891. All of their children were born in Alabama and probably in Fayette County, Alabama.

(Kimbrel Foster Tucker served in the Confederacy in Indian Territory, now Oklahoma.)

Nancy Harper was born in 1855 in Alabama and was sick most of her young life. My step-mother was so busy with the rest of the family but she took the time to cook whatever she thought Nancy might eat; however, she would not or could not eat much of anything. Papa would kill and pluck chickens for us to make chicken soup and broth but Nancy would only drink a few sips. The doctor was not able to figure out what was wrong with her. He had left some medication for Nancy but she did not respond to it. I lived next door to Papa so was able to go over and help with her as I could. I would hold her little thin body in my lap and rock her while I was reading the Bible and story books to her, but she seemed too sick to be interested. She was only about ten years old when God called her home. He had gathered one of his fairest flowers of the garden of life. That was only one of the many times my heart would be broken because God saw fit to take many other family members before me. Everyone has a purpose in life and we just have to believe that whatever Nancy's purpose was, it had been fulfilled and God wanted her to be with Him. I had a difficult time dealing with my little sister's death. The hurt was so intense and my chest felt so heavy I found it difficult to breathe at times, but by this time, I had my children to think of and care for, but it was quite difficult to keep my mind off of Nancy.

Malissa A. Harper was born in June 1857 in Alabama, married Elijah J. "Lige" White and died June 28, 1888 in Arkansas. Elijah was born April 14, 1860 in Marion County, Alabama and died March 23, 1842 in Lawrence County, Arkansas.

In the 1900 Marion County, Alabama Census, it shows Elijah White, age 44, born in July 1855, Malissa White, age 42, born June 1857, Mary J. White, age 7, born December 1890, Martha A. White, age 8, born Dec 1891, William H. White, age 6, born July 1893, John T. White, age 5, born September 1894, George I. White, age 2, born May 1898, and Elijah J. White, age 5 months, born Dec 1899. Elijah J. White served in the 2nd Regiment, Arkansas Mounted Rifles, CSA.

Jesse H. Harper was born in 1861 in Marion County, Alabama. He married Sarah, "Sallie" Whitehead, daughter of Drury H. Cox and Mary Jane Anthony. Jesse and Sallie had fifteen children: Green, born 1883, died 1902; Drury Thomas, born 1885, died 1885; Mary Jane, born 1886, died 1950; George Houston, born 1889, died 1961; Martha Bell, born 1891, died 1975; Florence, born 1893, died 1967; Icy Elizabeth "Belle", born 1895, died 1945; Rhoda, born 1897, died 1985; Virgil, 1899, died 1986; Myrtie Chloe, born 1901, died 1976; Iowa "Owie", born 1903; Annie, born 1906, died 2000; Raymond, born 1909, died 1915; Lula, born 1910; and Orlena Harper, born 1914, died 2000.

(A picture of Jesse and Sarah "Sallie" Whitehead Harper taken on their 50th wedding anniversary, holding their wedding cake can be found in the back of the book.)

The Agonizing Death of Henry Tucker (sic)

...Light a candle of prayer in the quiet chapel of your soul....

The following is a true story of one horrendous atrocity (comparable to any done generations later by the Nazis). Such acts were committed by both sides in the guerilla hill-country war. This event was reconstructed from interviews with about a dozen "old-timers" interviewed by Wesley S. Thompson as source material for his various books. The following is largely drawn from Tories of the Hills, 3rd Edition, 1960, beginning on page 131.

Henry Tucker had enlisted in the 1st Alabama Cavalry, USV on March 11, 1863 in Glendale Mississippi. For reasons unknown, official "mustering-in" did not occur until October, 5, 1863. He had enlisted for a year but was released a little early - mustered out on February 5, 1864. His military duty completed, he returned home to his rugged hill country (Winston County/Marion Counties in Alabama between Natural Bridge and O'Mary's) to wait out the war, although he was also considering re-enlistment in the Union army. Little did he know, there would be no peace for him, for the dog-calvary rangers and "homeguard" of the CSA were out to get anyone they considered a "traitor" that they could find.

Led by Stoke Roberts, the vigilante homeguard began scouring the country commiting atrocities in the name of enforcing the Confederate's best interests, forcing men into the CSA army and punishing those who would not join them. They finally reached the home of Henry Tucker on a March or April day during the spring of 1864. As the vigilantes rode into his yard, Henry shouted to his wife, "Lord God, there's a bunch of them homeguards coming up the road now. What can I do?"

"Here, hide quick in this meat box!" Callie, his wife ordered, pointing to a big box of rough planks in the cook room.

Henry leaped into the box as the men rode up to the house and Callie threw an old worn quilt over the top of it.

"Whar is that man ye hid around here, woman?" Stoke demanded as he and his bunch of ruffians forced their way into her home.

"How do you suppose there is a man here?" she replied trying to be calm.

98

"We seed ya bang that door shut, woman! And there ain't no woman agonna be abangin' that door shet like that lessen thar is somebody around summers they air a'tryin' to hide," Stoke declared sharply.

"Men, I don't see why you'd be coming to my house looking for anybody," the poor woman tried to argue.

"Woman!" Roberts snapped, "They ain't no use to be alyin' about it cause thar's plenty of folks round here that try to hide them Tories when they git a chanct - and that Henry Tucker is bound to be around here summers and we're gonna ketch him fore we quit!"

Callie bit her fingernails nervously - she felt she must have turned pale when they called Henry's name. "Oh! I am grieved enough already! Won't you please go on and leave my home alone?" she cried pleadingly.

"Hell No! Men, git busy and hunt every crack in the place for that snake!" Roberts commanded the men.

They began to search under the beds and under the floor and in the loft of the house and in every box and barrel on the place. "Here he is, Stoke! Here he is!" Gibson shouted finally, pulling the old quilt from the meat box in the cook room.

Stoke ran to the door and saw with gloating eyes the form still crouched in the box. "Git him, men! Git him!" he shouted. Henry Tucker leaped to his feet and tried to run, but was grabbed by half a dozen men.

"Whar's the rope, Ham?" Roberts called to Carpenter. "Here ye air!" One of the men held up a heavy rope. Stoke grabbed it and began tying Henry at once.

"Oh, please, men, don't!" he begged in tones of anguish as Roberts drew the rope about him.

"Thay ain't no use to whimper and beg, Henry Tucker, ye damned Tory you! You'll be damned sorry ye ever shot at me fore I git through butcherin' on ye!" His language was vile and abusive. "Take him to the woods, men! We've got a lot of work on this fool fore he gits out uv his misery!" Stoke finished.

99

Henry was tied from his shoulders to his waist. The men threw him across a big horse and threw another rope around his neck and tied it so that one could hold it on each side. Then the group went galloping off with the prisoner jolting along on the horse. Callie had tried to save Henry, but was unable to do a thing. She buried her head in her hands and cried hysterically as the men rode away with their prisoner.

"Carry him to old Ball Rock," Roberts shouted. "I want to take the devil right back nigh the place where he shot at me a year or two ago!" By the time the group arrived to where Stoke was leading them, it was already dark. When they stopped, they found Stoke already off his horse beside an old dead pine tree on the ground.

"Split us up some pine and build us a fire fust. We're agonna take a long time fer this," Roberts told the man with a chopping ax. Four of the others were dragging Tucker by the rope around his neck. Others were bringing limbs for the fire.

"Oh, Lord, Lord, Stoke, don't torture me, please don't! Kill me with your guns or your ax or any other way you want to, but please don't torture me to death!" Henry pleaded pitifully.

"Pull his clothes off," Roberts directed. The men went to work tearing Tucker's clothes from his body, until he stood shivering bare naked. Stoke was getting out a big long knife. Grinning fiendishly, he proceeded to cut the prisoneer between the heel, like fixing to hang a hog, paying no attention to Henry's screaming as loud as he could.

"Now, hang him on this limb, men," he ordered, pointing to the limb he had cut off. With the prisoner stripped and hanging head down like a hog ready to be gutted, Stoke stepped back and in a cruel pretense of a magnanimous Judge, said, "Now, you damned Tory - if ye got anything to say, ye can say it!"

"Oh Lord, men, please have mercy! Shoot me or knock me in the head or something!" he pleaded. Stoke laughed. "Skin him, men!" he commanded. Several of the men began at once, but found their knives too dull. "Castorate the devil, cut his whole ___ and all off!" Stoke ordered. "I want to poke them in his mouth!"

"Now punch the devil's eyes out! No - let me have that knife!" Stokes cried, his eyes glowing with fanatical, saddistic fury. "I want to punch-out his eyes!" He seized the big knife and started boring in

100

the sockets of the miserable man's eyes. Directly, he flipped the eyeballs across the leaves on the ground. "Now I want to cut the bastard's tongue out next!" he rasped. "Here, give me that ax!" Maliciously, with the ax, he broke Henry's jaw on both sides, then pulled out his tongue from his mouth as far as he could and proceeded calmly to cut it off, paying no attention to the man's screams.

Stokes grinned barbarously. "Now I want to cut his hide around his head and pull it over his face and tie it! And I want you men to split up a bunch of long pine knots and drive them into his kidneys and his bowels and heart. The men dutifully did this. Then, when the struggling in death finally commenced, Stoke bashed his head in with the chopping ax.

William Rowell heard the prisoner's screams for a mile and a half. Tom Johnson and Andy Ingle found the body four days later, still hanging, and buried Henry Tucker north of O'Mary cemetery which is on the Marion and Winston County Alabama border.

(This story adapted and contributed by Joel S. Mize, descendant of Daniel Tucker, grand- father of Henry Tucker, Pvt. Co B; 1st Alabama Cavalry. Rev. 7/97.)

Captain Joseph Hornback

...Seek me in the sunrise or in the pounding surf,
See me in the autumn leaves....

Joseph Hulings Hornback, now spelled Hornbeck, was born March 12, 1823 in Champaign, Ohio and died October 4, 1904 in San Bernardino, California. He married Cecelia Amanda Gulick, who was born November 12, 1826, and died March 4, 1928 in Santa Rosa, California.

He first enlisted in Company K, 21st Ohio Volunteers, on August 24, 1861 in Wood County, Ohio and transferred to the 1st Alabama Cavalry, USV on July 24, 1862 in Huntsville, Alabama, and was a carpenter by trade. He was captured at Stone's River in Murfreesboro, Tennessee on December 31, 1862 and again March 21, 1864 in Arkansas. He was exchanged and reported for duty June 7, 1864 at Decatur, Alabama. He was wounded in action March 10, 1865 at Monroe's Crossroads, NC suffering from a gunshot wound to the left leg. He served as 1st Lieutenant while in the 1st Alabama Cavalry, USV, and mustered out July 19, 1865 in Nashville, Tennessee. He is buried in the Santa Rosa Rural Cemetery in Santa Rosa, Sonoma County, California.

Hornback must have been a good leader as appeared to be liked by the soldiers in his company. He is the one Jackson McWhirter liked so much and escorted home to Ohio after he was wounded at the Battle of Monroe's Crossroads in North Carolina. On December 30, 1863, Hornback wrote the following letter from Camp Glendale, which was about ten miles from Corinth, Mississippi. He wrote it to the Perrysburg (Ohio) Journal and will give you some idea of their camp life:

"Letter from Glendale, Mississippi

Camp Dairies (Davies), Miss. Dec 30, 1863.

Ed. Journal: Since we have been here (early in November) we have been recruiting - receiving about 309 into the regiment. This regiment was composed of twelve months' men, except companies I and K, so that the time of four companies has already expired, and they have been mustered out' but now companies are rapidly forming on the three years' basis. Company K has mustered in

102

thirty-four men since we came to Mississippi, and is a full company again; and it keeps its only commissioned officer present for duty very busy indeed.

We do considerable scouting, and have had several skirmished this fall, but such work has got to be an old story with us, and creates no excitement. Our principal want is good horses.

The holidays create quite a demand for salt and groceries, among the inhabitants' and the only place where they can be obtained is at some post or camp.

Bad as they hate the Yankees, the ladies have visited us in considerable numbers of late, all claiming to be loyal, of course, which I think is doubtful, as they never give us any information of the guerrillas, when in the neighborhood. I take every occasion to tell them of it, too. I feel like doing everything in my power to assist the loyal people of the South, and there is a great deal done for them in this regiment, but we are sadly imposed upon by the rebel women; but they are so polite and well bred, that a Yankee officer cannot always resist their eloquent appeals. They have been so very sociable of late, that one of the officers concluded to get up a party. Accordingly, on the evening of the 29th inst., a number of them assembled at the residence of Mr. George, nearly half a mile from the fort and were enjoying themselves in a "little-john shin-dig, or break-down," - vulgarly called a cotillion party. They had taken the precaution to post a strong guard about the premises, but taking pity on the poor fellows, dismissed them about 11 o'clock P.M., and within an hour there was a heavy firing at the outposts, which created great alarm. There were probably fifty or sixty shots fired, and of all the skedaddling that ever was seen, that which followed was a little the tallest. A party went down to the scene of action, but found all quiet. The casualties, as officially reported are:

One very much frightened 1st Alabama Cavalry Regiment;
About twenty-five pairs of badly "skeert" shoulder-straps;
Several pairs of muddy pants, (U.S. uniform);
One Major with a sprained ankle'
One Lieutenant driven into a swamp, (he reported next morning, however); and Two officers' hats left in the house.

One officer reports seeing four mounted rebels about three hundred yards from the house' another says he was shot at near the fort.

103

Opinions differ as to the cause of the alarm - some insisting that it was rebels' other, that it was our own boys. The most reasonable conclusion is, that some evil-disposed person or persons, with wicked intent and malice aforethought, being instigated by the devil, did, on or about the night of the twenty-ninth of December, in the year of Grace 1863, by the firing of sundry and various guns, pistols, and other weapons, hideous screams and demonic yells, disturb the peace and quiet of a whole regiment, and entirely break up and scatter a social party, in the eternal disgrace of the managers thereof; thereby inflicting a great social and moral evil on the party aforesaid. Further, deponent saith not. Respectfully yours.

J.H. Hornback,
1st Lieutenant Company K, 1st Ala. Cav
P.S. The Journal arrives promptly; a welcome visitor it is, too.
J.H.H."

Back to the 1st Alabama. The regiment remained in Nashville at Camp Campbell through Christmas, 1862. They were learning the ways of the military while they were part of a post command at headquarters. It was during this period that the men met their most deadly enemy of the war......disease. It was devastating and it not only claimed the life of my beloved husband, Andrew Ferrier McWhirter, and my brothers, Robert and Tennessee Polk Harper, but my precious eighteen-year old son, George Washington McWhirter. It also claimed the lives of many others from home.

The trouble kept getting worse and worse and the Confederate Home Guard was running rampant looting, murdering, burning homes, barns, crops, etc. of Union families left behind, raping the wives and widows of Union soldiers and terrorizing their young children. It became so violent that in June 1863, a number of Union families and sick and convalescent soldiers, consisting of about 300 persons, mostly women and children whose husbands had joined the Federal service, under the care of Jefferson Milner, a Private in Company B of the 1st AL Cavalry, USV, was selected to escort the "squad" to Cairo, Illinois at which time he was then ordered by General Beaufort who was commander at Cairo, Illinois, to go further north and take them to Centralia, Illinois, which he did. This was to protect them from the marauding Confederate Home Guard imposing so much destruction on Union families, up to and including murder. I might add, here, that after the war many of the families remained in Illinois where their husbands joined them and lived the

104

rest of their lives and are buried there. Many of them were in Marion County, Illinois.

Death left some survivors under almost unbelievably sad and tragic conditions. Union widows were left with small children and no way to provide. They were also left at the hands of the Confederate Home Guard who were determined to wreak havoc on any Unionist or Union sympathizer they could find. (More on this later)

I want to be sure to include my son, Thomas A. McWhirter's, Civil War Diary that he kept up with during the war. He didn't have much to write on but had a little tablet and it gave him something to do when they weren't busy. (See picture of Hornback in back of book.)

THOMAS A. McWHIRTER'S CIVIL WAR DIARY
(Sic)

...And so, despite the emptiness, honor the void
In tribute to what once was....

Thomas A. McWhirter wrote a small diary while he was in the 1st Alabama Cavalry, USV about their movements and some of the things that happened, including General William Tecumsah Sherman's march to the sea. I will include what he wrote in his diary in quotation marks and then add a little history, as I learned about it later, in parentheses after each of his brief statements.

"Thomas A. McWhirter was in the following battles and skirmishes."

"Oct. 20 1862, was in skirmish with Dibbly Cavalry at Neelys Bend 10 miles above Nashville, Tennessee." (This was actually George G. Dibrell's Cavalry.)

"Nov. 5, 1862, was in battle with the Rebbels 5 miles from Nashville, Tennessee on the Frankling Pike. Was in the Stones River Battle commencing Dec. 27th 1862 and ending January 5th 1863."

(On December 26, 1862, the Union Army of the Cumberland left Nashville to engage Braxton Bragg's Army of Tennessee. General William S. Rosecrans sent the three wings of his army on different routes in search of the Rebel army. Many Federal units lost more than one-third of their men at Stone's River. Many Confederate units fared little better. Union soldiers recalled the carnage as looking like the slaughter pens in the stockyards of Chicago. As night approached, the Union army was bloody and battered, but it retained control of the pike and its vital lifeline to Nashville. Although Confederate cavalry would wreak havoc on Union wagon trains, enough supplies got through to give General Rosecrans the option to continue the fight.

"Van Cleve's Division of my command was retiring down the opposite slope, before overwhelming numbers of the enemy, when the guns ... opened upon the swarming enemy. The very forest seemed to fall ... and not a Confederate reached the river."

The cannon took a heavy toll. In forty-five minutes their concentrated fire killed or wounded more than 1,800 Confederates.

106

A Union counterattack pushed the shattered remnants of Breckinridge's Division back to Wayne's Hill.

Faced with this disaster and the approach of Union reinforcements, General Bragg ordered the Army of Tennessee to retreat on January 3, 1863. Two days later, the battered Union army marched into Murfreesboro and declared victory.)

"March 1, 1863, was in battle with the Rebbels at Bradyville, Tennessee."

"April? 3rd, 1863, was in battle with Rebbels Morgan's Cavalry at Snow Hill, Tennessee."

(On the 2nd of April, Companies C,D,E, & F went on a scout with the 1st Cavalry Brigade to Snow Hill skirmishing with Morgan's Cavalry. DeKalb County in Tennessee furnished almost as many Union troops as it did Confederate troops in the Civil War. Fighting occurred around Liberty and included the battle of Snow's Hill on April 3, which engaged about two thousand men on each side. After the armies left, guerrillas, or "bushwhackers," terrorized both Union and Confederate sympathizers in the county. Bitter feelings about the war lasted for decades and were especially strong at election time. Not long after the war, Dowelltown grew up one mile east of Liberty and became the home of several Union army veterans not long after the war.) The distanced they marched was **85 miles,** returning to camp on the 6th. On detached duty from April 8th, 1863.) Note: When the cavalry uses the term, "march", it means in the saddle, not on foot.

"April 8th, 1863, started to Ala. and GA on a raid under command of Col Streight of 51st Indiana."

(The goal of Streight's raid was to cut off the Western & Atlantic Railroad, which supplied General Braxton Bragg's Confederate army in Middle Tennessee. Starting in Nashville, Tennessee, Streight and his men first traveled to Eastport, Mississippi, and then eastward to Tuscumbia, Alabama. On April 26, 1863, Streight left Tuscumbia and marched southeastward. Streight's initial movements were screened by Union Brig. Gen. Grenville Dodge's troops.)

"April 30th 1863, was in Battle at Day's Gap in Alabama in the ???? in and at Crooked Creek in the P M?"

107

(On April 30 at Day's Gap on Sand Mountain, Forrest caught up with Streight's expedition and attacked his rear guard. Streight's men managed to repulse this attack and as a result they continued their march to avoid any further delays and envelopments caused by the Confederate troops. This battle set off a chain of skirmishes and engagements at Crooked Creek (April 30), Hog Mountain (April 30), Blountsville (May 1), Black Creek/Gadsden (May 2), and Blount's Plantation (May 2). Finally, on May 3, Forrest surrounded Streight's exhausted men three miles east of Cedar Bluff, Alabama, and forced their surrender. They were sent to Libby Prison in Richmond, Virginia. Streight and some of his men escaped on February 9, 1864.)

"May 1st 1863, in skirmish with Rebels at Blountsville, Ala. at noon and at 3 o'clock in the afternoon. Fought these again 6 miles from Blountsville."

(Arrived at Blountsville, Alabama on May 1st, 1863. About six miles from the last skirmish, word was passed through the Confederate line that the enemy was at hand. It was about 1:00 AM. The enemy's position was strong, the southern bank of a swift stream, the Mulberry Fork. But again, the ambush failed to surprise, and after another short engagement, Streight withdrew. It was now 2:00 AM, and Forrest ordered all hands to dismount, unsaddle, feed what corn they had left, and lie down for two-hour's sleep. This was a short nap, considering the fact that out of the last 48 hours, they had either ridden steadily or fought for 44 hours. While the Confederates slept, Streight's tired and weary band was winding down the eastern slope of Sand Mountain. They reached Blountsville at 10:00 AM. The citizens had not seen visitors in blue before and had the pleasure of furnishing corn for 2,000 hungry animals as well as seeing every horse and mule in that region gathered up and carried away. It was ten miles from Blountsville to the Locust Fork of the Warrior River and Streight and his men had been dogged by Forrest the whole way. While crossing the river, two of Streight's pack mules drowned and some of Forrest's men pulled them back on their side waving a box of hardtack.)

"May 2nd 1863, was in Battle with the Rebels 6 miles above Gadsden, Ala. Coosey (Coosa) River."

(After leaving Gadsden, it became apparent to both commanders that the bridge over the Coosa River before reaching Rome could be decisive. Streight determined to make one mighty effort to get to Rome first, and towards this and dispatched Captain Russell with

108

two hundred of the best mounted of the command to seize and hold the bridge. Forrest dispatched a single courier to hasten to Rome, warn the citizens, and have the home guards protect the bridge. As night fell on the 2nd, Forrest sent a skeleton squadron ahead to "devil" Streight all night while his own depleted regiments lay down for an all night's rest. Not until daylight did Streight manage to get across the river and when he did, he left the bridge in flames.)

"*May 3rd 1863, was surrendered by Col. Strait to Gen. Forist.*" (Forrest)

(Streight was barely out of sight when the rebels were seen inspecting the ruins of the bridge. Not to be outdone, they forded the creek holding their ammunition high above their heads. As Streight's men lay sleeping, Forrest and his men surrounded them. Colonel Streight wrote in his official report: "Nature was exhausted. A large portion of my best troops actually went to sleep while lying in line of battle under a severe skirmish fire." This is where Thomas A. McWhirter was captured again.)

"*May 4th 1863, was paroled by the Rebels at Rome, Geo. and sent to City Point, VA and then to Camp Chase, Ohio by the way of Fort? Monroe and Anapolis, Maryland, Baltimore, Maryland and return to our Regt. June 8th 1863 for duty.*"

(Next line is illegible and begins with...) "*...in one at Miller, GA and one near Savannah, GA.*" The next whole page is illegible.)

"*June 27th 1863, was in Battle with the Rebels at Shelbyville, Tennessee.*"

"*July 13, 1863, was in skirmish with the Rebels at Pulaski, Tennessee.*"

"*Oct. 19, 1863, skirmish on raid in to Ala. and advance to Walker County and returned on account of high water. We was under command of Col. Spencer 1st Ala.*"

"*Oct 26th, 1863, on ???? returned and fought the Rebels at Vincent's X Roads and there I was captured and was prisoner two months and made my escape.*"

(Colonel George E. Spencer had been made Commander of the 1st Alabama Cavalry, USV when Spencer was given orders by Gen. Hurlburt to take his cavalry on a raid into Alabama. He was to proceed through Jasper and to Columbiana. It was a month before the regiment numbering 650 men, with two light steel guns and supplies, moved out of Corinth in a SE direction. There was considerable doubt that Col. Spencer was leading them to their intended destination for they apparently wandered about in several NW Alabama counties. Nine days after departure, on October 26, they were at Vincent's Cross Roads, only some 30 miles from Corinth, when Brig. Gen. Samuel W. Ferguson and 2,000 Confederate Cavalry attacked them. According to Gen. Ferguson's report to Richmond, he scattered the Alabama Tories over the country, killing 20 including two captains, the adjutant, and a lieutenant, and capturing the two light steel guns, a large number of horses, many supplies, and 40 prisoners. On its return to camp, they were moved from Glendale, MS to Camp Davies in Corinth, MS.)

(Thomas was wounded and taken prisoner at Vincent's Crossroads with several other 1st AL Troopers. They were taken to Cahaba Prison in Alabama, where Thomas made his escape and walked back to Decatur, Alabama where he thought his regiment was.)

"June 25th 1864, I was on the raid with Gen. Sherman in Miss."

"Oct 15th 1864, was in a skirmish with the Rebels right/fight Mis. From Rome, GA over the ???? Spring Road."

"Nov. 11th 1864, move from Rome with Gen. Sherman's expedition from Atlanta to Savannah and was in one skirmish near ???"

More Abuse Inflicted On Sarah

...in God's great plan they had to die,
There is no peace, no rest, no light,
Nothing but an endless night....

This is a letter I received from my son, Thomas, after the Battle at Stone's River in Murfreesboro, Tennessee. That was one more bloody battle.

"Dear Mother, I know it has been hard on you since Papa and George died. It really hurt me to have to leave them behind in Nashville and continue the war without them. However, during the battle we just went through, I was glad they didn't have to participate in it. It was so disastrous that it is difficult for me to describe it. We left Nashville, Tennessee on December 26th after hearing Braxton Bragg and his Rebel army were at Stone's River in Murfreesboro and they were trying to keep us from getting through to Chattanooga. We had already had a small skirmish about five miles out of Nashville, but nothing to compare to what I am about to tell you.

The weather has been terribly dreadful the past few days and it is so cold, foggy, and raining with a mixture of sleet. We have been marching in all of this mess for several days. On December 30, we met up with the Rebels and it was like nothing I had ever seen before and hope I never see again. Mother, there were all kinds of projectiles whistling by our heads, men and horses were falling all around us, and the deafening sound of all the cannons from both sides was unpleasant to say the least.

I have never seen such a gory mess in my life, the ground was crimson with blood and it was nothing but fields of carnage, dead men and horses as far as the eye could see, with captured cannons all jumbled together. The ground was literally covered with blue coats of the dead and wounded Union soldiers. I assumed the gray coats of Confederate dead would be on the other side of the hill. One of the soldiers stated it looked like the slaughter pens in the stockyards of Chicago.

We hadn't even rested from that until they charged us again late that afternoon and we had it to do all over again. The next day, we walked around and it was the same picture of blood and carnage everywhere we looked. We hauled our wounded into the makeshift hospitals in Murfreesboro. We also lined up the dead soldiers side by side in long rows with barely room to walk between the rows. Then we penned a piece of paper on their breast with their names, regiment and state written on the paper, but we couldn't find out who some of them were and had to write "unknown" on them. Some of the men started digging a long narrow ditch to bury them all in. A buddy of mine and I walked into town to see if we could find Bill Hefner, a fellow soldier who had been badly wounded. It was a chaotic scene everywhere we looked with everyone running around trying to find their loved ones. The streets were full of wagons bringing in more wounded. They had turned the courthouse and churches into hospitals and morgues.

After the make-shift hospitals were filled beyond capacity, teamsters loaded the wounded soldiers in the wagons and hauled them to Nashville. The screams of the wounded solders could be heard from a long distance away, as they were in extreme pain. We could hear those blood-curdling screams even after they were out of sight and I will most likely continue hearing them for a long time to come. Also, when we walked in the courthouse, the surgeons were amputating arms and legs as fast as they could and throwing them over to one side. Some were throwing them out the open windows piling them up outside on the ground. One of the soldiers was screaming for them to please not amputate his leg but they continued, explaining to him he had no choice, he would die if they did not amputate. He screamed at them in no uncertain terms that he had rather be dead than go home half a man. The surgeons held something over his nose and mouth and kept sawing.

Mother, I want to tell you a sad story I experienced when we walked in the courthouse hospital looking for our fellow trooper. Over on one side, there was a wounded Rebel soldier and while he had been waiting to be treated he looked around and saw the body of an officer being carried in with blood all over his face. When they placed the dead officer on the floor close to him, he noticed it was his colonel. Even as wounded as this Rebel soldier was he stood up, found a vessel of water, kneeled by his dead Colonel's body, took out his handkerchief and began washing the blood off his face every so gently as if he were still alive. Tears were streaming down his face uncontrollably and his hands were shaking so he could hardly clean the officer's face. Even though he was the enemy, I could not help but feel sorry for him. I went over and kneeled down beside him and asked if it was a relative and he shook his head and begin telling me what a wonderful officer he had been and how good he was to the soldiers. The Rebel soldier had been invited to a grand ball a few nights before but didn't have anything to wear. He told his Colonel why he couldn't go and the Colonel pulled off his jacket and handed it to him telling him to wear it. He was thrilled to have something so nice to wear and when he looked over at the officer, he was wearing that same jacket he had loaned to the soldier, but it was now saturated with the officer's blood. The soldier continued cleaning the blood from his dead Colonel's face and then started trying to clean the blood from his jacket as best he could. He then took out his comb and combed his Colonel's hair and whiskers. He placed his hands across his body and positioned him like he was asleep.

Mother, I believe that was the saddest sight I saw all during the war. When the Rebel soldier finished cleaning and grooming his dead officer and stood up. I leaned over with tears in my eyes and hugged him while telling him how fortunate the officer was to have a soldier like him. He thanked me and my buddy and I left without finding Hefner. We continued walking and looking in different hospitals until we both were sick from the carnage so we went back to camp. We had not had anything to eat in two days but crackers and wanted to see if we could find something. Yours truly, Thomas"

The more I thought about Andrew and how wonderful he was, the more I wanted to write about him so that when the children grew up they would know just how wonderful he really was.

There is a feeling of great insecurity in the tough quarters across the region, the objectionable element having scented the trouble and it is not that unlikely that bloodshed will ensue. The ones proposing to secede showed their ire on some of the Unionists and we knew there would be more to come. While Andrew Ferrier, as well as Andrew Jackson, called "Jackson", and George Washington McWhirter didn't disregard the threats made against their lives, they did not let them weigh upon their minds. They considered them the natural consequences of the political attitude and took a philosophic view of the situation.

Andrew Ferrier McWhirter was a man who could be trusted by day and by night. He was capable of the strongest and best friendships and entered into life with his friends and family and reciprocated heartily and cheerfully every good sentiment they entertained. He was an honorable man and the family, area, state and country was poorer after he died than before. He had before him as bright a future as any young man in the area. His McWhirter genes ran as deep as his ancestors before him. They were great pioneers, scholars, teachers, college professors, doctors and preachers. I ask that when you see his children who survived the war, you will know and remember they are the sons of Andrew Ferrier McWhirter, a great man whom you will see no more, but whose memory will be embalmed in your hearts as long as you live. The consciousness of his death will never be forgotten by the citizens of Marion and surrounding counties in Alabama. When you see his children looking through their father's eyes, it will bring up many an unpleasant thing about the Civil War, and in your memory, you will know their father passed away untimely, that his sun went down when it was yet noon in a vigorous manhood, when he was just entering upon a long career of usefulness in our midst. If not for the dreaded war, his son, George Washington McWhirter, could have also been a great man, but he lost his life long before his time should have ended, before he even had a chance to marry and have children. Andrew Ferrier McWhirter was courteous and considerate to his brethren and faithful to his family and friends. He entertained the profoundest convictions with reference to the church. He loved his God and made sure his children did, also. His manner, speech, and how he raised his family indicated clearly that he had been in the hands of a father and mother who knew how to train children and to make gentlemen and ladies of them. His heart was in the right place and he passed that along to our children.

I'm sure if he could speak to us from Heaven, he would tell his children, friends and neighbors to commit their souls for time and eternity unto the hands of Him who doeth all things well. In early life he was baptized in the Primitive Baptist Church, and had the utmost respect for the teachings of the Church. Our son, Jackson McWhirter, was also baptized in the same faith and after he returned from the war he took up the teachings and later became a Primitive Baptist Circuit Rider, preaching in Alabama, Mississippi, Tennessee, and Texas. He preached in each county in Texas with the exception of three.

I was living in a secluded area of Marion County, Alabama with three young children at home to care for and no one to work the farm. The children and I did the best we could but there were many times I wished Andrew and the older boys were there to help. Andrew would have known what to do when something went wrong with the plow or if a shingle blew off the roof. I was afraid of storms and always worried about them because on February 24th 1860, a

114

tornado hit south of here and demolished homes and a church. We had a lot of wind from that tornado. Then later on May 5th 1868 a bad tornado started in Lowndes County, Mississippi and came through Pickens and on to Tuscaloosa County, Alabama, which was right next to us. At that time, that was the strongest tornado I had ever been in. It killed seven people on the same farm. However, on February 24, 1875, the strongest tornado came through Pickens and Lamar County, Alabama, which was even closer to us and it was terrible. Several homes and four plantations were completely destroyed. There were three deaths in one family and many people were injured. There was a lot of damage done to my roof during that tornado. The last tornado I remember was on April 22nd 1883, when several tornados went through Alabama, the worst one was not far from us in St. Claire County where at least 20 homes were unroofed or destroyed. Although we had a lot of wind from that one, it didn't do any damage.

Things were getting worse and worse as the war progressed. We had no income but we got by with the meat in the smokehouse and the vegetables I had put up and saved in the cellar. Papa had a water-powered grist mill so he ground our corn into meal so I could have it for cornbread, "Johnny-Cakes, and cornmeal mush. He also gave us flour so I would have it for biscuits, bread, and pie crust. We ate a lot of beans, potatoes and cornbread during the war, but since the potatoes didn't keep as long in the cellar as other root vegetables, we usually ran out of them before the next time it was time to dig them. I also made a lot of fried pies from the apples I had dried because the children loved them so. We had fried chicken or chicken and dumplings occasionally but we needed the most of the chickens for the eggs so I didn't cook them very often.

Speaking of apples, beans, and such, I have mentioned my aprons a few times and will tell you a story about why aprons are used so much. I made several aprons because I wore them everyday for more reasons than to keep my dress clean. They were a lot easier to wash than dresses but they also had many different uses and I don't see how any housewife can get by without them. Many times I have dried the eyes of my small children when they cried for one reason or another. Sometimes when I am outside working in the garden, I won't have my egg basket with me, but I will check the chicken coop, find a few eggs and bring them back to the house in my apron. In the hot summertime, as I cook over the burning hot wood stove, my aprons were used to wipe the perspiration from my face, and they have carried a many an apple I have picked up off the ground that

115

had fallen from the apple trees, and vegetables I picked from the garden. I sit on the porch shelling peas and beans, dropping the hulls in my apron and when finished, I picked up the bottom corners of my apron and carried the hulls out to the pigs. That is unless they were purple-hull peas, in which case I sometimes made jelly out of them.

To make the purple-hull jelly, I would wash the hulls good, boil them in a pot of water until they were tender, strain the juice and then boil the juice with sugar, lemon juice and pectin if I could get it. A lot of times pectin was scarce so I had to boil apple peelings and cores until soft and then strain them and mix the juice with the purple-hull pea juice, in order for it to jell. Apples have natural pectin in them but the pea hulls don't so it has to be mixed for it to set up. You can see it's a lot easier and faster to make if you have the pectin to start with. However, we had several apple trees that Andrew planted so apples were plentiful in the fall.

Papa also tanned hides for people, which was a nasty job. After people killed and processed an animal, they would remove the hide from the carcass and take it to Papa to tan for them. He would have to lace the hide to a strong frame. The hide is scraped from the outer layer of skin and the fatty tissue was scraped from the underside. He had a scraper, which was a tool he used for doing that. He would convert the raw hide into leather which then would be used as a fabric for everyday living needs such as garments and accessories, bags, rugs, utility items, or simply cut into strips for straps and ties. Sometimes these would be nailed across windows in houses when glass wasn't readily available.

Once he scraped the hide clean he applied a substance to it and smeared it into the hide until it was thoroughly coated. This had to be done within just a few hours after it was removed from the animal or it would start to decompose. He also had what he called a buffing stick that he used to smooth out the surface as well as stretch it. The stick had a large bulb-type thing on the end so it wouldn't tear the hide. After that, he would stretch it more and tan it by smoking it until it turned a golden brown color. That would cure the hide so it would stay soft and pliant even after getting wet.

I was getting to where I looked forward to hearing the mail carrier coming because I always loved getting letters from my sons and brothers, but at the same time, I was also afraid it might be bad news that I didn't want to hear. I was in the garden one day when I heard

116

him coming and I tensed up when I saw him slowing down, but he handed me a letter and I recognized Thomas' handwriting. I went inside to read it and couldn't believe what all my boys are going through. The following is what Thomas had to say:

"Mother Dear, I have witnessed the most horrible, gruesome site of my life, and I am almost sorry I ever saw this part of the country. I wanted to write to let you know I am alright because I knew you would have heard about the horrendous Battle at Day's Gap here in Alabama and be worried.

There is so much to tell that has happened but I will try to make it as short as I can. On April 26, 1863, General Dodge supplied mules, wagons and rations to Colonel Streight at Tuscumbia, for his men in expectation of a battle with Nathan Bedford Forrest, but when the "mule brigade" set out in the dark of midnight, 150 men had no mounts and had to walk beside mounts who were barely able to carry their saddles. The next day, April 27th, we moved in a blinding rain, a pitch-black night, and on such a muddy road we only made about five miles by daylight on account of the badness of the roads and depthness of the streams swollen by all the rains. The Confederates kept after us until we hardly had any sleep. On April 28th we moved on through mud and rain to Moulton where we arrived about sunset and bivouacked about 9 PM but we were up again by 1 AM on the 29th, mounted and off toward Blountsville, having all kinds of trouble with the mules along the way.

Colonel Streight had assigned Captain Smith and the Alabama boys to be his rear guard and we were saddling up when we heard this loud explosion and someone yelled "What happened?" It was an exploding shell fired from an artillery piece barely 500 yards from us. It was from Nathan Bedford Forrest and his "rag-tag" army and they yelled "HOWDY". No one could believe Forrest had gotten that far! We were chased up the mountain, several of our soldiers were wounded, six were taken to the home of Unionist James Turrentine, who was 86 years old and blind and was the father and grandfather of some of our Union soldiers.

I will skip all the small stuff that happened but the rebels finally caught up to us and we were in the worst fight you can imagine. Several were killed and wounded and the rebels made off with most of our provisions including medical supplies. There our wounded men lay all over the place half-naked, starving and going though the agonies of all types of wounds, broken bones and going untreated.

117

Several needed amputations but the instruments had also been carried off.

If that was not horrible enough, the local men, women and children came from many miles around to see "the wounded Yankees", and we shockingly watched some of the loathsome people make off with the last remnant of our bread and bacon the Confederates left behind because they didn't have room to carry it all!

Mother, I was fortunate not to be one of the ones killed or wounded and just wanted to let you know so you would not worry. Please let Grandpa Harper know. This war is so bad I cannot begin to describe it's horrors, and I can only imagine what might have happened to our state if so many of us had not kept to our beliefs and fought for our country. I want to get this in the mail to you and I will write more as I have time. Love Thomas"

As the sun rose in another chapter of the pandemonium in the area, I knew I needed to get the hoe and chop the weeds in the garden. As I pounded the hoe in the ground, I heard this pinging sound of the hoe striking something hard and kept digging around until I turned up a perfect arrowhead. I picked it up and looked at it for some time wondering who made it and how it got there. I leaned against my hoe and got lost in my thoughts. I kept rubbing the arrowhead thinking about the Indians who used to own this land before Andrew Jackson came through here in 1838 and rounded up almost 20,000 Cherokee Indians like sheep and herded them off to Oklahoma to a reservation, where they would no longer be free as they had known freedom. They didn't have time to get anything except their children and a lot of them walked all the way with no shoes, and their feet bleeding and sore but they had to keep walking and keep up. He had already caused the Creek Indians to lose twenty-two million acres of land in southern Georgia and central Alabama.

Almost 4,000 Indians died on this abhorrent forcible march, and were buried in shallow graves along the trail.

One of the people watching them leave stated, "There was a silence and stillness of the voice that betrayed the sadness of the heart."

This was not the first time they had removed the Indians from their own lands. In their ancestral homeland in parts of North Carolina, Tennessee, Georgia and Alabama, some 100,000 American Indians were forcibly removed from what is now the eastern United States to

118

what was called Indian Territory included members of the Cherokee, Chickasaw, Choctaw, Seminole and Creek Tribes. Their journey by water and land was over a thousand miles long, during which many Cherokees died. The Cherokee struggled to hold on to their land and culture in the face of overwhelming force.

I began thinking of one of our friends and neighbors, Andrew Jackson Ingle. His mother was a beautiful Indian and when Andrew Jackson came through, he met and apparently fell in love with her. It was rumored he lived at her house while here. She was so afraid of having to go on the march that she did everything she could to make him comfortable, so he agreed to let her remain in Alabama. Nine months later, she gave birth to a baby boy. However, Peter Ingle took him in, named him Andrew Jackson Ingle and raised him as his own. He grew up to be a respected citizen of the county and served in the county court system.

While I was standing there leaning against my hoe and thinking about all of this and feeling sorry for the thousands of Indians who had to walk all that way, I heard several hoof beats riding through the woods toward the house and it frightened me. I screamed for the children to get in the house but before I could get to the door, the Confederate Home Guard rode up between me and the front door. They were yelling all kinds of obscenities and one of them literally herded me toward the barn where he drug me inside, threw me down on the hay running his filthy hands provocatively all over my body while I was shivering like the weather was extremely cold outside. It literally made me sick and I was absolutely terrified but didn't want to let on. I tried to get back up while calling him "a trashy mule-headed, gater-bait Rebel". He pushed me back down and my right hand hit something hard. My shivering quickly abated as I looked to the side to see what my hand had hit, and it was a pitchfork. I grabbed for it and tried to hit him with it but he yanked it out of my hand and threw it across the barn. He then laughed saying he liked spirited women and to keep up the fight. All I could think about right then was the children and I was so afraid they might do something to Mary Caroline. Even as young as she was, that wouldn't stop them, as mean as they were. I was thankful they had made it inside the house. The other men must have gotten what they came after because Ham Carpenter, the leader, stuck his head in the barn door and yelled, "Get outa there, you hot-headed reprobate", and they rode off, bound for some other sort of debauchery, leaving this savage beast behind. He stood there with his hair mussed and was raking the hay off his nasty, smelly clothes. As

119

he reached for the door latch, he turned to me with a laconic smile on his face telling me I could expect him back anytime. I looked at him laboriously thinking he said that like it was something I would look forward to. He meant what he said because it was not to be the last time he would display his haughty arrogance around here.

Before the Confederate Home Guard left, one of them went in the smokehouse and ran his bayonet through a ham and rode off with it leaning across his shoulder still on the bayonet. I could see them through a crack in the barn, and I knew they had been stealing everything they could get their hands on. Papa had helped me hide most of the meat Andrew had already smoked and it was a good thing we did. I also had a lot of corn in the corn crib and they had already taken what they could carry of that. I crawled to the door of the barn and peeped out to make sure they were gone, and could see that cowardly beast walking toward his horse. Just then I heard the thundering approach of horse's hooves coming from the opposite direction, and thought it was Papa. While the brute that attacked me was walking to his horse, he was yelling something back at me but his words were drowned out by the rhythmic rattle of the horse's hooves. Just as the uncivilized brute was mounting his horse, the flamboyant Union cavalry officer rode up, dismounted, jerked off his gauntlets and slipped them under his belt. I collected my dignity, brushed the hay out of my hair and stumbled outside, somewhat embarrassed. The blue-clad officer saw me coming across the yard, disheveled and almost in a stagger. I was trying to hide the trepidation I felt but am afraid I didn't do such a good job of it. Standing there with his arms akimbo and a perplexed look on his face; he asked debonairly if that man had bothered me. Before I could answer, the savage turned his horse around and riding toward the officer, he yelled from his horse, "Hell yes, I did, do you think you are big enough to do something about it? I ought to shoot you where you stand, you bluebelly ………." The officer lunged and with one hand, he yanked him off his horse to the ground while drawing his weapon with the other hand which he pointed at him and sternly blurted out, "Don't get cocky with me, you sorry Rebel loving contemptible bastard, the entire area is under Martial Law and that, my dear sir, suspends any of your civil affairs, if you have any. I can hold you and your gang of outlaws personally responsible for what has transpired here and ought to take you in as a prisoner." This almost avenged my sense of outraged justice. I told the officer that the rest of the lecher's miming jackanapes had already ridden away after they raided my smokehouse, and he said he had heard them leaving as he rode up. Before the officer could get back to him, he had mounted his horse and rode off as fast as he could while uttering obscenities at the officer. The officer asked me if I was alright and apologized for his language. I told him I was a little shaken and perturbed, and then explained what had just transpired. He asked where my husband was I told him he and three of my sons had joined the Union Army, and he said, "Good for them". He asked if there were any other men in the area to help protect the women and I advised him they had all joined the Union Army except Mr. Hallmark and Mr. Rice who were deemed too old to fight. He wanted to know if there was anything he could do and went on to say he was looking for an escaped prisoner, described him in depth and asked if I had seen such a man in the area. I assured him I had not. He pulled his steed around, told me to be extremely careful and keep my doors locked, and bid me good day. I was happy he had ridden up when he did, but I surely was sorry to see him leave. His short presence made me feel safe and protected. However, I just wanted to be alone where I could unleash the agonized sobs that were near to bursting forth. I didn't think I would be able to contain them until the officer left. After he rode off, I went down to the creek, buried my face in my apron and sobbed until I could cry no longer.

I wanted to hitch the landau to the horse Papa had given me and go see him where I would feel safe but was afraid to be out with just the children and I, in case we should run across the dreaded Confederate Home Guard or the escaped prisoner. I felt like a prisoner in my own home!

The Confederate Home Guard had left many Union wives, widows and other Unionists in extremely dire circumstances by stealing their food. What they couldn't take, they usually burned. The husbands and sons were not only being killed while in the war, but the home guard was killing the Unionists they found to be aiding the Union soldiers and their families. When they decided to secede from the Union, they had no idea there would be so many men in Northwest Alabama would want to fight for their country they loved, rather than against it.

Maybe, just maybe my other two sons and brothers would soon return and they could help protect us and help with the farm. Jasper Green, one of the neighbors with Union ties helped out as much as he could but finally he had to join the 1st Alabama Cavalry USV in December 1863, to keep from being conscripted into the Confederacy. Jasper and his brother, Samuel rode 90 miles from their home in Marion County, Alabama to Camp Davies,

Mississippi, just out of Corinth, to join the Union Army. Jasper was promoted to Sergeant in January 1864. Of course when he joined the Union Army, it left his wife, Martha Burnett Harper, vulnerable to the Home Guard and she had four young children at home to feed and care for. Martha's brother, Payton Burnett, went with Jasper Green to Corinth and also joined the 1st Alabama Cavalry Union Army, but was captured and taken prisoner of war just three months later.

We had planted a good garden which was filled with the delicacies of spring and I worked in it every chance I got. It was therapy for me to get out there and hoe, dig, plant or pick vegetables. I was thinking about how the blackberries would be blooming soon and I could make a blackberry cobbler and some jelly. The crab apple trees were already blooming and they make good jelly, also. I was out working in the garden one day wondering how my sons and brothers were when I heard a noise, looked up and a dove had lit in one of our apple trees. I remember the Cherokee lore which said the dove is sent from the spirit world to coo for those who feel alone, and sing for them. Their song is said to tell them they are loved and have a rare soul. I thought about that for a while and it actually made me felt better. I just kept on hoeing around the vegetables, and fortunately I had planted and preserved enough vegetables for us to eat until next summer, hopefully.

I couldn't help but think of Andrew dying in Nashville and I couldn't be with him and hold his hand. That must have been a lonely death for not only him but for our son, George. I missed Andrew and wished for a simple touch of his hand. It was not a time when rest came easy to me, my family, or any of the other people in northwest Alabama.

Papa had to get back home to grind some corn for someone who had hid their corn well enough the Confederate Home Guard wasn't able to find it or they would have taken it.

122

Children of Andrew Ferrier McWhirter and Sarah Harper

...can we truly hope to find
among our tears
God's healing power, among our fears....

Thomas Andrew McWhirter

Thomas Andrew McWhirter was born July 10, 1843, married Mary Jane Hallmark, daughter of George Hallmark, on February 13, 1866 and had the following children: Sarah Elizabeth, born December 18, 1866, married Benjamin Franklin Miles and died November 13, 1935 in Marion County, Alabama; Nancy Mahaley, born 1872, married Thomas Head July 28, 1887; Susan Angeline, born February 10, 1874, married William Curtis Sexton June 29, 1890 and died January 29, 1921 in Marion County, Alabama. Thomas and Mary Jane had several children who died in infancy. Thomas died August 26, 1917, and is buried in the old Poplar Springs Primitive Baptist Church Cemetery in Marion County, Alabama. Mary Jane died August 1, 1904. Thomas was 5' 8" tall, had hazel eyes, black hair, and light complexion.

Thomas A. McWhirter chose to remain in Marion County, Alabama. At least seven of his and Mary Jane's children died at birth or shortly after, including one set of twins. He is buried in the Old Poplar Springs Primitive Baptist Church Cemetery in Rock City, Marion County, Alabama.

He was enrolled in the 1st Regiment Alabama Cavalry, USV on the July 24th 1862, at Huntsville, Alabama for 3 years, and is reported on Roll to October 31, 1862, present & so reported to June 30, 1863. However, Prisoner of war Records also show him captured at Rome, Georgia May 3, 1863, but he also escaped from there and made it back home.

June 30, 1863 to Oct 31, 1863, (4 mo muster) Missing in Action at Vincent's Cross Roads October 26, 1863. Company was in action at that place & date. December 31, 1863, to February 29, 1864, name not borne. April 30, 1864 to December 31, 1864, present. From December 31 1864 to April 30, 1865 at Annapolis, Maryland. Paroled Prisoner of war, wounded in battle. May & June 1865, present. Mustered out with company July 19, 1865 with remark

123

"Wounded in Skirmish near Richmond, North Carolina, April 1, 1865." Company was in action at Faison's Depot North Carolina March 30 & 31, 1865. The reason he was sent to Annapolis, Maryland was because as the war was winding down, they sent wounded POW's, who had been exchanged or released, there for medical treatment and processing to be sent home. Thomas had been wounded and then captured two weeks later.

Prisoner of war Records also show him captured at Rome, Georgia May 3, 1863 and confined at Richmond, Virginia. May 9, 1863, paroled at City Point, Virginia, May 15, 1863, reported at Camp Parole, Maryland May 16, 1863. Disposition not given. Reported at Camp Chase, Ohio May 22, 1863. No later record. No evidence of such ....?...

This is one more letter Sarah Harper McWhirter received from Thomas asking her to keep it to go with his Civil War Diary he wrote:

"Dear Mother, I haven't been able to write much in my diary lately but rather than writing all of this in the diary, I thought I would just write and tell you what has been going on since we left Savannah and let you know what a week or few weeks are like in the army. Please save this for me so I can add it to my diary when I get home. You can also show it to Mary Jane, if she wants to read it because I won't have time to write all of this to her, too.

We finally broke camp near Savannah, Georgia, on January 28, 1865, and moved on the Springfield road leading to Sister's Ferry on the Savannah River. We arrived at Sister's Ferry on the evening of the 29th, where we camped until February 3rd, when we crossed the river and commenced our march in South Carolina in the direction of Lawtonville. On the 6th we had some skirmishing with Crews' brigade, of Wheeler's command, capturing some prisoners. On the 7th we assisted in destroying Charleston and Augusta Railroad, and then on the 8th we moved from Blackville on the road to Williston, and we were in advance. We came to the rebel pickets just before reaching the village. We routed, and drove them through the town, and established a picket-post half a mile west of the village, awaiting the arrival of the rest of the troops. The regiment soon arrived, and as we were about to establish camp the picket-post was attacked. Captain Latty, in command of two squadrons, was immediately ordered forward with instructions to ascertain, if possible, the force the enemy had in the vicinity. As he advanced the firing became rapid, and we were ordered to Captain Latty's assistance. We drove them one mile and a half, where we found they had established a strong line. We drove them half a mile, where they had another line. We were re-enforced with the Fifth Kentucky Cavalry and then ordered to resume the chase. On advancing we found the enemy in a strong position in the woods near White Pond. On being ordered, we charged them and there followed the most complete rout I ever witnessed. Guns, sabers, canteens, haversacks, saddle-bags, hats, and everything left behind by the fleeing enemy were abandoned and completely strewn over the ground. We continued the pursuit over five miles, capturing quite a number of prisoners, with five stand of colors. We were then ordered to abandon the pursuit, and returned to camp at Williston. We had been contending against a greatly superior force of the enemy. We were praised in the highest degree for our actions, but we lost four men, wounded, one mortally, who afterward died.

On the 11th we again resumed our march and participated in all the different scenes through which we passed, crossing the Edisto, Saluda, Broad, Wateree, and Great Pedee Rivers, via Lexington, Alston, Black Stocks, Lancaster, and Sneedsborough, nothing of special importance occurring. After crossing the Great Pedee River and going into camp at 8 o'clock on the evening of March 6, we were ordered to proceed to Rockingham, N.C., about twelve miles distant, and, if possible, take the place and secure the mail. We advanced to within three miles of the place without meeting any opposition, but found the road strongly picketed by the enemy, and were immediately ordered to charge. We drove the enemy from post to post until we reached the edge of the village, where we found a line too strong for us to break, so we slowly fell back and returned to camp, arriving there at 4 a.m. on the 7th. We leave later on for Monroe's Crossroads and will probably be skirmishing with them all the way. This is all I have time to write, so give my love to Mary Jane and Papa Harper. Love Thomas"

It was right after this that they camped at Monroe's Crossroads, and Kilpatrick's Calvary attacked them early the morning of March 10th while they were still asleep.

George Washington McWhirter

George Washington McWhirter was born in 1844 in Eldridge, Walker County, Alabama and enlisted in Company K of the 1st Alabama Cavalry, USV on July 24, 1862 in Huntsville, Alabama along with his father and two brothers. He was sent as far as Nashville, Tennessee where he contracted measles and died in Army Hospital #14, on October 8, 1862, just two weeks after his father died in the same hospital. He is buried in the Nashville National Cemetery in Nashville, Davidson County, Tennessee.

Andrew "Jackson" McWhirter

Andrew Jackson McWhirter was born June 23, 1847, in Marion County, Alabama to Andrew Ferrier and Sarah Harper McWhirter. He was barely fifteen (15) when he joined the 1st Alabama Cavalry, USV. Andrew Ferrier and Sarah were extremely upset about his decision to join but he was determined to go along with his father and two brothers. He was in Nashville when his father and brother, George Washington McWhirter, died, and he was on General William Tecumseh Sherman's famous March to the Sea, along with his brother, Thomas.

Jackson McWhirter married Nancy Jane Whitehead in 1867, in Marion County, Alabama. Nancy was born August 1, 1848, and died March 12, 1936, at the home of their son, George Franklin McWhirter, in Marion County, Alabama. After Jackson's death, she left Eagleville, Tennessee and went back to Marion County, Alabama to live with her son, George Franklin McWhirter and his wife. Nancy Jane Whitehead was the daughter of Archibald Whitehead, Jr., and his wife, Martha G. "Patsy" Anthony. Archibald, Jr. died an untimely death on August 8, 1861 and it is thought he was killed by what he called the "Confederate Dog Cavalry" because of his loyalty to the Union. .Archibald's brother, Drewry "Drew" Henry Cox Whitehead, was also a Unionist and he and three sons served in the 1st Alabama Cavalry, USV.

Andrew Jackson McWhirter was so very young when he enlisted, but he proudly served out his time and after several close calls he was able to return home to his family. Jackson applied for a pension and it was denied. After he died, his widow applied for a pension and Andrew D. Mitchell gave the following statement:
"When I became a member of Company L 1st Alabama Calvary, Andrew J. McWhirter, was then a member of Company K 1st Alabama Calvary. Captain Hornback was the Captain and Andrew J. McWhirter was with his Company and Regiment in Tennessee, Alabama and Georgia, I was with this Regiment ONE YEAR EIGHT MONTHS AND FIVE DAYS, Andrew J. McWhirter was with this Regiment all the time I was with it, Andrew J. McWhirter

126

just prior to the close of the war went to Ohio and did not return until the Company was disbanded, I know this of my own personal knowledge." Other affidavits state he served in Co. K of the 1st AL for almost two years and was present and served as an artilleryman during the Battle of Monroe's Crossroads in North Carolina. The request for a pension was denied stating Andrew Jackson McWhirter was a Servant, which was a Civilian position and was not a pensionable classification. George W. Whitehead signed an affidavit in a request for pension trying to help his sister, Nancy Jane Whitehead McWhirter, draw a pension from her husband's service in the 1st AL Cav. US. "I know of my own personal knowledge that Andrew J. McWhirter was an Orderly under Captain Hornback, United States Army. I know that Andrew J. McWhirter served more than eighteen months in Tennessee, Alabama and Georgia. He fought with the Artillery in the battle of Monroe's Cross Roads, North Carolina, March 10, 1865, in this battle Captain Hornback was wounded, a day or two after this battle Andrew J. McWhirter got on a boat with Captain Hornback at Fayetteville, North Carolina, and went home with Captain Hornback some place in Ohio, where he remained until late in the summer of 1865 when he returned to Alabama. During the absence of Andrew J. McWhirter, Company K 1st Alabama Cavalry was disbanded, I was a member of Company K 1st Alabama Cavalry and was discharged and returned home, I know this of my own personal knowledge." Signed George W. Whitehead on October 11, 1928, J.T. Curtis, Notary Public. There was another note in the file stating A.J. McWhirter had escorted Hornback home to Ohio because he was worried about him being wounded and afraid he might not make it by himself."

Andrew Jackson McWhirter's daughter, Martha Elizabeth McWhirter Letson, submitted a letter October 12, 1928 stating the following: "Enclosed find application blank for my mother's pension. I have two affidavits from two of my father's comrades. These two men were raised with my father – they were friends before the war and knew each other intimately. My father left home to join the army before either Mr. Whitehead or Mr. Mitchell did. There is no doubt of my father's service in the army. Possibly his going home with Captain Hornback may be the reason father did not get his discharge papers. If this is allowed can it be fixed so Mother can get back pension as is done sometimes? Very Truly, Mrs. W.P. Letson" (Mrs. W.P. Letson was Martha "Mary" Elizabeth McWhirter, daughter of Andrew Jackson McWhirter and Nancy Jane Whitehead. She married William Palestine Letson.)

127

On November 29, 1867, Andrew Jackson McWhirter married Nancy Jane Whitehead in Glen Allen, Alabama. The marriage was performed by John Beasley, Justice of the Peace. Nancy was the daughter of Archibald Whitehead and Martha G. "Patsy" Anthony. Jackson was a Primitive Baptist Circuit Rider, preaching in Alabama, Mississippi, Tennessee and Texas. He was the minister of the Old Poplar Springs Primitive Baptist Church in Rock City, Marion County, Alabama and also preached in the old New Hope PB Church in Hatley, Mississippi on alternate Sundays, riding his horse back and forth from Rock City to Hatley. He moved to Eagleville, Rutherford County, Tennessee sometime before 1900 and he preached at the Eagleville Primitive Baptist Church until shortly after he suffered a debilitating stroke. He is buried on his farm about a mile out of Eagleville, Tennessee with a large tombstone. His widow, Nancy Jane, died March 12, 1936 in Marion County, Alabama and is buried in the old Poplar Springs Primitive Baptist Church Cemetery in Marion County, Alabama along with their son, John Crow McWhirter, who died at the age of 13 after being kicked in the head by a horse. Jackson's brother, Thomas A. McWhirter is also buried there as well as several other relatives. One of Jackson's granddaughters stated he was preaching in church one Sunday when a baby began crying and its mother stood up to take it outside. Jackson told her to sit back down stating he could preach louder than any baby could cry.

Robert McWhirter

Robert McWhirter was born in 1848 in Marion County, Alabama and died between 1850 and 1860.

William Hamilton "Hamp" McWhirter

William Hamilton "Hamp" McWhirter was born July 19, 1852 in Marion County, Alabama. He married Sarah Jane Hallmark, who was born March 14, 1854, and died July 23, 1911 in Marion County, Alabama. Sarah Jane was the granddaughter of their neighbor, George Hallmark, who was murdered by the Confederate Home Guard during the Civil War. William Hamilton and Sarah had the following children: Mary Ann, born January 20, 1880, died February 24, 1916, Thomas Andrew, born October 1881, died in 1907, John Lewis, born March 1, 1883, died October 14, 1960, George Washington, born October 10, 1885, died December 27, 1929, Margaret Jane, born July 31, 1888, died June 25, 1925, Martha Emilene, born April 7, 1891, died June 8, 1929, and Phoebe Drucilla

128

McWhirter, born February 8, 1898, and died July 12, 1959. Their son, Thomas Andrew, was killed in a coal washer accident in Carbon Hill, Marion County, Alabama.

William Hamilton was roofing a house, had a stroke and fell to the ground. He never recovered. Two of his daughters died in the 1920's, one daughter died during childbirth in 1916 and is buried in Buttahatchie Cemetery.

Mary Caroline McWhirter

Mary Caroline McWhirter was born May 17, 1855 in Marion County, Alabama and died December 16, 1934, in Quitman, Wood County, Texas. She married George Washington Harbin November 29, 1873, in Marion County, Alabama. George was born February 22, 1846, in Cherokee County, Georgia and died November 29, 1920, in Quitman, Wood County, Texas. Mary Caroline and George had seven children: Robert Andrew, born February 16, 1875, died October 19, 1946 in Dallas, Wood County, Texas; Alonzo Alexander, born November 3, 1876, died February 21, 1962 in Childress County, Texas; Nancy Alice, born January 1880, died 1910 in Quitman, Wood County, Texas; Jessie Jackson, born 1883 and died December 5, 1945; William Thomas, born March 1886, died 1960 in Wood County, Texas; Walter Franklin, born March 1893, died 1952 in Hollis, Harman County, Oklahoma; and Ida Mae Harbin, born October 15, 1897 and died January 1974 in Egypt, Wharton County, Texas.

Mary Caroline McWhirter Harbin's Pension record states she died 16 Dec 1934 from cerebral hemorrhage (apoplexy), at the home of her son, R. A. Harbin. Mary Caroline and George are buried in Ebenezer Cemetery in Oak Grove, Wood Co., TX. They moved to Texas some time between 1893 and 1897. After Jasper Green McWhirter and his wife died leaving small children, Mary Caroline and George petitioned the court for guardianship of the children.

According to George Washington Harbin's Pension Records, #30706 he was born in Cherokee County, Georgia, enlisted in Company K, 2nd Georgia Cavalry, CSA in Cherokee County, Georgia in the summer of 1863, and stated he was surrendered at Kingston, Georgia in May, 1865. In 1915, he stated he was 69 years old and had been living in Wood County, Texas since 1893. He listed his Post Office as Quitman, Texas, RFD #5.

129

Mary Caroline McWhirter Harbin, filed for a Civil War pension December 16, 1920, stating they were married 29 November 1873 in Marion County, Alabama.

John Madison McWhirter

John Madison McWhirter was born February 15, 1858, in Marion County, Alabama and died January 10, 1907 in Marion County, Alabama. He married Georgia Ann Elizabeth O'Mary, daughter of Thomas Christmas O'Mary and his wife, Elizabeth Oma Arnold. John and Georgia had the following children: Sarah Elizabeth, born May 29, 1878, died June 16, 1940; Susan A. "Susie", born February 9, 1879, died October 6, 1880; Savannah Belle, born June 20, 1882, died March 31, 1965; William Blaine, born February 19, 1893, died September 24, 1934; Thomas Benton, born June 16, 1896, died March 28, 1921; John Crow, born September 6, 1898, and died February 5, 1975; and Thomas B. McWhirter, born June 1896.

Children of Sarah Harper McWhirter

Nancy Ann McWhirter

In 1865, Sarah gave birth to a daughter, Nancy Ann McWhirter. (On January 5, 1888, Nancy Ann married George Washington Miles on February 5, 1888 in Marion County, Alabama. George W. Miles was born February 22, 1867. He was the son of Calvin and Livinia Ann "Viney" Matthews Miles. Calvin Miles was the son of William Miles, whose widow, Mary, later married Thomas Harper, Nancy Ann's grandfather. Nancy Ann McWhirter Miles died in 1892 during childbirth. They had two other children, Grant Miles, born 1889 and Andrew J. Miles, born April 2, 1892, and died February 6, 1976.)

On August 18, 1868, Sarah gave birth to Jasper "Green" McWhirter. "Green" McWhirter married January 5, 1888, in Marion County, Alabama to Mary Silvania Tucker, born March 19, 1870 in Marion County, Alabama. Green died around 1902 in Quitman, Wood County, Texas. Mary Silvania Tucker was the daughter of Kimbrel "Kimber" Foster Tucker and Martha Ann Harper, daughter of Thomas Harper. Kimber was born July 11, 1847 in Marion County, Alabama and died June 30, 1922 in Talihina, Leflore County, Oklahoma. They had married July 1, 1869 in Fayette County, Alabama Jasper Green died in 1902 in Winnsboro, Wood County, Texas and is buried in a "pauper's grave" with no marker. Jasper's children were: James Edgar,

Alonzo, Claude, Lafayette, Andrew, and Laura McWhirter, and at the time of his death, the oldest child was only twelve (12) years old. His wife, and the mother of his children, had died the previous year, leaving him to care for those six children. Mary Caroline McWhirter and her husband, George Washington Harbin, applied for guardianship of the children so they could care for them.

Jasper Green McWhirter

Jasper "Green" McWhirter was born August 18, 1865 in Marion County, Alabama and died in 1902 in Winnsboro, Wood County, Texas. He married Mary Silvania Tucker on January 1, 1888 in Marion County, Alabama. Mary Silvania was born March 19, 1870 in Marion County, Alabama and died in 1901 in Wood County, Texas. After Mary died, Green married Mollie E. Voorheese June 20, 1901. Just a few months later, Green was killed by a train, leaving six young children. Mary Caroline McWhirter, daughter of Andrew Ferrier and Sarah Harper McWhirter, petitioned the court for guardianship of these children and they were later found in the census records living with Mary Caroline and George W. Harbin.

Children of Jasper Green and Mary Silvania were: Alonzo L, born November 1, 1888, died January 21, 1964; Lafayette, born June 18, 1890, died August 23, 1974; James Edgar, born December 18, 1893, died February 28, 1976; Claude, born October 9, 1895, died October 6, 1971, and Laura McWhirter, born September 20, 1898, and died October 31, 1960.

Sarah's son, Jackson McWhirter, thought so much of Jasper Green McWhirter, above, that he named one of his children, Jasper Green McWhirter.

131

Thomas Andrew McWhirter in Battle of Stone's River

...With every ounce of faith confessing
Hope for a better life tomorrow
In our mourning we find blessing....

On December 26, 1862, about two months after his father and brother, George, died in Nashville, Thomas A. McWhirter, along with the Union Army of the Cumberland, left Nashville, Tennessee to engage Braxton Bragg's Army of Tennessee. One wing of General William S. Rosecrans' Army was sent in search of the Rebel army. According to Thomas McWhirter's Diary, they battled with the Rebels about five miles out of Nashville on the Franklin Pike, but they had no idea what they would be facing at Stone's River in Murfreesboro, Tennessee where General Braxton Bragg and the Confederate Army of Tennessee was camped. Bragg had chosen this area in order to position himself to stop any Union advances toward Chattanooga and to protect the rich farms of the Middle Tennessee area that were providing food for his men.

Union General-In-Chief, Henry Halleck had telegraphed Rosecrans telling him that the Government demanded action, and if he could not respond to that demand, they would try someone else.

The cold of the winter bore down with the fog and abundance of sleet and rain which hindered Rosecrans and his men, but by the evening of December 30, 1862, the two armies met and faced off. Bragg had ordered Breckinridge's troops to regain control of the Nashville Pike so he ordered them to charge again for one last assault. J. Morgan Smith of the 32nd Alabama Infantry, CSA, stated they charged to within fifty yards of them and had not the timely order of retreat been given, none of them would have been left to tell the tale. His regiment carried two-hundred and eighty into action and came out with fifty-eight.

As night approached, the Union army was bloody and battered, but it retained control of the pike and its vital lifeline to Nashville.

Faced with this disaster and the approach of Union reinforcements, General Bragg ordered the Army of Tennessee to retreat on January 3, 1863. Two days later, the battered Union army marched into Murfreesboro and declared victory.

132

The Battle of Stones River was one of the bloodiest of the war. More than 3,000 men lay dead on the field. Nearly 16,000 more were wounded. Some of these men spent as much as seven agonizing days on the battlefield before help could reach them. The two armies sustained nearly 24,000 casualties, which was almost one-third of the 81,000 men engaged.

On New Year's Day, wagons carrying the Union wounded off to Nashville as civilians from the area ventured cautiously onto the battlefield searching for their husbands, sons, brothers and friends. One civilian stated they spent the entire day looking for her fallen brother, but it was all in vain. She stated, "He sleeps among the unknown dead."

Sarah Harper McWhirter did not have the privilege of traveling to Tennessee from her home in Marion County, Alabama to walk the fields searching for her son, Thomas McWhirter, but as it turned out, Thomas was one of the ones to survive.

Different yards were filled with rows of dead Federal soldiers with narrow aisles between rows where relatives and friends could walk and read the name, company, regiment and state of each, and oftentimes just the simple word "Unknown" was pinned on the dead soldier's breast. On one edge of the yard they were digging a narrow but extremely long ditch for the burial of the fallen soldiers.

Thomas A. McWhirter had escaped harm during this battle, but it was just the first of others to come where he would not be as fortunate. As stated earlier, Thomas fought in this battle along with the ones at Vincent's Crossroads in Red Bay, Alabama, and others along the way as he marched with General Sherman's Army on his march to the sea, including the one at Monroe's Crossroads in North Carolina on the way back.

The First Alabama Cavalry, USV

...The One who fashioned us from stardust and seashells
and breathed in us a living spirit
creates, comforts and calls us still
to rise higher and become more.

During the war over two thousand loyal Southerners served in the 1st Alabama: farmers, mechanics, traders and others, from 35 counties of Alabama and eight other Confederate states. There were men from the border states of Kentucky and Missouri, from seven northern states and eight foreign countries. The "1st" WAS diversity 130 years before it became "politically correct."

During most of its operational life, the 1st Alabama was part of the 16th Corps, Union Army of the Tennessee. In its early months, the unit filled traditional cavalry roles of the time: scouting, raiding, reconnaissance, flank guard and screening the army on the march. It fought mostly in actions associated with those missions: actions no less deadly for being small. Names on the regiment's battle flag such as Nickajack Creek, Vincent's Crossroads and Cherokee Station among others, were hardly known at the time and are all but forgotten today. But there are better known places too, such as Streight's Raid through north Alabama; and battles at Dalton, Resaca and Kennesaw Mountain in the Atlanta campaign. Men of the 1st fell on many fields in their country's service.

By the time Sherman's forces entered Atlanta in late 1864, the "1st's" reputation was secure. One general called the Alabama troops "invaluable...equal in zeal to anything we discovered in Tennessee." And Major General John Logan, commanding the 15th Army Corps in Sherman's forces, praised the troopers as "the best scouts I ever saw, and (they) know the country well from here to Montgomery." General Sherman, knowing the value of his Alabama troops as soldiers and symbols of the loyal South, chose them as his escort on the march from Atlanta to the sea.

The honor of guarding the Army's commander, however, did not keep the 1st Alabama Cavalry from the line of fire. On March 10, 1865, soon after entering North Carolina, the 1st was embroiled in its hardest fight. At Monroe's Crossroads the regiment was surprised in its camp by the dawn attack of Confederate cavalry underGenerals Joseph Wheeler and Wade Hampton. A bloody hand

134

to hand conflict followed, lasting more than three hours.

After the Battle of Monroe's Crossroads, Thomas had the following to say later on that day when they went into town foraging. He had told about the battle and then stated:

"There were still horse-drawn ambulances bringing in the wounded, some crying out in pain, and they descended upon the town along with hundreds of grim-faced Union soldiers, many still in a state of shock. The horrific aftermath of the battle was evident everywhere as a dark gloom wrapped the city. Men fired into each other's faces, not even five-feet apart. There were bayonet thrusts, saber strokes, pistol shots with men falling backwards, to their knees, spinning around like tops, throwing out their arms, some with dangling parts. There were ghastly heaps of dead and wounded men all over the place.

Jackson and I (Thomas A. McWhirter) were both caught up in this horrendous battle and Jackson was awakened from a sound sleep as were most of us. He had been sleeping by the big guns, grabbed them and started firing, serving as an artilleryman after the Confederates attacked. Only the timely appearance of a section of field artillery enabled us to drive the Confederates from their camp and hold them off until help came. More on this battle later.

When the smoke cleared, the Third Brigade of Judson Kilpatrick's Union cavalry division, including the 1st and two other regiments, about 800 men, had routed 5,000 Confederates. The rebels lost 103 dead and many more wounded at a cost to the Federals of 18 dead, 70 wounded and 105 missing. Will write more as I have time. Love, Thomas"

Thomas and Jackson had apparently escaped with their lives but just a few days later on April 1, 1865, Thomas was wounded. On April 15, 1865, Thomas was out with some other soldiers foraging when they were caught and taken Prisoners of War by the Confederates. In the meantime, their Captain, Joseph Hornback, was severely wounded during the battle so Jackson asked for and received permission to help him to a ship and escort him home in Ohio. He had to remain with him for a few weeks to care for him and by the time he returned to his regiment, they had already mustered out so he returned home. Thomas was home a few days later.

I had a disturbing letter from Jackson after the Battle of Monroe's Crossroads. It really bothered me and I worried about it for some time. It was not like Jackson to concern me like he did in this particular letter. He had the following to say:

"My Dearest Mother, fighting is all around us and I feel compelled to write again to express my love for you and to thank you for the Christian life in which you and Father brought us up. The severe conflicts we are experiencing could bring death to me at any time, but if that should happen, it shall be God's will. If my death should be my fall on the battlefield for my country, then so-be-it, as I am ready. I have absolutely no misgivings in the cause for which I am engaged and my courage and love for my country does not falter. We owe a great debt to those great Americans who went before us through the blood and sufferings of the American Revolution, so I feel as though I am picking up where they left off to maintain the freedom of the country I love. I really hated to go against the wishes of you and Father when you begged me not to join the Army and you know I always did as you said, but I knew I would not be able to hold my head high if I did not fight to do all that I possibly could to help maintain this government and help pay the debt I felt I owed. At the same time, I realize that should I lose my life to the enemy, your life will be filled with sorrows and cares. I do want you to know, my dearest Mother; I am most grateful for having had the best loving parents in the world and am grateful to God for you.

No matter what happens, you will know that I love my country more than I fear death.

I will write again as time permits, your loving and grateful son, Jackson."

Thomas A. McWhirter was wounded April 1, 1865 in Richland, NC and taken POW on April 15, 1865 from Faison's Station, NC

HEADQUARTERS FIRST ALABAMA VOLUNTEER CAVALRY
FAISON'S DEPOT, N.C. MARCH 28, 1865
Report of Major Sanford Tramel, First Alabama Cavalry, of operations January 28 - March 24

LIEUTENANT: I have the honor to report that, in obedience to orders received from your headquarters, my regiment, under command of Maj. F.L. Cramer, numbering 18 officers and 292 men for duty, broke camp near Savannah, Ga., on the 28th day of

January, 1865, and moved with the brigade on the Springfield road leading to Sister's Ferry on the Savannah River. We arrived at Sister's Ferry on the evening of the 29th, and camped two miles from the river, where we remained until the 3rd day of February, when we crossed the river and commenced our march in South Carolina in the direction of Lawtonville.

On the 4th Capt. J.J. Hinds, commanding Second Battalion was ordered back to Sister's Ferry to report to Major-General Slocum, in obedience to orders from the colonel commanding brigade. This left only one battalion of 170 men in the regiment. On the 6th we had some skirmishing with Crews' brigade, of Wheeler's command, capturing some prisoners. On the 7th assisted in destroying Charleston and Augusta Railroad, on the 8th we moved from Blackville on the road to Williston, my regiment in advance. I, with two squadrons, was ordered in the advance, and came to the rebel pickets just before reaching the village. We routed, and drove them through the town, and established a picket-post half a mile west of the village, awaiting the arrival of the command. The regiment soon arrived, and as we were about to establish camp the picket-post was attacked. Captain Latty, in command of two squadrons, was immediately ordered forward with instructions to ascertain, if possible, the force the enemy had in the vicinity. As he advanced the firing became rapid, and I, with the remaining three squadrons, was ordered to Captain Latty's assistance. We drove them one mile and a half, where we found they had established a strong line. Major Cramer was soon on the ground and took command of the main body in the center, while I, with twenty men and Captain Latty with the same number, moved on each flank of the enemy, Major Cramer advancing with the center. This movement routed them. We drove them half a mile, where they had another line. This we broke also, and halted for a short time, when Colonel Spencer, commanding brigade, re-enforced us with the Fifth Kentucky Cavalry. We were then ordered to resume the chase, and on advancing found the enemy in a strong position in the woods near White Pond. On being ordered, we charged them, when followed the most complete rout I ever witnessed. Guns, sabers, canteens, haversacks, saddle-bags, hats, and everything which would impede the fight of the affrighted and flying enemy were abandoned and completely strewn over the ground. We continued the pursuit over five miles, capturing quite a number of prisoners, with five stand of colors. We were then ordered to abandon the pursuit, and returned to camp at Williston. We ascertained we had been contending against a greatly superior force of the enemy.

137

The conduct of the officers and men of my regiment on this occasion was praiseworthy in the highest degree. The loss of the regiment was four men wounded, one mortally, who later died.

On the 10th of February Captain Hinds joined us with his battalion, and the regiment was present at the fight near Aiken, but took no active part, except to build a barricade and hold a position on the right. On the 11th we again resumed our march with the brigade, and participated in all the different scenes through which it passed, crossing the Edisto, Saluda, Broad, Wateree, and Great Pedee Rivers, via Lexington, Alston, Black Stocks, Lancaster, and Sneedsborough, nothing of special importance occurring. After crossing the Great Pedee River and going into camp at 8 o'clock on the evening of March 6, I was ordered to take fifty men and proceed to Rockingham, N.C., about twelve miles distant, and, if possible, take the place and secure the mail. I advanced to within three miles of the place without meeting any opposition. I there found the road strongly picketed by the enemy, and immediately ordered my men to charge, which they did in a gallant manner, driving the enemy from post to post until we reached the edge of the village, where we found a line too strong for us to break with the small force at my command; consequently I ordered the men to fall back slowly, which they did in good order. I then returned to camp, arriving there at 4 a.m. on the 7th. We again moved with the brigade on the evening of the 9th camped at Monroe's Cross-Roads, having marched during the day in close proximity with the enemy. At the sounding of reveille on the morning of the 10th instant, we were aroused from sleep by the whistling of bullets and the fiendish yelling of the enemy, who were charging into our camp. Then followed a most bloody hand-to-hand conflict, our men forming behind trees and stumps and the enemy endeavoring to charge us (mounted) with the saber. While gallantly cheering his men Maj. F.L. Cramer was wounded and taken prisoner.

The fighting was most desperate for an hour, when we succeeded, in connection with the Fifth Kentucky and Fifth Ohio Volunteer Cavalry, in driving the enemy away from our camps.

During the fight I was captured by the enemy and held as prisoner until the 14th instant, when I succeeded in making my escape, and after three days lying in the swamps and traveling nights, I succeeded in rejoining my command. After my capture Capt. J.J. Hinds took command of the regiment and retained it until my return, and I am indebted to him for the gallant manner in which he handled the command during the remainder of that severe and terrible fight. Captain Peek deserves special mention for his gallant daring and coolness during this struggle. The loss of the regiment in the affair was 4 men killed, 27 wounded, and 41 missing.

My regiment moved with the brigade, and was present when the cavalry encountered the enemy on the evening of the 15th, also in the fight of the 16th instant, but sustained no loss as it held a position on the left. We next encountered the enemy in strong force on the 18th, but evaded him by taking a road leading more to the right, while a portion of the Fifth Kentucky Cavalry attracted his attention at a certain point. We encountered the enemy again same day, but he was easily repulsed and driven away. My regiment continued with the brigade; was present and assisted in guarding the left flank of the army during the hard battles of the 19th, 20th and 21st instant. The enemy then being routed and the campaign ended, my regiment moved with the brigade to Faison's Depot, where we arrived on the 24th instant and have remained in camp since that time. During the campaign my regiment has captured something over 100 prisoners and over 200 horses.

The regiment has lost during the campaign: Maj. F.L. Cramer, severely wounded and a prisoner; afterward paroled on account of wounds. Capt. John Latty, Company C; First Lieut. George W. Emerick, Company A; First Lieut. Joseph H. Hornback, Company K; Second Lieut. George C. Jenkins, Company M, wounded severely; Surg. J.G.C. Swaving and First Lieut. John P. Moore, Company E, captured. Moore afterward escaped. Four enlisted men killed, 28 wounded (2 or 3 mortally, who afterward died), 46 captured; 215 horses - some by being captured, others by being worn out and abandoned.

I have the honor to be, lieutenant, very respectfully, your obedient servant.
S. TRAMEL, Major, First Alabama Volunteer Cavalry, Comdg. Regiment.
(Extracted by Glenda McWhirter Todd)

A potential disaster had become a clear cut victory. A few weeks later, the 1st was present at the surrender of General Joseph E. Johnston's Confederate army and "Sherman's March" was at last complete.

When the 1st Alabama Cavalry (U.S.V.) mustered out for good on October 20, 1865 only 397 men remained with the colors. In three years' service the regiment lost 345 men killed in action, died in prison, of disease or other non-battle causes; 88 became POWs and 279 deserted. There is no accurate count of wounded. Bitterness between secessionists and loyalists in Alabama remained for years after the war. It soured state politics for over a century and traces of it can still be seen. Many old troopers suffered for their loyalty, legally, politically and socially. But they're remembered, and honored, by their descendants today.

Andrew "Jackson" McWhirter was not the only boy to enlist at age fifteen, more than 100,000 who enlisted were fifteen or younger. Three-hundred were thirteen or under, some drummers and some fighters, and unbelievably, 25 were ten or under. At age thirteen, T.G. Bean of Pickensville, Alabama organized two companies of soldiers in 1861 from the University of Alabama.

Sarah Continues Talking About Her Life

...All the love God has to give
All the love we need to live
In a world of sorrow and pain
To lose ourselves, ourselves to gain....

The reason I'm telling you all of this is because of how involved the McWhirter and Harper families were in the 1st Alabama Cavalry, Union Army. My heart felt as though it was absolutely broken and I felt completely helpless as I watched my husband, three oldest sons, one barely fifteen, and three brothers ride off to fight against our southern neighbors and in some cases, friends who had chosen to fight for the Confederacy rather than the flag of their country.

The life seemed to drain right out of me when Andrew Ferrier, Thomas, George Washington and Jackson McWhirter along with my brothers, Tennessee Polk, Josiah Houston, and Robert Harper all joined the 1st Alabama Cavalry of Union soldiers. I knew from the atrocities the Confederate Home Guard had done already, they would kill anyone who served in the 1st AL if they had a chance. As I was thinking about this, it came to my mind that my brothers would probably be fighting and shooting at each other since some of them chose to join the Confederacy. I never understood their reasons but I couldn't stand to think about them facing each other on the battlefield, and couldn't help but wonder what actions they would take if that happened. I wouldn't be able to stand it if my brothers did come up against each other on the battlefield and one shot and killed the other. I wanted to think they wouldn't do that but feelings were so high, I knew in my heart they probably would.

I lived in a secluded mountainous area in Marion and Walker County, Alabama with no real close neighbors, and it was lonely. My neighbors and I used to visit back and forth freely but it got to where we were all afraid to leave our homes. The people on one side of me were the William Head Family, James and Susan Killenworth, Washington & Mary Hallmark, George and Sarah Hallmark, whose daughter, Mary Jane, was our son, Thomas Andrew's girlfriend , and Thomas and Phebe Hallmark. On the other side were John and Nancy Amerson, William and Harriett Rice, Jackson and Anny Tucker, Jesse and Rebecca Grigg, and on up from there were Archibald and Martha Whitehead, whose daughter, Nancy Jane, would marry our son, Jackson after the war was over. Then there were Drury and Mary Jane Anthony Whitehead, more on Drury later, but he hid out in a log to keep from being captured by Carpenter and his gang and forced into the Confederacy. Then there were Archibald, Jr. and Nancy Whitehead. The houses were spread out through the woods and while we used to visit by riding horseback or hitching up the wagon and riding in it, most of the men were gone and the women were afraid to go through the woods alone because of the Confederate Home Guard.

Since I have already mentioned Drury Whitehead, I might as well go ahead and tell you his war story. To begin with, he was a brother to Archibald Whitehead, whose daughter, Nancy Jane Whitehead, had been sweet on our Jackson McWhirter and they would go on to marry right after the war was over, so living so close to Drew for a long time, and then this closeness between his daughter and our son, Drew seemed like family to us. Needless to say, I was upset when I heard he had been captured.

Drury Henry Cox Whitehead was born on September 5, 1831 in Lauderdale County, Alabama. Drew, as he came to be called, was the youngest child of Archibald and Nancy Smith Whitehead. Archibald and Nancy moved the family to Fayette County, Alabama in the 1840's in order for Nancy to take possession of her inheritance from her father, William Smith. Nancy Jane Whitehead later married Jackson McWhirter in 1867.

Drew was a free spirited lad with an independent mind. When talk of secession began in 1860 the Whitehead family decided to steer clear of the "secesh" movement. As the situation became more heated, the boys decided that they were not going to join the Confederate Army. One can envision the lively conversations that probably took place at Aston's Store in Glen Allen, the local gathering place for the citizens.

At first Jefferson Davis asked for volunteers. Then a conscript law was passed making service mandatory. When this scheme didn't work, especially in Northwest Alabama, a Home Guard unit was created to find these slackers and "Tories" (a derisive term referring to the Tories that remained loyal to Britain in the Revolutionary war) and force them to sign up, be imprisoned or they were given the choice of joining with them or being shot!

Hartsook Prison was constructed just south of Winfield to house the Tory prisoners. The fear of capture was a daily occurrence as the

142

Home Guard roamed the countryside searching for them. Several of Drew's, as he was called, relatives were just as opposed to serving as was Drew. His older brother, Arch, Jr., suffered an untimely death in 1861, and it is assumed by many that he may have died of injuries received because of his opposition to the war.

Feelings on both sides ran high. As the war dragged on, these feelings turned to persecution and what followed was some of the worst brutality against private citizens suffered anywhere in the country. Drew's neighbor and friend, Benjamin Northam was ruthlessly murdered because he was considered to be AWOL from the Confederate Army.

Drew was arrested by Confederate conscript officers and taken to Tuscumbia, Alabama where he was forced to begin his service in the Confederate Service. He was there about two weeks when he made his escape and made his way to the Union Line in Corinth, Mississippi where he joined the Union Army on January 16, 1863. He was captured at least once but managed to escape and return to his unit in the Union Army. He served until he was mustered out January 22, 1864.

As I said earlier, the men who were opposed to the war began to 'lay out' in the woods and hills to avoid capture by the hated home guard. Daniel Smith, a neighbor and possible relative, helped Drew and some of these men while they were hiding out. He provided them with food, clothing, guns, ammunition and information. He suffered persecution for it and some people state he was supposedly hanged by the home guard he referred to as "Dog Cavalry" because they used dogs to hunt the men down, but he survived. Drew would later testify for Daniel Smith before the Southern Claims Commission on his behalf and Daniel testified for Drew on his pension claim. Smith had three sons who died while serving with the First Alabama Cavalry, USA. Drew's nephews, George W. Whitehead, Joseph Pinkney Whitehead and William Mack Guess along with the Smith boys, as well as a likely kinsman, Ephraim Whitehead, joined the 1st Alabama Cavalry-USV.

After he was discharged, Drew made his way back home and resumed his life with his wife, Mary Jane Anthony, and five small children. Because of the friction in the family, I will tell you that Mary Jane Anthony was the second daughter and the ninth child of William Anthony and Jennie McMinn. Her family remained loyal to the Confederacy during the Civil War. Several of her brothers, uncles, and cousins enlisted in the Confederate army, which caused tensions between family members that would last for years, if not forever. Her brother, Nathaniel, was wounded at The Battle of Fredericksburg in 1862, and died of his wounds a few days later.

Mary Jane's family was avid in their support of the Confederacy, one even naming his son John Wilkes Booth McMinn, in honor of the assassin of President Abe Lincoln. Drew had some of this same fire in him for he named two of his sons after famous Northern Generals, Drury Grant and John Sherman.

One can only imagine the sorrow and heartbreak this terrible conflict brought to Mary Jane and her family. Her older sister, Martha, had been married to Drew's older brother, Arch, Jr., who died earlier in the war. It is unknown if these family relationships were restored after the war. It has been said in times past that, "Women and children suffer most from the ravages of war." It is more than a guess that Mary and her sister certainly qualified in this respect.

Drew would suffer reprisals from some of his neighbors and former friends after the war. He and Mary Jane went on to have thirteen children and became respected citizens of their community and live long and productive lives. They are buried at Morris Cemetery in Glen Allen, Alabama.

Unionist, Drewry D. McMinn Shot By Confederate Home Guard

...how can we, made of billions of atoms, ever be forgotten?...

This is another story of the atrocities committed in northwest Alabama during the Civil War. It was written by Joel S. Mize and adapted from Thompson's Tories of the Hills, and an alternate account by Dodd & Dodd in Winston: "An Antebellum and Civil War History".

Drewry Dallas McMinn was born 1817 in Robeson or Rutherford County North Carolina, eighth child in a line of eleven born to William Abraham and Mary Margaret Byers McMinn. Both his grandfathers, Robert McMinn and William J. Byers were Revolutionary War soldiers as was his great-grandfather Abraham Kuykendall, Captain of North Carolina Militia. As a very young boy his father entered land in the new State of Alabama and at age 5, the family settled on that land located just a few miles southeast of the present town of Winfield Alabama.

Young Drewry grew up surrounded by families who also had migrated down from North Carolina and his grandfathers had fought in the Revolution alongside the patriots and patriarchs of those neighboring families. Another linkage many of these families had was a religious heritage formed from association with the Quaker religion of Pennsylvania that was carried south into Virginia and North Carolina. Those neighboring families included Anthony, Smith, Mills, Berryhill, Tucker, Brown, Tidwell & Guess.

Some of these families had made the compromise and bought slaves, others had not. When the issues of slavery and States Rights were debated hotly in the 1850s and early 1860s, some took one side and other families took the other side. The prevailing view of each family was often shaped by whether one's land was well suited for large abundant crops which needed much human labor. Often, intermarriage with families having extensive crop lands might be a deciding factor on ones views. Drewry's McMinn clan generally favored the call for secession while many of the neighboring families were strong in favoring union loyalty. His family and numerous others became caught in the crossfire of competing ideology - and they split and divided leaving emotional scars which created animosity of greater than normal intensity. This was war!

145

And the war in northwest Alabama got very brutal (see the story of the brutal death of Tory Henry Tucker). The Confederate Home Guard was vicious in treatment of loyalist families and retaliation in kind was the norm. Home Guard leader Stoke Roberts who had led violence against the Tory families operated out of a log-house jail known as Hartsook Prison, located just south of present day Winfield Alabama. A band of Tories caught him near there and quickly pronounced his death sentence then took a long iron spike and drove it completely through his mouth and out the back of the head and nailed him to the root of a big oak tree.

During the War Between the States, some of the Tories of Marion County Alabama formed a "bandito association" which numbered 60-100 men under leadership of John Stout, "a desperate and bad, though bold and not unskillful man". From their headquarters north of Pikeville, they rode almost daily in raids across north Alabama, often robbing local Confederate families of goods and money. It was into this scene that the tragic end of Drewry McMinn unfolded. Drewry is said to have joined the CSA Army and been promoted to Lieutenant in the CSA Army. With all the trouble being caused by the Tory uprising, he was assigned to pose as a Tory who had lately come home from the Yankee lines. After a few days of returning home in late September or early October 1864, Drewry was told of Stout's whereabouts. Stout was reported to be staying with a group of women a few miles west of Helving's Toll-Gate.

McMinn went to Helving's Toll-Gate and found the women but no George Stout. Instead, he found that Stout had beaten the women in a drunken rage and left their place. In his sympathy for the women, Drewry told one of the women that it was his intent to get in with Stout and then kill him. This was a big mistake as one of the women at that place was George Stout's sister, Parmelia.

Stout heard the report from his sister and was on full alert for Drewry McMinn. He sent word and invited Drewry to join him in a raid he was planning. An hour or two later, Drewry along with his confederates Lt. Coudroy and three other men came to the ford in the river, where in crossing, they found themselves covered by Stout and a half dozen other men. There by the riverbank, swift Tory justice was enacted as Drewry and his four confederates were tied to trees and summarily shot through the head.

Captain A.J. Stewart of the Conscript Cavalry (Home Guard) had gotten word of the capture but not of the fate of these men, took

146

Lemuel Burnett (age 54), an "aider and abettor of the Tories" as hostage in retaliation. The cycle of brutality continued.

Left behind to survive as best they could without their father were the family of Drewry Dallas McMinn: wife, Elizabeth Martin born 1818 Alabama and their seven children, all born in the family home located along the Marion/Fayette County line - John, Nancy Jane, Mary Ann, Abram M., Emaline F., Sarah D., and Sintha C.
[Drewry Dallas McMinn's older sister, Jane, married William Pickens Anthony - grandparents of George W. Whitehead, Company K, 1st Alabama Cavalry (Union Loyalist Regiment)]

Postscript: The death of Stoke Roberts was taken from Thompson's work and may have been an archetype story, as Stokely Roberts died of natural causes aft 1900 in Itawamba Co MS.

Sarah Endures More Abuse and Heartbreak

...Yet know the love and life we shared remain....

I awoke a little after 6:00 one morning, to the sound of heavy tramping of horse hooves, the rattling of wagons and the sound of voices uttering the most appalling curses I had ever heard. Frightened, I sprang out of bed and looked through the shutters to see what was going on and it was several members of the Confederate Home Guard. These men were yelling all types of obscenities. I grabbed a blanket and wrapped it around me and hoped they would ride on by but something told me they wouldn't. They started banging on the door and I reluctantly opened it, knowing they would kick it down if I didn't, to see several angry men saying things I wasn't used to hearing. They were looking for two soldiers they had forced to join the Confederacy but not long after they joined, they had deserted and gotten away. These vigilantes thought some Union sympathizer would be hiding them. After they told me who they were looking for, I tried to assure them they weren't there but they wouldn't take my word. One of them shoved me in my bedroom and shut the door while the others looked in the loft where the children were sleeping. I screamed at them, begging them not to bother me or my children but they paid no attention to anything I said. I didn't know the one who pushed me in the bedroom, but I could see the anger in his eyes and knew he was furious. He shoved me down on the bed with a determined look on his face, and I was so terribly frightened my hands were shaking. He looked under the bed and started throwing everything in the floor and then when he realized no one was there, he turned toward me with a scowl and stared at me for what seemed like ten minutes. Just as I started to stand up, he lunged toward the bed, landing right on top of me pushing me backward. He was filthy and his breath smelled as if he hadn't brushed his teeth in a year. On top of that, he reeked of whiskey and the stench coming from him almost made me throw-up. I fought the repugnant beast off as long as I could but his body was too heavy for me to push him off and while he was trying to kiss me, one of his hands was running all up and down my body. The more I fought, the more enraged he became. I was terrified, but when he started to run his hand up my nightgown, my animosity turned to absolute hysteria and I fought him like a wildcat. I bit him on the chin as he tried to kiss me and then I started screaming at the top of my voice. The leader came rushing in, jerked him off of me and told him to get out of the house and back on his horse, they had

148

work to do and were leaving. They had turned over ever thing in the house, even snatched the children out of their beds to make sure there wasn't anyone hiding in there. They looked under the bed, in my blanket chest, and anywhere they thought was large enough to hide someone, they really made a mess. The miscreants finally left cursing and saying they knew the traitors were around there somewhere and they assured me they would be back. The reprobate who shoved me around yelled at me and assured me he would most definitely be back.

As soon as the children heard the door close they rushed down the steps and into my room to make sure I was alright. I assured them I was and that I didn't want to frighten them with my screams but thought if I screamed loud enough, maybe one of the others would come to my rescue. I felt dirtier than I had ever felt in my life, even after I had been out plowing all day. I wondered if I would ever be able to wash the filth and stench from that monster off of me.

Christmas came and went and it was all I could do to keep from crying in front of the children. I thought about what a sad day it was for not only me, but for the children, because Andrew and George were gone to be with God. I was separated from my two oldest sons and brothers under most trying circumstances and I have no idea for how long. Also, the cares and needs of three young children rested entirely with me and the outlook was gloomy. It was certainly depressing but I just prayed for God to get me through this and bring the rest of my family back home safely.

I hated this war, I hated the enemy, I hated the vicious men who had been roaming the country-side taking advantage of the poor defenseless wives and widows whose husbands loved their country enough to go to war and try to protect the same country for which their forefathers before them had so bravely fought.

Each day brings with it such terrible startling events, and we never know what to expect.

It was the end of December and the coldest weather I can remember. The rain has turned to sleet and the wind cuts right through anyone unfortunate enough to have to be outside. I thought about my sons and brothers out in the weather and wondered how they were. I knew within reason they weren't keeping warm, because even if they had a tent to sleep in, they wouldn't have enough cover to keep warm. I worried about the animals being outside and wondered if they had enough to eat, so I decided to appease my curiosity by wrapping up as well as I could, braving the cold to go out and see about them. Hamp either hadn't fed them enough that day or they had eaten more than usual because I didn't see any hay out there for them to eat. I just rounded them all up and put them in the barn. It seemed like it took forever to get them in there and by the time I was back in the house, my feet and hands were numb from the cold. I was glad I had done that because I wouldn't have been able to rest wondering if they had anything to eat and knowing they were out in this weather.

I decided to draw a bucket of water from the well and bring it inside and William Hamilton had left some water in the bucket the last time he drew water, and it was frozen. I turned the bucket upside down and pecked it against the well but it didn't come out. It was so cold I was afraid my feet would get frost bitten so I just dropped the bucket in the well, filled it up, pulled it up and carried it in the house, knowing what had frozen would thaw during the night. I certainly didn't want to have to wrap up early the next morning and go out in that frigid weather to carry it to the house. Besides that, the water wouldn't be as cold when we got ready to bathe as it would be right out of the well, especially in this cold weather.

I took the water in the house, stoked the fire in the fireplace and got ready for bed. I missed Andrew so much and couldn't imagine living the rest of my life without him. I thought about all the happy times we had had and longed for a simple tender touch from him. I thought so much about our lives together and how much we enjoyed snuggling up in the bed under a warm quilt, and I just felt like I could reach over and touch him. I cried myself to sleep as I did most every night.

The weather began to moderate and the long cold winter was turning into a nice spring with cool mornings. I wanted to take advantage of it and decided to go out and start getting the garden ready to plant the early vegetables that needed cold weather to grow. William Hamilton was barely eleven years old but he could be a lot of help when he wanted to. We had almost finished cleaning off the garden spot when Papa rode up and I didn't even want to look at him I was so afraid he would have that same look on his face as he did when he brought me the news about George and Andrew. I immediately thought about Thomas and Jackson and wondered if something had happened to them or maybe one of my brothers. He walked up behind me and when I heard him say "Sis", I knew in my mind that someone else had died before he said anything else. He went on to tell me that my brother, Robert, had died in Corinth, Mississippi, and had also died of measles. I was stunned beyond speechlessness and so worried about Papa because he hadn't been well and the war had been so hard on him with his sons fighting on different sides, and everything else that was going on. He also had brothers in Tennessee who fought on different sides. I decided I needed to console him rather than think about myself and what all I had lost to this hellacious war. I put my arms around Papa and he cried like a baby. That just broke my heart; I don't remember him crying that hard when my brother, Thomas Wade, died in Knoxville, Tennessee. He kept saying over and over, "When will this hell on earth ever end, how many lives have to be lost before someone comes to their senses and ends this torture and murder?"

I asked Papa to come in and sit down and talk for a while but he said he needed to get back home. I knew he wanted to get off to himself and have a long cry so I didn't insist.

I knew I needed to keep busy, so William Hamilton and I went back to the garden while Mary Caroline sat on the front porch and colored with John Madison. We hitched the mule up to the plow and plowed several rows; however, we were a long way from being through. We had to plant vegetables such as lettuce, cabbage and onions early and I didn't even have the plants to set out, but was sure Papa would get them for me and I needed to turn the garden spot, anyway. We unhitched the mule, put it and the plow up and went in to cook supper.

It was late October of 1863, and word had gotten around about the 1st Alabama Cavalry, US being involved in a pretty large battle at Vincent's Crossroads which was in Red Bay, Alabama, and not too very far from where we lived. We were also told the battle was fought over such a long, large wooded area the troops from both sides left in such a hurry that they left some dead and wounded soldiers in the woods. However, no one knew who these soldiers were that they left behind. Of course Papa and I couldn't help but worry about it and I could just see my sons, Thomas and Jackson lying out in the woods wounded or even worse, lying out there dead!

I tried to keep busy and keep my mind off the war but it was difficult. I busied myself during the day in the fall garden, pulling up turnips and cutting the turnip greens off of them. I still had my three youngest children at home and worked on my quilts at night. I thought about the hundreds of thousands of husbands, sons, and brothers whose lifeless bodies lay strewn all over northwest Alabama and the south in battlefields everywhere. I thought about the unwanted cruelty, but these visions sharpened the pain.

Then in a couple of weeks, I received word that my son, Thomas, had been wounded in the Battle of Vincent's Crossroads October 26, 1863, and while wounded, he was captured and taken prisoner of war by the Confederate Soldiers. I feared for his life after all else that had happened. William Dwyer was also captured and they were taken to Cahaba Prison, which was a horrifying Confederate Prison. The battle was fought fiercely over a two-mile long area that was so densely wooded that some of the wounded soldiers and the dead bodies of soldiers were left behind. After about two months in Cahaba, Thomas and William were both able to escape from the prison and started walking for the Union lines at Camp Davies, MS. After traveling six days, William Dwyer became exhausted and unable to travel any further and Thomas was forced to leave him at a Union sympathizers' home about 150 miles from their line. There are several documents on file that state how William tried to get back to his regiment but due to weather conditions and his illness; he was not able to return until January 5, 1864. When he did return and reported to Major Shurtleff who was the only officer left, the rest of the regiment, including Thomas McWhirter, had gone with Major General W.T. Sherman on his march to the sea. Thomas was captured again about 150 miles from home but managed to escape again and walk back home to Alabama. On March 10, 1865, on the way back from Savannah, Georgia, both of my sons, Thomas and Jackson, were right in the middle of the early morning Battle of Monroe's Crossroads. See the account of this gruesome battle in another section of this book. On April 1, 1865, Thomas was wounded in a skirmish at Richland, North Carolina and then captured with some other soldiers while out foraging on April 15, 1865 at Faun's Station, North Carolina. They were held POW at Annapolis, Maryland. I wasn't aware of all of this when it happened and was actually thankful I didn't know at the time, after everything else that had happened.

About mid to late November, Papa had ridden into town just to see what all was going on and if there was any word of who was killed, wounded or captured at the Battle of Vincent's Crossroads. No one seemed to know anything other than what we had heard. However, he ran into the mail carrier who had had a letter for me from my son, Thomas. He handed it to me and I stood there frozen, afraid to

152

open it. So much had happened I was afraid Thomas was telling me that something happened to Jackson at Vincent's Crossroads. Papa just stood there looking at me and could tell I was upset. He asked if I wanted him to read it and I told him that I would read it.

I slowly opened the letter from Thomas and the first thing I saw was "Cahaba Prison". My heart felt like it vaulted to my feet and my hands were shaking so bad I could hardly hold the letter. The tears started flowing and I couldn't even see to read what he wrote so I handed it to Papa to read to me and sat down in the nearest chair. He said Thomas had been wounded and taken prisoner at the Battle of Vincent's Crossroads in Red Bay, Alabama and they were keeping him at the so called hell-hole of Cahaba Prison, but he didn't even say what his wound was or how bad it was. I had heard from some of my neighbors about Cahaba Prison and how bad it was.

The Confederate government acquired an abandoned cotton warehouse in Cahaba Prison was an old abandoned cotton warehouse the Confederates were using to house captured Union prisoners of war. It was near Selma in Dallas County, Alabama. Colonel Samuel M. Hill originally owned the warehouse, and had constructed the building as part of a complex to provide storage for the Cahaba, Marion, and Greensborough Railroad. The railroad failed in the 1850's and the warehouse was abandoned. Cahaba was selected after an extensive search throughout Alabama for suitable locations for a prison to handle excess prisoners from the main Confederate prison at Andersonville, Georgia. Cahaba was selected due to its relatively secure location in the deep South, which would permit freedom from potential Union raids.

Inmates sarcastically named the prison "Castle Morgan" after Confederate cavalryman John Hunt Morgan. There were two co-commanders at Cahaba, with Captain H.A.M. Henderson sharing command with Lieutenant Colonel Sam Jones. Henderson took charge of the prison facilities, while Jones directed the prison's guards. The prison guard totaled 179 troops, with a number of them coming from established Alabama reserves. These troops were additionally armed with two small caliber artillery pieces.

The original warehouse part of the prison complex covered approximately 15,000 square feet, and was located along the bank of the Alabama River. A wooden stockade fence was built around the warehouse to secure the prison yard. There was a covered water supply that ran through town and into the center of the prison building, with a pipe system set up using old wooden barrels.

However, there were areas where it could be uncovered, and the Confederate sympathizers would urinate in the trench, knowing it flowed right into the prison area. Towards the end of the Civil War, only about half of the building's original roof remained. Conditions within Cahaba were common among Civil War prison camps. There were problems with lice, rats, and dysentery. However, Cahaba had access to ample medical supplies, firewood, and food. This contributed to the substantially lower death rate among Cahaba prisoners.

The prison had been intended for only approximately 500 prisoners. Its population had grown to 660 by August of 1864. Previously, Union General Ulysses S. Grant had suspended the practice of prisoner exchange with the Confederacy. Therefore, by October of 1864 the prison's numbers had swelled to 2,151. Many of the Union prisoners came from Northern states such as Illinois, Michigan, and Iowa. There were also substantial numbers from Southern states, with those who had served in Union units from states such as Tennessee and Louisiana.

As the fortune of the Confederacy continued to deteriorate on the battlefield so did the conditions within Cahaba Prison. The Alabama River flooded, leaving Union prisoners to survive by floating on makeshift rafts or sitting on ceiling rafters. These terrible conditions directly contributed to a prisoner revolt, which was quickly put down. With the approach of the end of the Civil War, Jones negotiated the exchange of Union prisoners from Cahaba for captured Confederates. This exchange took place at Vicksburg, Mississippi in April 1865. Once exchanged, many of the newly freed Union soldiers were placed on the extremely overcrowded steamship *Sultana* for the journey north. Unfortunately, the overburdened ship exploded, and many of the 1100 people who were killed were former Cahaba and Andersonville prisoners.

I'm getting ahead of myself talking about the prison and the Sultana so I will get back to that later, but I couldn't help think of how bad, not only Cahaba Prison was, but Andersonville Prison in Georgia was supposedly worse. These poor soldiers were drug into a war they did not want to have anything to do with, and forced to fight against their southern neighbors, (and brothers) which they didn't want to do.

Thomas left a lot out of his letter that I would have liked to have known. I couldn't believe he didn't mention how bad his wound was or if it would be alright and I was upset with him for not writing about that. However, I assumed if it had been too bad, he wouldn't have been able to write so I tried not to worry about it. He didn't mention his brother, Jackson, and I was left hanging in the wind, worrying about both of them.

I was peeling potatoes for dinner and thinking about the war that had torn up so many lives and caused so much hardship and pain. These men and boys were dying and being killed and it had gotten to the point I was afraid to answer a knock at the door. Just about that time I heard someone open the door and heavy footprints coming toward the kitchen. It was Papa and when I heard his voice, I jumped and cut my finger with the knife I was using. I wrapped my cut finger in my apron as I turned to look at Papa and it only took one glance to tell that something was dreadfully wrong. He came over, hugged me, started crying and said he had just received word that my brother, Tennessee Polk Harper had died of measles in Hospital #9 in Nashville, Davidson County, Tennessee on March 9, 1862. My little brother was only nineteen years old, just a mere child. He wasn't married so he didn't leave a wife and children to mourn his death. Papa and I stood there embracing and crying for several minutes. Anytime he brought me this type of news, it hurt me almost as much to see him cry as it did to hear the information of the death he was bringing me. It appeared our whole family was being wiped out in this dreaded war. Our boys and husbands were being killed or dying of disease every day and my mind was always focused on who would be next. What added to the hurt was the fact they weren't sending our sons, husbands and brothers home, they were burying them and the Confederate dead in mass graves in the hospital cemeteries and the old City Cemetery in Nashville, Tennessee, sometimes just throwing them in a hole and covering them up because there were so many to bury.

(Several of the 1ˢᵗ Alabama Cavalry, US soldiers are still mistakenly buried in Confederate Circle in Mt. Olivet Cemetery in Nashville. When they were moving the bodies to the Nashville National Cemetery, these were identified incorrectly as CSA soldiers rather than Union. The 1ˢᵗ Alabama Cavalry soldiers still buried in Confederate Circle are: James W. Downum, Isaac R. Perrett, Jeremiah Russell, Henry Senyard, and John West)

In early March 1864 I received a letter stating my son, Andrew Jackson, was in Adams USA Hospital in Memphis, Tennessee. I was frantic with worry and walked the floor day and night for weeks until I heard he had been dismissed from the hospital and had returned to the regiment. He was with the regiment on General Sherman's march to the sea, as was my son, Thomas A. McWhirter. General Sherman was very proud of the men in the 1st Alabama Cavalry, USV and used them as his escort in his march. (More on Jackson, later)

My brother, Josiah Houston Harper enlisted in the First Alabama Cavalry, Co. B, USA on January 20, 1863 in Glendale, Mississippi, and was mustered in January 22 in Corinth, Mississippi. On February 8th he was on detached service working as a scout, which was also a very dangerous job. He mustered out January 22, 1864.

Josiah had married December 25, 1856 to Nancy Jane Berryhill and they had four children, Mary E., born October 1, 1858; Thomas Wade "Tom", born December 14, 1859; Rebecca Jane "Becky", born October 25, 1861; and William Jefferson "Jeff" Harper. Josiah was also serving as a Home Guard for the Union Army as well as a Scout and they were both dangerous jobs to be in. He also made shoes for the Union Army. We were so pleased to hear he had mustered out of the army and was on his way home, however, he had to make another trip and on his way home, he was captured, brutally tortured, murdered by the Confederate Home Guard and left hanging from a tree. He had pleaded with them to let him go because he was out of the army but they knew he was a Union sympathizer and dragged him into the woods and killed him, anyway. He not only left a large family devastated but a wife and four young children. Below is the copy of a Southern Claim filed by John Lyons after the war which tells about Josiah's horrific death.

Nancy Jane Berryhill Harper signed the following document in 1874 for a claim from the Southern Claims Commission, for John Lyons. (Sic)
"Nancy J. Harper, 43 years of age and a resident of Fayette County, Alabama for one year testified, Before that, I lived in Marion County from my childhood. I am no kin to the claimant and am not interested in the success of his claim. I have been living a close neighbor to him 18 years and have known him intimately all that time. I lived after the year 1862 in 1/4 mile of him. Before that time, I lived about in 4 miles of him. I saw him after the year 1862 most every day during the war, that he passed by my house in going to his

156

fields. I conversed with the claimant and heard him converse about the war frequently, its causes, its progress and results. He and my husband talked together frequently. They both voted against secession, done all they could against it. After the war came up, I heard claimant tell my husband that he was here and had to stay here, that we must hold our peace and do the best we could.

I know that claimant done all he could and dare to do during the war for women and children whose husbands was in the Union army. He went to the salt works and got salt and let the Union women have it. He done everything he could to keep the Confederate cavalry off of them and saved their property all he could. My husband was in the Union army. He treated me as above stated and as far as I know, he treated other Union men's wives the same way. I have heard nothing more than above stated except similar things and favors for Union women and their families by claimant for the Union Cause. I have heard or know nothing he has ever done for the Confederate cause.

I can't say that I know his public reputation. He was reported to the Cavalry as a Union man. James Tucker, George S. Tucker, John P. Lyle and Thaddeus Walker are his neighbors and was during the war. They perhaps can testify to his public reputation."
The witness testifies that some prominent Union men in the area were George S. Tucker, John P. Lyle and Samuel Roberts.

"I don't know whether or not they could testify to claimants loyalty." The witness states that the claimant knew she was adherent to the Union cause, "he knew it by my talk, and my acts and deeds, and by my husband being in the Union army."
Witness testifies that "the Confederate cavalry came to the house of Claimant and cursed and abused his daughters and said that they would take claimant in out of the wet and put him where the dogs wouldn't bite him, and called him a damned old Tory traitor and everything else that was mean. My husband, Josiah Harper, went into the Union army. Served out his time and came home. Claimant after my husband came home, saw him several times. My husband was at Claimants house. Claimant and him were on the best of terms up to his death. The Confederates caught him and hanged him. Claimant and his family help look for him until he was found. Claimant took his wagon and stears (and) hauled him to the grave yard and help bury him." Nancy J. Harper (Her mark), John C. Moore, Special Commissioner

John Lyons, Marion Co., Alabama 1874, Southern Claim # 20850

This claim, totaling $458, is for one bay horse, 7 or 8 years old, valued at $100, 150 bushels of corn valued at $300, 200 pounds of bacon valued at $50 and 800 pounds of fodder valued at $8. This property was taken by Union forces commanded by General Wilson on or about March 26, 1865.

The claimant called as witnesses George S. and Martha Tucker of Fayette County, John P. Lyle of Walker County, Nancy J. Harper and Harvey and Adaline Brown of Fayette County, and H.W. Farris and Sarah (Harper) McWhirter of Marion County.

Testimony was taken by Special Commission John C. Moore at the home of John Lyons on October 22 and 23 and on November 14, 1874. The claimant states that he is 66 years old and was born in Augusta County, Virginia. Claimant is a farmer and a resident of Marion County for 30 years. "I did not change my occupation or residency from the beginning of the war to the end. I was on the side of the Union at the beginning and was so to the end, though I had to act different and talk different before some. I never did do anything or say anything willingly against the Union cause. After the war started, living where I did, I had obliged to talk to suit the ground that I was on."

"40 out of 80 men in my beat went to the Union army. I aided their wives and family all I could. I cut and hauled wood for them. I went to the salt works and got salt for them. This was done during the war. *Josiah Harper, a Union soldier, went to the war, served out his time and came home. While here I protected him from being caught by the Confederates all I could without being found out at it. They at last caught him and hanged him. Myself and family looked for him after he was hanged until found. I hauled him to the graveyard and help bury him, and other like favors I done for the Union cause and its defenders.*

The claimant states that he "lived in a section of the country where I dare not contribute anything to the Union cause and let it be found out on me. I worked against secession and opposed it with all my mind, heart and strength." Claimant testifies that because of his Unionist stance that, "The Union raiders would always pass my house without pestering or taking anything I had or mistreating me or my family in any way." Some of the leading and best known Unionists in claimants area were T.P. Harper, George Hallmark, Joseph Harper, Doc Smith, Aron Bolin (?), William Miles and many others. They are all dead, most all died in the Union lines."

Claimant states, "I have never taken any oath to the so-called Southern Confederacy." Because of his views he was, "Threatened and abused by talk and the taking of my corn and threatened to be hanged and called a damned old Union man because I was protecting and assisting Union men and their wives and children."

John Lyons, Marion Co., Alabama – 1874, Union Claim (SIC)

Harvey Brown, 58 years of age and a resident of Fayette County, Alabama testifys, "I have lived here all my life. I am a farmer. I am here in favor of the claimant. I have known him thirty years intimately. I lived in three miles of him. I met him frequently, sometimes 2 or 3 times a week. I did not hear the claimant say anything as to how he voted before the war came up, he and I talked about it, and I heard him talk about it to other people, he always talked against the war, and was opposed to it, talked in favor of the Union.

Josiah Harper was a Union man and went to the Union army. He, claimant, cut wood and hauled it for his wife while her husband was in the Union army. The Confederate soldiers caught said Harper and hanged him. Claimant and his family hunted for said Harper until he was found. The claimant always told me he was a Union man but he had to ly low and keep the thing dark, he was severely treated by the Confederate Cavalry, and strongly suspicioned by them of being a Union man. I have heard him speak against the Confederate cause....his public reputation was that he was loyal to the United States." Those who could testify to his public reputation are, "George S. Tucker, William Tucker and Joseph Roberts." Prominent Union men in the area were, T.P. Harper, A.J. McWhirter, George M.D. and Josiah Harper, James Mills and Peyton Burnett.

"I know the Confederate cavalry threatened him heavy and talked about killing him, said he was carrying news to the Union people. His property was taken as was said by the Confederate Calvary."
Harvey Brown (His mark)
John C. Moore, Special Commissioner

Murder or political assassination was a constant threat for Alabama Unionists who chose to remain at home. Three sons of Solomon Curtis were all killed in Winston County. Joel Jackson Curtis was killed in 1862 for refusing to join the Confederate Army. George Washington Curtis, home on leave from the union army, was killed by the Home Guard in his yard while his wife and three children watched. Thomas Pink Curtis, the probate judge of Winston County, was arrested near Houston by Confederate authorities in 1864 and taken to a bluff on Clear Creek where he was summarily executed with two shots to his right eye.

Henry Tucker was a private in Company B, of the 1st Alabama Cavalry, USV, and when his military duty was completed, he returned home to his rugged hill country of Winston County, Alabama between Natural Bridge and the O'Mary's house to wait out the war. He was considering reenlisting in the 1st Alabama Union Army. Little did he know there would be no peace for him, because the dog-cavalry rangers and Home Guard of the Confederacy were out to get anyone they considered a "traitor". He was arrested by the Home Guard at his home in Marion County and tortured to death. (See story of Henry Tucker's death earlier in this book.)

The War and Abuse Continue

...And only when you are ready, let go of even this,
Do not be afraid. I shall live on in your heart as you do in mine
And as we do in God's....

This war was the most tragic thing I had ever heard and I wondered if we had remained in Smith County, Tennessee if I would still have my husband, all of my children, brothers, cousins, uncles and other relatives who had died and been so brutally killed during this horrific war, but the people in Smith and Warren Counties in Tennessee also sent their loved ones off to the same war and are probably having the same problems as we are.

One day the last of June in 1863, I believe it was, Papa came over with a letter he had gotten from Josiah and he sounded very upset. It wasn't like Papa to get this upset so I knew it must be bad. He started off, Dear Papa and all, I am still in Corinth, Mississippi and we don't have much to do around camp but criticize and speculate on the operations of our fellow soldiers in different parts of Dixie, and curse the double dyed traitors on the other side.

All we want is a little perseverance, a little energy and a lot of conscripts with a lot of ammunition. On the 14th of April, a large body of Rebels crossed Bear Creek and made an attack on one of our out posts, at Glendale, about ten miles from Corinth, Mississippi. Part of our 1st AL Cavalry was there, along with Yates Sharpshooters and they were able to repulse the Rebels, reinforced by the 81st Ohio and 9th Illinois. We lost six or eight killed with 18 to 20 of our men taken prisoners. Josiah

Things kept getting worse and worse and it wasn't safe for any of us to go outside for fear of the Confederate Home Guard or the guerrillas, who were as bad if not worse than the Home Guard.

One of my friends' husband was plowing his fields during the war when the CSA Home Guard came by, drug him into the woods, hung him from a tree, slit his throat, drove an iron wedge down it and disemboweled him. They left him hanging in that condition and his wife, being worried about him went out on horseback looking for him and found him still hanging in that condition. She rushed to one of her neighbors and told him and he took his wagon to where he was hanging, cut him down, took him back and buried him. She not only told me this, she wrote this in her daily diary she kept all through the war, and probably longer.

I just happened to think that in December 1863, my son, Thomas, was wounded and taken prisoner of war during the battle of Vincent's Cross Roads, which wasn't very far from Marion County. His cousin, Joseph Harper, was also taken prisoner during that battle. I imagined all kinds of things those rebels would do to Thomas while he was in captivity. We heard later that Thomas had been taken to Cahaba Prison and were told all kinds of horror stories about that prison. It had a tall brick wall and prisoners were contained in old decrepit buildings which held no provisions for bedding so they had to sleep on bare floors. The building had four open windows and only one fireplace in the whole building to keep them warm. To give you some idea of how large the building was, it had been built as a 15,000 square foot cotton warehouse but was taken over and used by the Confederacy as a prison for Union soldiers. From 1863-1865 it housed over 5,000 prisoners, so you can imagine how cold the prisoners got with only one fireplace. There were so many prisoners that they hardly had room to lay down. We heard later that they only had six square feet of living area when the army regulations stated they had to have forty-two. The supply of water for drinking, cooking, washing and bathing was conveyed from an artesian well, along an open street gutter for two-hundred yards into the prison. In its course the stream gathered the washing of Confederate soldiers and citizens, the slops of tubs and the spittoons of groceries, offices and hospitals. It was an open sewer in the midst of a small town and the receptacle of the filth, solid and liquid, which the careless, indifferent, or vicious people might throw into it.

According to the stories we heard, the river often flooded and covered the same floors the prisoners had to sleep on, sometimes with waters running one to four feet deep. It became so crowded they installed bunks, five tiers high, which were built along the walls with room for 432 men. However, by the end of March 1864, 660 prisoners were held there. There was a 12-foot high fence built around the 1/3 acre.

When I heard all of this I cried and cried thinking about my son living in those conditions, and I couldn't sleep at night. So many lives were being ruined and I was losing my husband, sons, brothers and other family members just because they didn't want to fire on the flag of the country they loved so much. How could that be reason to take a life, especially so many lives? My brother, James, was wounded in battle and was in the hospital but sent home to die, which he did three years after the war ended. He left a wife, Drusilla Byers Harper and six small children.

Unbeknownst to me, about two months after Thomas and a fellow soldier, William Dwyer, who had also been captured, had found a way to escape their Confederate captors at Cahaba Prison and they started walking back to the Union lines at Camp Davies, Mississippi. After traveling six days, William Dwyer became exhausted and unable to travel any further. Thomas left him with a Union family and started walking the other 150 miles to where his company was stationed.

On December 9, 1863, at the tender age of 19, my brother, Tennessee Polk Harper, died in US Army Hospital in Nashville, Tennessee. My precious family is being eliminated one by one and there is absolutely nothing I can do about it. God has blessed me with a fine husband and with these wonderful boys and one by one they are being taken away from me. I wondered how much more I could stand but when I thought of how strong they were and stood up to fight for what they believed, I knew I had to stay strong and do what I could for the rest of my family.

As stated, General Sherman was so impressed with the 1st Alabama Cavalry, USV that he used them as his escorts on his march to the sea. My remaining two sons in the regiment were included in this march. My brother, Josiah, was on detached service as scouts.

Not only was my family dying, one by one, the Confederate sympathizers and Home Guard were marauding, burning houses, barns, and crops belonging to Union families and killing for no other reason than some men didn't want to fight against their country they loved. Things became so bad that hundreds of people in the area were forced to flee the devastation of their homeland. Fortunately the US Army stepped in and escorted the Union families to Illinois for their protection. I couldn't bring myself to pack up the children and leave everything behind that Andrew and I worked so hard to have. I just couldn't figure out how I would ever start over in a strange state with no husband and three small children, surrounded by strangers. All of the hardships caused the children to grow up instantly and the widows to grow old much sooner than they ordinarily would have.

163

I tried to plow but all I had to plow with was the old iron plow that was supposed to be pulled by a horse or mule. Andrew, George, Thomas and Jackson had all ridden off on what horses and mules we had but one and the Confederate Home Guard stole that one. I just had to push as hard as I could to plow and it was very difficult doing that and keeping up with the children at the same time. Papa finally brought me a horse to use and I was thankful. After he brought it over to me, we stood there for some time talking about the war and about it tearing up families and killing so many young men, including several in our family. This war touched every family in northwest Alabama and beyond.

The mail carrier brought me two letters, today, one from Thomas, and the other from Jackson and I was thrilled to hear from them. Jackson doesn't write as often as Thomas does but when he does write, he writes long letters. I will give you the one from Thomas, first.

He mentioned again that General William Tecumseh Sherman was so proud of and impressed with the 1st Alabama Cavalry Regiment of Union men that he chose them as his escort in his march to the sea. I was shocked to read what Jackson, Thomas and all the other men were having to endure on this trip.

"Dear Mother and all, sorry I haven't written but we have been marching day and night in the cold rain. It has been raining for three weeks, seems like, and the swamps are so deep we can not get through in some places. You would not believe how deep the mud is in the swamps and they aren't good for anything but frogs and alligators, would not even grow rice. Speaking of rice, we have lived on rice for over a week and before that, we were on half rations for over a week. All I had for supper last night was a cup of coffee and cracker, and you know we don't drink coffee, so I gave mine away.

We have encountered mud the depths I have never seen or known to exist. Besides all this, we are in icy water up to our armpits, and our shoes get stuck in the mud. At first we could reach down and fish them out but now the swamps have gotten so deep that we can't even do that. Sometimes my feet and legs get so numb from the cold water that I can hardly walk. They have had to carry a few of the soldiers out because of that. Some of the troopers took their pants and socks off and tied them to the top of their bayonets so they could hold them up and keep them out of the water. I saw one poor fellow climb up on a cypress stump to get his feet and legs out of the water and he sat there and shivered until someone had to pull him off and carry him to the other side. I believe he would have sat there until he froze to death. Under different circumstances, there would be a haunting beauty about these swamps with their cypress stumps and the wildlife, but it's difficult to see the beauty under these conditions.

Talking about socks, Mother, I don't know what I would have done without the socks and gloves you knitted for me. They are so much warmer than the ones we are issued and there actually weren't even enough to go around to everyone. You probably wouldn't know me if you met me on the street, now. You know how particular I always was about my clothes? Now, my clothes are ragged, the hem is out of my pants, my shirt hasn't been washed in over two weeks, and my boots are three sizes too large. I can't wait to get home to you, Mother, and eat some of your fried chicken, plum pudding, and strawberry short cake.

Actually, about half of us are barefoot and many wear wrappings of old blankets or quilts. Socks disappeared months before and trousers are tattered, with a lot of the men only wearing breechclouts. So many of us have had to rip off the sleeves from our coats to make patches for our trousers because they were so tattered. Again, Mother, your little sewing case you made for us came in handy, much more so than I ever imagined it would. I was reluctant to take it with me thinking some of the men would make fun of me for carrying a sewing kit around with me but as it turned out, several of them have asked to borrow it. Shoes have actually been the biggest clothing problem in General Sherman's army. I surely could use a pair of boots or shoes if it's to where you or Grandpa Harper could see your way clear to send me a pair. I will draw off a picture of my foot on a piece of paper so you can see what size I need. Don't worry if you can't because I'll make do, they would just be ruined in these swamps if I had them right now. Hopefully we will be to the coast in a few days and it is thought a ship will be there with some rations, clothes and other supplies.

South Carolina is as full of swamps and bayous as a sieve is full of holes and they really make our march difficult. One thing that really bothers me is, as the engineers are having to corduroy almost every foot of the roads to admit the passage of wheels, and in order to corduroy them, they chop down some of the most splendid magnolia trees to use for the roads or bridges. Each time I see them cut one, I think of the beautiful magnolia trees we have back home and you know how I cherish them.

165

Some of the soldiers are burning everything they come across in South Carolina, not by orders but in spite of orders. They were so angry with the men in South Carolina because this is where the war started and they blame them for it. They want to make it so hard on them they won't think of starting another war.

If it wasn't for the games and pranks the troopers play for fun, this situation would probably be worse than it is. We were amused at a drunken soldier who shaved off the tail of the 17th Ohio's Commander's favorite gray stallion. He was livid with rage and offered a $500 reward to anyone who would tell him who did it. The boys got a good laugh over the prank, but not in front of the Lt. Colonel, of course. I don't think he ever found out who did that.

We finally got through the swamps, but it rained all night last night and is still raining, cold and so disagreeable. The rain ran under our beds last night and our tents, blankets, and overcoats were all wet and muddy, making them much heavier to carry. Some of the soldiers who are up for reenlistment have decided not to do so because of all this. We heard heavy cannonading for some time this afternoon.

You know I'm no hero-worshipper but what I have seen out of General Sherman convinces me that he is a leader, of genius equal to that of Napoleon in the field. None but an unusually bold man would have undertaken this campaign, and none but a man of genius could have succeeded as he has. Sherman says that Savannah is virtually his, and we tend to agree with him. Of course there is still the march back that we still have to contend with.

Mother, it pains me to even complain to you about what is going on here because I have heard how bad it is at home and I know within reason the Confederate Home Guard will be, if they haven't already been, harassing you just because we have different beliefs and love our country. I wish we could have left a gun behind for you in case you need one but knowing you could never shoot anyone, no matter what happened, it's just as well we took them. We are fortunate to have such a loving, caring mother and I pray for God to take care of you and keep you safe. I hated to go off and leave you but my feelings for our country are so deep that I felt like I had to do something to try to help protect it, not only for us, but for generations to come. I knew Grandpa Harper would be close by to help if you needed him, although he does live some distance away.

I must tell you how pretty the palm fans are and the Spanish moss which drapes several feet from the trees. I wish you could see it because as much as you love flowers, you would really enjoy it.

I will sign off for now but promise to write again the first chance I have. Please know I love you and give my love to Hamp, Mary Caroline, John and all.
Yours truly, Thomas"

The following is what Jackson wrote.

"Dearest Mother, I want to start by telling you how much I miss you, and also your cooking. What I would give to be able to see you, if just for a few minutes. As you know this is the first time I have ever been away from you and I am so lonesome and homesick I could cry. Right after our regiment left Rome for Atlanta, I walked by a pear tree and couldn't believe all the pears which still hung so temptingly from the tree. I would have thought they would all be gone or on the ground rotting. I remembered the pear cobblers you used to make and wished I had watched how you made them but I'm sure someone in camp will know how. I picked as many as my haversack would hold and took them with us. One of the cooks made them for us but they were not as good as yours.

When we were just outside of Rome, a buddy of mine and I attended a Negro meeting one night and there was one sermon by a white soldier and one by a Negro field hand, both were excellent and the singing was beyond description. At first it brought tears to everyone's eyes and then the shouting began. It was very moving.

We are finally in Savannah and General Sherman is happy about that, but not as happy as all of us are to get out of the swamps and icy water. When we reached Savannah, General Sherman telegraphed the following message to President Lincoln, "I beg to present you as a Christmas gift the City of Savannah, along with one hundred and fifty guns, plenty of ammunition, and about twenty-five thousand bales of cotton." Sherman is a good warrior and is good to us. We all love and respect him. The people in Savannah were afraid he would burn their town when we arrived but he had friends who lived here and promised them he wouldn't do any damage to the city.

We were hindered coming out of the swamp when one of the wagons got stuck and was almost all under water. About seventy-five men

167

had to go back in the frigid water, unhitch the team of horses, lead them in and go back to carry enough of the load on the wagon in until it was light enough they could pull it out of the mud by hand and onto the road.

From the time we left Rome, Georgia, marched to Atlanta and on to Savannah, we had marched 350 miles, and a lot of that was through the swamps.

The march to the sea was actually four armies marching parallel routes making the march sixty-miles wide and we were mostly able to live off the land. Some of the Rebel deserters had found Union uniforms, probably took them off Union soldiers they had killed. They foraged and scoured the countryside taking everything in sight they could carry. I'm sure they dined sumptuously. Our regiment had skirmished with the Rebels almost daily all the way to Savannah, one being at the Oconee River Bridge on the November 23rd. Our Company, K, had a pretty good skirmish at the burned Oconee Bridge and Georgia Central Railroad on the 30th, one near Millen, Georgia on the 2nd of December and near Savannah on December 9th.

The hundreds of miles marched and in the saddle deemed several of our soldiers unfit and they were sent back to northwest Alabama.

Savannah had originally been defended by 10,000 Rebel troops but knowing they would be no match for Sherman's 60,000 soldiers, they retreated and moved on up into South Carolina.

I don't think I told you what happened when we were camped around Columbia, South Carolina. Some degenerate set fire to some dead grass at the far end of the island and drove a herd of rattlesnakes down in our camp. As you can imagine, it got kind of intense in camp with people scattering everywhere shooting at them, but no one was bitten, to my knowledge.

Some people are accusing Sherman of burning Columbia, but what actually happened was, the Confederates knew we were on the edge of town and would be in Columbia soon. There were several large bales of cotton sitting all over town and they set fire to them and then rode off in the opposite direction. When we arrived, General Sherman ordered us to dismount and start putting out the fires. He even got off his fine steed, Sam, and started fighting the fires, himself. At the same time, the people of the town acted like they were happy to see us and they offered whiskey to any of the soldiers who wanted it. Of course they started drinking and partying and some began fanning the fires, which made it extremely difficult to extinguish. We fought that fire until we finally got it under control and extinguished.

I can't wait to get somewhere and get some good food. Some of my buddies and I are tired of sweet potatoes and hardtack and are going into town to get oysters tonight. We will be so happy to have something decent and different to eat.

I attended preaching Christmas Day at the Presbyterian Church in Savannah, because it was within walking distance. The preacher, Reverend Doctor Axson preached a splendid sermon. We are supposed to be here two or three weeks and if we are, I may go back and hear him again if it's to where I can. It helps ease the troubled mind to hear someone like him after all we have been through. I think God is leading me in the direction of preaching and I want to do something with my life that will help others. I can't think of a better way of helping people than leading them to Christ. Mother, your teachings and love of God have led me to make this decision and we are so fortunate to have a God-loving Mother like you and parents like you and Papa who took us to church all of our lives. I have talked to some soldiers who have never been in a church, and they are the type that will go out foraging and take everything a family has without leaving them anything to eat. They also spend enormous prices for whiskey so they can get drunk and party. Apparently it doesn't bother them to ride off with their wagons full and hear the women and children crying and begging them to leave just enough food so they won't starve. The soldiers who rode off ignoring these pitiful people are the very ones who are bitter because they are having to fight in this war and do everything they can to hurt the southerners down here, including leaving them hungry.

Talking about church, I heard they have had to close our Poplar Springs Primitive Baptist Church, down there, because of all the interruptions during services by the Rebels. I was actually glad to hear that because no telling what the Confederate Home Guard would do to you and the children going to and from the church.

Well, the time slipped up on me and I didn't get your letter mailed in Savannah, as I had originally planned so I will write a bit more. We have now left Savannah and on the way back, through South Carolina, North Carolina, Georgia and hopefully on back to

Alabama. The roads are so muddy and the more horses and wagons that travel them, the deeper the ruts get. General Sherman called out his engineers to corduroy the roads, but it's going to take a while for them to cut all the trees they will need to put across the road. The engineers are going to have to corduroy about 400 miles of road during the Carolinas campaign and the entire army will have to rework nearly 800 miles of road, so we have a huge chore ahead of us before we can even start back home.

We will have to travel slower because those trees can roll and get horses' hoofs caught between them.

I'll be so glad when this war is over; we have lived off the land since we started this trip. Several people have to go out in different directions each day to forage enough for the 60,000 or so soldiers we have with us because there is no way the army could provide or carry enough rations to feed everyone. Most of the men go easy on the southerners and leave enough for them to live on but then, as I said, there are those who disobey orders and take everything they can find. It doesn't appear to bother them in the least to leave the women begging them to leave food for their children. The boys I have gone out foraging with have even helped the women hide what we left them so other Union soldiers couldn't take it from them. It was amusing to see where some of them hid their food and valuables, some have hung their hams and other things from trees, some buried it, but I have seen the soldiers poke any freshly dug earth with their bayonet or prod pole to see if there was something under there. You would be amazed at what they have unearthed. One slave in Georgia said Union soldiers had noses like hounds. He said they stopped at his master's house one time, one of them sniffing and sniffing until he started toward the swamp where the owner had tried to hide his horses and mules by tying them up to the trees down by the swamp rather than leaving them in the barn.

More than once, Sherman has given his orders to leave the women, children and poor people alone and gave them specific orders not to enter their homes, but there are a few soldiers who are so angry at having to be in the war they want to punish anyone they think had anything to do with starting it. My conscience would bother me too much to leave anyone without food, no matter how hungry I was. They send out fifty or so foragers from each brigade and expect them to bring back enough food for thirty men to have three meals a day and this happens every day. Some of them were caught by the Confederates and guerrillas and brutally murdered. We found about sixty-four bodies of Union soldiers who had been hanged, had their throats slit or shot from close range, all lined up on the side of the road. Some had signs on them saying "Death to Foragers". One of the Confederate prisoners said Sherman's army had stripped the country so bare that a crow couldn't fly across it without taking a haversack. Speaking of haversacks, Mother, I don't know what I would have done without the haversack you made for me and the little needle-case you fixed and put in it. I have had to use that several times. As I told you earlier, there were so many men from Alabama who joined the Union that they could not outfit all of us and were not prepared for this.

I don't think I told you but General Sherman sent out four separate foraging expeditions of 650 wagons each and they were filled with almost 2 million pounds of corn and 140,000 pounds of fodder, sweet potatoes, live stock and syrup. On the way back to camp, we had to defend the "corn wagons" from the attacks against the hogs and fowl.

I know all this sounds like we had plenty to eat, but no matter how many went out foraging or how much we brought back, it was never enough to feed the entire army. I also know you must be tired of reading by now but before I go, I must tell you one other thing. Sherman was clear when he told his soldiers not to enter the houses and the Union authorities responded swiftly to acts of plunder committed by the troops. Senior officers issued orders that strictly prohibited men entering houses and specified that punishment for arson or plunder would be execution by firing squad. However, I don't know of anyone who was killed by a firing squad for arson or plundering.

An Illinois surgeon was so disgruntled about the war and all of the men wounded and dying and he stated the following: "There is no God in war. It is merciless, cruel, vindictive, un-Christian, savage, and relentless. It is all that devils could wish for." After all we have been through, it would be easy for me to believe that but I still remember what you and Papa taught us and I know there is indeed a God during war, and everywhere, or it would be worse than it is, if that's possible.

Well, Mother, I didn't mean to write this much but get started and can't find a stopping place, there is so much that has happened. I am so homesick and want to see you so badly. I need to get some sleep and will try to get this mailed off to you tomorrow. Please write and let me know how you are. I'm sure Mary Caroline is growing, as well as Hamp and John. Tell them I said to be sure and help you all they can. Hamp is big enough, now, that he can help you with a lot of the chores. I imagine you are teaching Mary Caroline how to cook and sew by now. Hamp can bring in the water and wood for you. I imagine Grandpa Harper chops your wood but if not, Hamp is even big enough for that. Just hope he will be careful and not cut his toes off with the axe. Make him plow the garden for you when it dries up a bit; you need to get the lettuce, garlic and onions out in February if possible.

You and the children stay safe and know I love you all. Give my love to Grandpa Harper and tell him I'll write him as soon as I can. Love, Jackson"

I had kept Hamp, Mary Caroline and John in the house and close to me since the war began and they were getting antsy, wanting to go somewhere and play with children their own ages. I didn't dare let them walk to the neighbors' house alone so I walked them over to William and Ellender Head's house so they could play with their children for awhile. They had several children around the same ages as my younger ones, William, Sarah, Joseph, Mary, & and Nancy Head were between the ages of 6 and 17 years old, so the youngest ones were the right age for my children to play with.

Just as I got back to the house, I heard a noise that sounded like several horses running this way from the opposite direction of the Heads, and I was so afraid it was the Confederate Home Guard, again. I waited for the dreaded knock at the door, and sure enough, my fears were realized, it was them. They shoved me backward, almost pushing me down and started calling me a "damn Yankee lover, blue-belly lover," and worse names. All of them but one went in the kitchen and I could hear them pilfering around, opening drawers, and doing as much destruction as they could. They delighted in ransacking houses of the Unionists, especially when there wasn't a man or older boys in the house. After we got inside, the same brutal one that molested me before shoved me in the bedroom, pushed me backward on the bed and told me not to utter a sound or he would kill me. About the same time, I uttered "Get your nasty hands off me, you vicious, bumbling Rebel." He bristled up like an enraged porcupine and his fingers bit painfully into my arms. He let loose a series of definitive expletives and reassured me he would kill me if I opened my mouth again. He asked me where my children were and I told him they had gone to visit Papa Harper but

172

that Papa would be bringing them home anytime. He was so brutal, pinching me on my breasts really hard and laughing when I flinched, acting like he was having a good time. He was like a madman and kept on molesting me and the more I fought him, the more he laughed. Every bone in my body ached, and they ached for days. I had always been taught not to hate anyone, but I absolutely hated this animal who called himself a man. I hated the war and I hated anyone having anything to do with the enemy. My first thought was that Ellender Head might walk the children home and I didn't want them to witness any of this, but just kept hoping the children were having a good time and wouldn't be back for a while. I laid there enduring all the torture and pain but never moved or made another sound except for a grunt or two from the pain, and he hurt me so bad I couldn't help it. These brutal monsters delighted in torturing the Union wives and widows and murdering any Union man they ran across. One who has never been through something like this cannot imagine how many thoughts can run through the mind in such a short time. While I was so thankful the children were not there, I was afraid these miscreants would leave here, go over to Ellender Head's and do something to her and the children because her husband was off fighting in the 1st AL Cavalry Union Army, also. While I worried about Mary Caroline, they could just as easily molest the boys and had, in some cases, but they were older than mine. I finally heard the door slam and eased up from the bed, Fortunately, I still had water in the pitcher sitting in the washbowl and didn't have to go to the well, so I scrubbed as hard as I could until I nearly scrubbed the skin off. I put some clean clothes on, combed my hair, and stumbled out in the living room. It took me the rest of the day to get the mess cleaned up and I was hurting so bad I could hardly walk or bend over, and already had bruises all up and down both arms. I didn't want the children to see the bruises on my arms when they got back so I had put on a long-sleeved dress.

Somehow I managed to make it through the day and walked back over to Ellender's house to get the children. Her husband, William, was also off fighting in the 1st Alabama Cavalry, Union Army and she was pretty much in the same shape as I was. The Home Guard thought all Union wives and widows were open game for them and they prayed on them mightily. I didn't feel like reading the Bible to the children that night like I always did. However, while sitting in Andrew's rocking chair, I reached for my Bible and called the children around a little earlier than usual. I started reading but my heart just was not in it and I could not get the happenings of the day off my mind.

After the children went to bed I went in my bedroom, got down on my knees, and prayed and cried like never before. I missed my beloved husband and sons, especially George Washington who would never return home again. I thought about how many of my loving family members I would never be able to feel their arms around me again, and it hurt. I prayed for God to bring what was left of my family home safe and sound, and very soon. I begged God to give me the peace and strength I needed to go on with my life and care for my young precious children.

With tears still in my eyes, I stood up, walked outside and sat down in one of the chairs on the porch. I looked up at the stars and full moon and thought about what a beautiful night it was. Andrew and I used to sit out there at night after the children went to bed. We had a nice yard with magnolia trees that were just beautiful. I always loved Magnolia trees. We had other large trees and I had a few flowers scattered around, including buttercups which are my favorite, but I had just not been interested in them since the war started. The sun had dipped low in the West and the evening was calm and quiet with only the sound of the tree frogs in the distance. A peace seemed to wash over me and I could feel God answering my prayers. I continued feeling better and more at ease as the night wore on.

Andrew and I used to talk about how beautiful the South was in the Spring with the gorgeous blooms of dogwood and red bud trees, the glow of a profusion of dandelions, wild violets, buttercups and other wild flowers scattered throughout the woods. The woods would be vocal with different species of birds Now our beloved South is being burned with intentionally set fires, and drowned with blood from hundreds of thousands of men, young and old alike, many of which are mere teenagers, scattered across several states

I finally went back in the house and got ready for bed. I had already changed sheets on my bed because I did not want to take a chance on smelling the horrendous, stinking uncivilized creature who had forced himself on me earlier in the day. I finally dozed off to sleep, but sat straight up in the bed and my heart took a frantic leap when the outline of a man appeared at the foot of my bed. He was the same size as Andrew. I could not figure out what I had seen but finally decided it must have been an apparition. Sleep didn't come easy after that and I laid there thinking about what all I had to do the next day. Finally peace came to me in the form of sleep and I slept the rest of the night.

174

I overslept the next morning and jumped up still thinking of the figure I had seen at the foot of my bed, and wondered if Andrew was trying to tell me something, but quickly dismissed that thought. I prepared breakfast and tried to act happy at the table in front of the children. Actually, I had a lot to be thankful for, but it was difficult to think about that when all hell was breaking loose around us. I left the dishes to Mary Caroline and "Hamp" while I went outside to the wash pot with my bed clothes. I put them down, hauled a couple of buckets of water from the creek to put in the wash pot and built a fire under it. I had just dipped up another bucket of water and started back from the creek when I heard fast hoof beats coming from the woods. I thought my heart was going to jump out of my chest, but by the time I got to the wash pot, I could see Papa Harper riding up. My first thought was that he was bringing more bad news but he quickly informed me he just came to see if I needed anything.

I poured the bucket of water in the wash pot; put the sheets, pillow cases and bar of lye soap in the pot to soak. Papa and I went up and sat down on the porch. Papa asked me after a bit why I was so quiet, and while I was thinking about telling him what had happened the day before, I quickly put that thought aside for different reasons. Anytime something like that happens to a woman, they fear if someone finds out, they might think they brought it on themselves. While I knew Papa would never think that, I decided not to bring it up at all. Besides, I really didn't want to even talk about it and was afraid Papa might be so angry he would hunt him down and try to kill him, and maybe get killed in the process. I decided the best thing I could do, was try to forget about it and not mention it.

Papa left and I continued my washing, getting the lye soap out of the then hot water, and started scrubbing the sheets. I could not help but think of what happened on these sheets the day before. How dare that brute come in my home and try something like that. I finished washing the sheets but rather than try to pour the hot water out of the heavy hot pot, I just put the fire out, took the sheets to the creek and rinsed them there. I then took them back to the yard and hung them across the fence to dry.

Maybe, just maybe my Thomas, Jackson and my brothers would soon return and protect us from these hooligans, and help with the farm. Jasper Green, one of the neighbors with Union ties would help as much as he could but finally in December, he had to join the 1st Alabama Cavalry USV to keep from being conscripted into the Confederacy. He rode 90 miles from his home here in Marion

County, Alabama to Camp Davies, Mississippi, just out of Corinth, to join the Union Army. I knew I was going to miss his help but knew God would provide and we would make do with what we had.

In January 1865, I received a letter from my son, Jackson, telling me about an incident that happened in Georgia December 9, 1864. It was about the wickedness of one of General Sherman's soldiers, and I could tell it really got to him and would be something he carried in his mind for years to come. He had a tender heart and couldn't stand to see anyone or any animal hurt and in pain. He said this was one of the most horrific acts that happened on the march, but he said he would first have to preface it with the following. "Several runaway slaves had enlisted in the 1st Alabama Cavalry, Union Army because they wanted to fight for their freedom and the freedom of their children, and they thought this was the best way to do it. Many of the others, men, women and children, got in line behind Sherman's soldiers in Atlanta and were marching behind him hoping he would lead them to freedom. Of course they had to eat off the land because he hardly had enough to feed his troops, much less that many followers and Sherman decided he would try to feed them in exchange for them cooking and doing some work, but he had no idea how many would get in line and follow behind them. However, the food became extremely scarce and he urged them to stay behind. Some turned around and left but many others refused and continued following them. They looked up to Sherman and thought of him as their savior. They carried babies, led small children and each town they went through, more would join in the march. Many of the soldiers resented this because they said they slowed them down and there just wasn't enough food to go around.

In December 1864, Sherman was only about twenty miles from Savannah when they reached the swollen, icy Ebenezer Creek in Georgia, which was about 165 feet wide and 10 feet deep. Jackson said it was estimated that about 5,000 freed slaves had been following them and working for food. It got to where the army was living off the land and did not have enough to feel the army and them, too. The army took their pontoons out of the wagons and put them across the swollen creek. It took a while for all of the soldiers to cross Gen. Davis had given orders to make the slaves wait until all of the soldiers crossed, but just about the time some of the so-called contraband had had started across, one of the soldiers looked up and saw Joe Wheeler's Confederate Cavalry coming, so he cut the pontoons loose, and the ones on the bridge, who were mostly slaves, fell into the cold, icy water, women, babies, young children and all.

176

Some of the others jumped in and tried to swim across, not wanting to be left behind. Some of the ones on the other side were afraid of what would happen to them if the Confederates caught up with them so they tried to flee them by jumping in and trying to swim across. However, the water was too cold and the creek too wide for them to make it and they drowned. Many of these could not even swim!"

This would have been difficult for me to believe had I not already witnessed so much inhumanity here at home and had so much already happened to me. Take care and please let me hear from you so I will know you are alright. Just send it to Sherman's Union Regiment in North Carolina and I should get it, and we should be in North Carolina by the time it gets here. Jackson"

I could hardly sleep that night for thinking about that and all that my sons had witnessed while fighting for their country. I got up in the middle of the night, got down on my knees and begged God to please take care of them and bring them home to me safely. I didn't think I could handle losing another child.

Jackson had already said that General William Tecumseh Sherman was so proud of and impressed with the 1st Alabama Cavalry Regiment of Union men that he chose them as his escort in his march to the sea. I was shocked to read what Jackson, Thomas and all the other men were having to endure on this trip. His letter wasn't dated but I think I received it about the first week of December.

The winds of March came as if they were blowing in more death and destruction. I remember Momma saying she tried not to worry about things she was not able to do anything about, and I tried to remember that. However, when so much was going on and I was losing so many loved ones, it was a difficult rule to follow, especially with my sons still fighting.

Raindrops softly fell on the roof and I was taken back to the time Andrew and I were alone and we both enjoyed listening to the soft patter of the raindrops. We used to lie in bed while it was raining and talk about how the raindrops sounded so peaceful dancing on the roof and little windows. However, they were just a prelude to the storm which came later.

The bright lights of the flames burning in the fireplace danced around the black pot hanging above them cooking the beans I had hung in there to cook. I had not yet decided what else I would prepare for lunch. My thoughts quickly turned from that to how Andrew loved beans and cornbread and as long as he had that and maybe potatoes fixed some way, he didn't care if we had any chicken, beef, or any meat. He was so easy to cook for and never complained about what I cooked. Anytime I asked what he wanted to eat, he would say, it didn't make any difference. I wondered if I would ever get over losing him. It continually bothered me that I was not with him or George when they died and I thought about what a lonesome death they must have died. Also, they were not buried where I could visit their graves and that bothered me. I could only hope Thomas or Jackson would take me to Nashville sometime to visit their graves, but it would certainly have to be after the war ended and then it was doubtful.

I spent a restless night and decided to get up early the next morning and see how the early vegetables I had planted were coming along. The spring days were growing warmer and as I walked close to the edge of the woods, I noticed the lush green hue of grass peeping through the ground. I also noticed the fresh scent of lilacs as the buds began to open into full blooms. The forest was dotted with wild flowers and the white and purple tiny blooms of the violets were peeking up through the dead leaves and limbs of the forest so bright they looked like tiny lights. The trillium was blooming and I stood there amazed at God's beauty. About that time the scent of the lilacs in my yard floated by and as I turned to admire their beauty, the fresh sweetness of apple blossoms filled the air and as I turned toward the orchard, I thought about how hard Andrew had worked to set out the apple trees. I looked at the forest on the other side of the house and the dark woods were brightened with beautiful redbud and dogwood blooms. The forest had come alive with beauty, and I knew I should be thankful for what I had rather than what I had lost because there were a number of people who had much less than my family and I had. It took God's majestic beauty to bring me to my senses and out of my doldrums, and I realized at that time that I had grieved long enough. Life was not going to be as easy as it had been before the war, but I knew with God's help, we would get by with what we had, and I was so thankful we were as fortunate as we were.

I'm getting ahead of myself, again, but after Thomas and Jackson got back home, they were telling me all about the war and about one of their friends, Jonathan Roach. Jonathan was a good fellow and the other soldiers liked him, but it seemed that if anything could happen, it would happen to Jonathan. He was captured and held prisoner of war at the horrid Cahaba Prison, for some time while in service.

Jonathan was born in 1818 in Cherokee County, Georgia and was 46 years old when he joined the 1st Alabama Union Army, not a young lad in any sense of the word. He and his family witnessed all the other atrocities that the other Union families witnessed but he was determined to fight for his country, a country his ancestors fought for and helped build, a country he loved just like all of the other Unionists did. He enlisted fairly early, in November 1863, and then was captured December 5, 1864, less than three weeks after he enlisted. He was taken to Cahaba Prison.

After going through all of the brutality and ruthlessness of the inhumane prison, the war was finally over and Jonathan was going to be able to go home and spend the rest of his life with his family he loved so dearly. I think we can all imagine how excited he was, along with the rest of, not only the prisoners, but all of the soldiers who had had such a difficult time fighting in this war. He couldn't believe he was free, and it had been a long time since he had been a free man or had a meal worth eating.

Jonathan had about twelve children, one of whom, Joseph, fought with in the Union Army. He was so excited about going home to see all of them. Joseph served in the 1st AL Cavalry., USV for two years.

Jonathan and about 1,700 other Civil War prisoners were loaded on the side-wheeled steamboat, Sultana, in late April 1865, and it was a joyous occasion for all of them. They were shouting with joy that they were finally free, the war was over and they were going home to their families. It was a wonderful day for all of them. Just boarding the vessel for home put new life in Jonathan. There would be no more fighting, no more destruction; no more starvation, he was free and on his way home to his family. However, what Jonathan and the other released POW's didn't realize was that by law, the Sultana couldn't safely carry more than 376 people including the crew. There were already several passengers on board before the prisoners were even loaded, and they would wind up with approximately 2,100 people on board. A disaster waiting to happen!

On April 26, 1865, the Sultana docked in Memphis, Tennessee. It was ironic that some of the former prisoners got off the boat to see the sights and sounds of Memphis after the hardships of war, but they didn't get back in time and the Sultana had gone off and left them. They were devastated, not knowing when they could ever catch another boat home.

Four years of war had ruined many levees and dikes and the banks of the Mississippi were covered in foamy water. The overloaded steamer chugged on toward Cairo with all of the freed prisoners of war, the boilers played out and there was a tremendous explosion on board the steamer sending flames up into the night sky which were visible for miles around. Hundreds of sleeping soldiers were blown into the river.

These poor soldiers had been starved for months and living in prisons not fit for vermin. They were on their way home to their loving families and now this. The water was icy cold and many of the soldiers could not swim. Actually, after all they had been through, they were too weak and in no condition to swim, even if they could have. The huge twin smokestacks wavered in the breeze before coming down and pinning some of the soldiers in what was left of the burning steamboat. Most of the men left on the boat preferred drowning to being burned alive so they jumped overboard.

The next daybreak, hundreds of soldiers were found all up and down the Mississippi River clinging to driftwood, planks from the boat, tree stumps, or anything they could find that might keep them afloat and save them until they could be rescued. Fortunately, Jonathan Roach was one of the soldiers and former prisoners of war who survived this terrible accident. He went on home to his family, recuperated and lived until 1905, naming one of his sons, Sherman Roach, after General William Tecumseh Sherman.

Jackson had written home about an incident which took place just outside of Savannah, GA. These troops had already been through the icy waters of the South Carolina swamps braving any beasts that might be swimming around, which could have been an alligator or any one of many poisonous snakes. A Michigan soldier described the swamps to his wife like this, "If you want an idea of the face of this country just think of the swampiest country you ever seen, and then imagine one a hundred times swampier, and you have it."

As I stated earlier, Thomas and Jackson were both with Sherman on his march to the sea. Some said General Sherman was crazy while others said he was crazy like a fox. But he knew what had to be done to win the war and he did it. While his soldiers burned a lot of houses and crops on the march to the sea, he gave orders before they started for his troops not to bother the women, children and poor people. However, many of the soldiers were still angry that they had to fight the war they felt South Carolina started, and that they had wanted no part of in the first place, that they went out on their own and did what they wanted to. Also, when they fanned out 60 to 70 miles wide, there was no way General Sherman could monitor everything they did.

This is a letter I received from Thomas around the first of January of 1865.

"Dearest Mother, On December 9, 1864, we were marching through Georgia as advanced guard for the 17th Army Corps, and were just seven to ten miles out of Savannah when we encountered torpedoes that had been placed in the road by the Rebels. Two had already been exploded and set off a series of blasts that flung bodies of men and horses across a sandy roadway. Lt. Francis W. Tupper, Adjutant, had dismounted and was going to mark the area to keep others from being injured. In doing so he stooped up to pick up a wire and as he pulled it back, his foot slipped and the torpedo exploded almost blowing off his right leg. When General Sherman reached the area and saw Tupper, a dead horse and several wounded men scattered around the roadway, he looked down at Tupper, just a lad, and asked how long he had been in. He told him he had been in three years and his time had expired three weeks ago. Tupper's leg was horribly torn and mutilated, was raw and bloody with bone and muscle protruding and his knee shattered. His left hand was cut and burned, his face and one ear considerable cut and burned. I will have nightmares, for weeks to come, of some of the carnage I have seen in this war. I could not imagine how much pain he must have been in.

They sent Sgt. Tupper to a farmhouse and then to a USA Hospital in Hilton Head, South Carolina in the horse-drawn ambulance and then he was transferred to an Officer's Hospital in Beaufort, SC on December 20, 1864. They had no choice but to amputate his leg above the knee. The torpedoes had been placed in the road with just sufficient earth and leaves over them to conceal them.

General Sherman was enraged, and said that was not war; it was plain out and out murder. He knew the Confederates had already been through there, knowing he and his troops would come along the same path which is why they had planted the torpedoes. We had just captured some Rebel prisoners the day before and they were bringing up the rear. They were ordered to go to the front of the line

181

and march side by side all the way across the roadway and told them they better find every torpedo the Rebels had planted because if they didn't, they would be the ones to either find them or step on them causing them to explode. They begged and begged saying they would be blown up, but he reiterated the order, saying he didn't care a damn if they were blown up, that he would not have his men blown up like that. Sherman followed right behind them as they marched to the front of the line. They uncovered seven more torpedoes; some of them copper cylinders over a foot long, triggered to blow up at the slightest touch. What was so ironic was the Confederate Sergeant who had supervision of the placing of these torpedoes was one of the prisoners and he readily found them all and carefully aided in clearing our way to Savannah.

Major Edwards was Commander of Company M and he rode with us. He stated Lieut. Tupper was a good soldier, gallant officer, and a meritorious gentleman, and in every way worthy of respect and confidence.

Mother, I don't like telling you about all this as I'm afraid it will just cause you to worry more, but I just had to talk to someone about it and you have always been interested in anything I had to say. You have always taken the time to sit down and talk to any of us when we had something on our minds, and I miss those times. I am homesick and ready to get back. Take care and I will write when I can. Please give Mary Jane my love. Thomas

(Lt. Tupper had to have the lower third of his thigh amputated, but this didn't keep him from doing what he wanted to do after the war was over. After his leg was amputated, he was sent home to Michigan. He moved his family to Denver, Colorado and in 1917, a newspaper article referred to him as "a one-legged veteran of the Civil War". Tupper wrote "The lead from the torpedo went in just above my knee and came out my ass". Tupper went on to become Clerk of the District Court in Denver, Colorado.")

This is one of the last and saddest letters I had from Jackson while he was gone, and I could only sit down and cry long after I read it. It is unimaginable what my boys have been through during this war. Sometimes I feel sorry for myself for losing my beloved husband, son, and brothers, but when I read what all my boys have been through, especially my boy who was barely fifteen-years old when he joined, it makes me ashamed for being so selfish as to pity myself.

182

My Dearest Mother, I sit here on this calm spring evening wondering how I could have wound up half way across the country from my loving family and comfortable home I love so dearly, fighting in a war that should have never begun. It never crossed my mind that a heart could hurt so badly as one so homesick. I have had to grow up in such a hurry that you will be surprised if God in His glory should see fit to spare my life.

My abounding love for you and my family is only in contention with my love for my country, which is why I am here in the first place. If the enemy had its way, our precious South would be an entirely different place and most likely would not be fit to live or raise a family. While I have many times sought for a wrong motive in leaving my family to fight for my country, I could not find one, and am satisfied I did the right thing. The principles you and father advocated, and my love of country, are the reasons I answered when my country called. The memories of you and father and the happy life you both worked so diligently to provide us is what sustains me on the battlefield and at night in the lonesomeness of silence.

Mother, I know your heart must break at the loss of Father and George, as mine does, but I pray that time will bring with it a healing influence and that God will give us a peace that passeth our understanding. I know the abounding love you had for father and him for you, but keep in mind that in time we will be with him again in the great hereafter.

I wasn't going to mention this, but it is bearing on my mind so, that I must tell you about it. Some of us went in a little place the other day to get something to eat and there were some old newspapers lying around. I picked up a couple of the "Richmond Daily Dispatch" Newspapers and when I began reading, I almost cried. It said the Rebels had captured some Union prisoners, many wounded, and said hundreds of sick Union prisoners had been unloaded from a boxcar in the pouring down rain, with no shelter, care or food. Then they were thrown into several cattle cars with no rations, straw, bedding or any protection from the hard cold floor of the train cars. What was worse than that was, the soldiers with fractured limbs had not been treated nor the limbs placed in splints, and many of the bones had worked their way through the wounds and were protruding in the open air with no protection from germs. The ones with amputations were still worse than that. The sutures had cut through the skin leaving the bones and muscles bare, and the majority of wounds had not been cared for and they were alive with maggots.

As if this wasn't bad enough, the Union soldiers were forced to endure the harassment of the townspeople when the train landed at the depot. The huge crowds of the curious had gathered to get a glimpse of the soldiers as they were almost thrown from the cattle cars, and they jeered and yelled obscenities at the wounded and dying soldiers.

The Union physicians began examining the soldiers and stated that the ones who had early amputations had done best. One problem was the delayed removal of the wounded from the battlefield due to lack of ambulances and continuing of firing from the enemy assured death to some who might have been saved had they been removed earlier and had the proper care.

Mother, I could not finish eating after reading this and wished I had not picked up the paper in the first place.

Please take care and I will write again as soon as I can. Your Loving son, Jackson

(I have read where some of the families who owned farms where the Manassas battlefield was, stated they picked up bones from soldiers who had fallen during this battle, for the next fifty years.)

The loyal men who served in the 1st Alabama Cavalry, USA followed their heart and fought for what they believed to be the right thing to do. They paid a terribly high price for their loyalty and convictions. Even after the war, some were threatened, some murdered, and all were scorned by their southern neighbors. Many of them moved west to escape the persecution. During the war the US Army had to escort many Union families, which totaled over 300, to Illinois for safe keeping because of the atrocities committed toward them by the CSA sympathizers.

This is one more letter Sarah Harper McWhirter received from Thomas asking her to keep it to go with his Civil War Diary he wrote:

"Dear Mother, I haven't been able to write much in my diary lately but rather than writing all of this in the diary, I thought I would just write and tell you what has been going on since we left Savannah and let you know what a week or few weeks are like in the army. Please save this for me so I can add it to my diary when I get home. You can also show it to Mary Jane, if she wants to read it because I won't have time to write all of this to her, too.

We finally broke camp near Savannah, Georgia, on January 28, 1865, and moved on the Springfield road leading to Sister's Ferry on the Savannah River. We arrived at Sister's Ferry on the evening of the 29th, where we camped until February 3rd, when we crossed the river and commenced our march in South Carolina in the direction of Lawtonville. On the 6th we had some skirmishing with Crews' brigade, of Wheeler's command, capturing some prisoners. On the 7th we assisted in destroying Charleston and Augusta Railroad, and then on the 8th we moved from Blackville on the road to Williston, and we were in advance. We came to the rebel pickets just before reaching the village. We routed, and drove them through the town, and established a picket-post half a mile west of the village, awaiting the arrival of the rest of the troops. The regiment soon arrived, and as we were about to establish camp the picket-post was attacked. Captain Latty, in command of two squadrons, was immediately ordered forward with instructions to ascertain, if possible, the force the enemy had in the vicinity. As he advanced the firing became rapid, and we were ordered to Captain Latty's assistance. We drove them one mile and a half, where we found they had established a strong line. We drove them half a mile, where they had another line. We were re-enforced with the Fifth Kentucky Cavalry and then ordered to resume the chase. On advancing we found the enemy in a strong position in the woods near White Pond. On being ordered, we charged them and there followed the most complete rout I ever witnessed. Guns, sabers, canteens, haversacks, saddle-bags, hats, and everything left behind by the fleeing enemy were abandoned and completely strewn over the ground. We continued the pursuit over five miles, capturing quite a number of prisoners, with five stand of colors. We were then ordered to abandon the pursuit, and returned to camp at Williston. We had been contending against a greatly superior force of the enemy. We were praised in the highest degree for our actions, but we lost four men, wounded, one mortally, who afterward died

On the 11th we again resumed our march and participated in all the different scenes through which we passed, crossing the Edisto, Saluda, Broad, Wateree, and Great Pedee Rivers, via Lexington, Alston, Black Stocks, Lancaster, and Sneedsborough, nothing of special importance occurring. After crossing the Great Pedee River and going into camp at 8 o'clock on the evening of March 6, we were ordered to proceed to Rockingham, N.C., about twelve miles distant, and, if possible, take the place and secure the mail. We advanced to within three miles of the place without meeting any opposition, but found the road strongly picketed by the enemy, and were immediately ordered to charge. We drove the enemy from post to post until we reached the edge of the village, where we found a line too strong for us to break, so we slowly fell back and returned to camp, arriving there at 4 a.m. on the 7th. We leave later on for Monroe's Crossroads and will probably be skirmishing with them all the way. This is all I have time to write, so give my love to Mary Jane, Papa Harper and all. Love, Thomas"

It was right after this that they camped at Monroe's Crossroads, and Kilpatrick's Cavalry attacked them early the morning of March 10th while they were still asleep.

Battle of Monroe's Crossroads in NC

...that simple faith to save our soul, that perfect love to make us whole....

Civil War sites are numerous in the southeastern United States, from major battlegrounds to the scenes of much smaller but still deadly actions that involved no more than a handful of troops on either side. Nowhere is a Civil War battle ground in so nearly original condition, however, as Monroe's Crossroads, North Carolina -- where a little known fight between mounted and dismounted cavalry units occurred in the early hours of March 10, 1865.

The primary reason for its well-preserved state is that Monroe's Crossroads lies today wholly within the confines of the Fort Bragg military reservation -- home of the United State's Army's elite 82nd Airborne Division. Even the approach roads used by Union and Confederate forces prior to the battle, for dozens of miles, are in the same unpaved condition as 133 years ago.

The 1st Alabama Cavalry (U.S.V.) played a crucial role in the fight. It was their timely stand behind a nearly impassable swamp that broke the momentum of the Confederate assault and bought time for their outnumbered comrades to rally and drive their attackers off with heavy losses. On another cold, rainy morning near the 133rd anniversary of the battle, two members of today's Company C, guided by topographical maps and a Fort Bragg archaeologist, walked the original field and stepped back in time...

Late on the evening of March 9, 1865, Brigadier General H. Judson Kilpatrick rode through a wet, black North Carolina night at the head of his 4,500-man cavalry division. His mission was to guard the left wing of Major General William Tecumseh Sherman's army as it ground its way north, wearing down Confederate resistance in this fifth winter of the war. Foremost in Kilpatrick's mind that night was his intended target, the city of Fayetteville -- which he'd been given permission to capture, along with any rebel troops unfortunate enough to be there when he arrived.

Kilpatrick -- "Kill Cavalry," as he was known to the troopers he pushed without letup -- had crossed into North Carolina with his Third Cavalry Division a week before. Since then, his force had battled heavy rains and nearly impassable roads. At one point,

Kilpatrick's artillery had taken seven hours to travel five miles through a sea of mud, manhandled by cursing gunners and equally unhappy troopers detailed to lend a hand with the guns. Confederate

Cavalry was all about the column. Skilled at hitting Yankee outriders suddenly and slipping away into the surrounding woods; they did not hesitate to make their presence known in frequent hit-and-run attacks.

The gray horsemen under Confederate generals Hampton, Wheeler, Humes and Butler, were determined to penetrate Sherman's cavalry screen and learn where he would turn next. Sherman had kept the Confederates guessing, however, in no small part because Kilpatrick's veteran troopers were good at their work.

Before leaving Savannah in late January, Sherman had told a confidante, "I know Kilpatrick's a hell of a damned fool, but that's just the kind of man I want to lead my cavalry on this expedition."

Kilpatrick was operating well forward of the Union main body as he approached Fayetteville, where Sherman planned to destroy the federal arsenal and rendezvous with supply ships coming up the Cape Fear River. He then planned to call in his cavalry screen and turn east for Wilmington. Meanwhile, as Kilpatrick's division neared Fayetteville, his brigades were separated by several miles along their line of march. Efficient scouting alone kept the components within supporting distance of one another.

About 2100 hours on the night of March 9th, Kilpatrick and his escort, riding southeast on Morganton Road, were planning to halt at nearby Monroe's Crossroads where the division's dismounted (4th) brigade was, by then, setting up camp. In pitch darkness and heavy rain, the riders topped a small rise about 50 yards west of the intersection with the Yadkin Road. Somehow, a sense of impending danger communicated itself to Kilpatrick and his bodyguard, and they left the road at a gallop, crashing into the nearby woods heading south. What had alarmed them was the capture of part of the escort by troopers of Major General Matthew Butler's Confederate cavalry division, which had been moving along the Yadkin Road nearly parallel to the Federals and reached the intersection first. Butler didn't learn until months later that his men had come within seconds of capturing Sherman's cavalry commander. Meanwhile, Kilpatrick and his remaining escort detoured crosslots toward their intended camp about three miles ahead, at the intersection of the Morganton and Blue's Resin Roads.

Later that evening, after his scouts had located and observed the enemy camp, Lieutenant General Wade Hampton, commanding the Confederate cavalry, realized his troops might defeat the Federals if he could get his force in close undetected. Given the rain and darkness, Hampton thought this could be done, especially since the scouts had reported the Federals had no pickets out north or west of their camp to watch their rear.

As he thought over his next move, Hampton considered three factors. First, Confederate forces in Fayetteville needed time to withdraw across the Cape Fear River and rejoin their main body further north. The Federals in his front were, at most, two brigades, with the remainder not close enough to offer much support. And within the confines of the federal camp was an undetermined number of Confederate prisoners who might also be freed. Even though his own force wasn't fully assembled, Hampton decided to attack the Federal camp at dawn. Accordingly, in total darkness, leading their mounts and ordered not to talk above a whisper, the Confederate troopers began moving into attack positions north and west of the Federal camp.

The Federal force at Monroe's Crossroads consisted of two cavalry brigades, one dismounted and one mounted -- altogether about 1,500 men.

The troopers had arrived by regiments, tired, wet and groping through the dark woods for places to pitch tents and find shelter from the incessant rain. Their camps ran from the Monroe house facing Blue's Resin Road, southwest about 500 yards to the sloping bank of a tiny stream called Nicholson Creek. After days of rain, the normally lazy stream had become a swamp, narrow, but long and deep, filling the little gully through which it flowed.

The camp of the Federal 1st Alabama Cavalry marked the farthest extent of the bivouac and was closest to the creek. A section of the 10th Wisconsin Light Artillery, two 3-inch ordnance rifles under Lt. Ebenezer Stetson, was posted on a slight rise about 250 yards behind the Alabamians' camp. Meanwhile, Kilpatrick's scouts under Captain Theo Northrup had bivouacked across Blue's Resin Road several hundred yards east of the main Federal camp. Northrup had been tempted by the comfortable Monroe house just south of the crossroads but thought it too exposed, and moved his men to what he considered a less vulnerable campsite.

As the Federals settled down for the night, Confederate scouts watched the camp. They had orders to locate General Kilpatrick's headquarters and the Confederate POWs. So close did they draw to the camp that four men from the 8th Texas Cavalry actually slipped inside the perimeter and made off with several horses. The scouts were surprised to learn that the Federals had no pickets north or west of the crossroads where Generals Hampton and Wheeler were assembling their men for a dawn assault.

Col. George Spencer, former commander of the 1st Alabama, now commanding the 3rd Brigade of Kilpatrick's Division, would later say that he placed his pickets to the east, facing Fayetteville, where he believed the greatest danger lay. A large Confederate force under General William J. Hardee still occupied the city, but hoped to get out before the Yankees arrived. It's likely that Kilpatrick and Spencer talked after the general's arrival in camp, and discussed Kilpatrick's narrow escape on the Morganton Road earlier that evening. Assuming that to have been the case, it's difficult to believe neither of the two experienced commanders sensed the presence of a strong enemy force in their rear. Nevertheless, no pickets or videttes were posted north or west of the Federal camp.

Throughout the night, more of Hampton's and Wheeler's units arrived and were assigned positions for the attack. As these assembled at the crossroads, one of Wheeler's divisions under Brigadier General William Y.C. Humes was posted to the Confederate right. Its task was to hit the Federals southwest of the Monroe house and either rout them, or keep them from coming to the aid of their comrades around the house. Humes's men were now directly across Nicholson Creek from the 1st Alabama and facing about 200 yards of swamp which they would have to cross in their assault.

Just before dawn the rain stopped and a heavy fog hung over the swamp, obscuring the Federal camp and screening the force assembled against it. Although their entire complement still had not arrived, the longer Generals Hampton and Wheeler waited, the greater grew the chance of discovery. Shortly after 0530, then, the word was passed to mount and the Confederates deployed into attack formation.

North of the Morganton Road, on the Federal right, General Butler's two brigades would strike the Monroe house and the Yankees camped on its grounds -- including, it was hoped, General Kilpatrick. Just south of the Morganton Road and west of the camp, behind a low rise of ground, Hampton had posted Brigadier General William Wirt Allen's division of Wheeler's Corps which had come up in the night. One of Allen's units was an all-Alabama brigade under Colonel James Hagan.

Another brigade under Brigadier General George Dibrell was there as well, being held in reserve. The assault on the west side of the Federal camp would be led by Shannon's Scouts, who would make straight for the POW compound they had located in their earlier reconnaissance. Meanwhile, some 300 yards further south and west of the camp Hume's division prepared to cross the swamp along Nicholson Creek and deal with the Federals posted there. Generals Hampton and Wheeler had a brief last-minute conference, in which Hampton rejected his subordinate's suggestion that the assault be made on foot. "As a cavalryman," said Hampton, "I prefer that this capture be made on horseback." Wheeler acknowledged with a salute, adding, "General Hampton, all is ready for action. Have your headquarters bugler blow the charge."

A late winter dawn in the Carolina sandhills doesn't break so much as filter reluctantly through the brooding pines and thick ground fog. But on this cold, sodden morning the blast of a Confederate cavalry bugle shattered the mist, and the peace of the Yankee camp, in a barrage of sound. The brazen notes poured forth, accompanied by General Butler's hoarse shout, "Troops from Virginia, follow me! Forward! Charge!" Before their commander's voice had died away, the troops north of the camp exploded from the woods and across the Morganton Road, screaming the Rebel yell and firing as they came.

The charge struck the camp of the dismounted brigade just as the first troops were stirring, overrunning the guards on the POW compound and setting off a stampede for the woods southeast of the Monroe house and across Blue's Resin Road. Those who didn't take to their heels surrendered or were shot down as they groped for their weapons to respond. Many of the Confederate prisoners dashed in the direction of the attacking force only to be taken by them for a Federal counterattack coming out of the mist. Several of the escapers were shot by their own men.

As Butler's men hacked and shot their way into the Federal camp, General Wheeler ordered his men to charge into the compound from the west. Wheeler, too, commenced the assault with his bugler blowing the charge -- as it turned out, just as the Federal bugler was preparing to sound reveille. Whatever notes the Yankee managed to play were drowned in the din of pounding hooves and yelling men.

At about that point, Kilpatrick emerged from the Monroe house in the face of what he later called "the most formidable cavalry charge I have ever witnessed." Coming from a man who spared little praise for his enemies, the words amounted to a high accolade. As the commanding general stood on the front porch clad, some said, only in his nightshirt, two flying squads of Confederate troopers pounded up and demanded to know the whereabouts of General Kilpatrick.

"Little Kil's" wits didn't fail him at that precarious moment. Glancing around quickly, he saw a figure on a black horse galloping into the mist. "There he goes," Kilpatrick replied, pointing, and the Confederates spurred their mounts in pursuit while their intended quarry watched them go. Thus, Sherman's cavalry commander narrowly escaped capture twice within ten hours -- at Monroe's Crossroad's Judson Kilpatrick's personal luck was definitely in.

"By this time," writes historian Mark L. Bradley, "the fighting around the Monroe house was a jumble of small battles at close quarters." So many men were fighting in that confined space that even wild or random shots hit living flesh. Those in the melee later wrote of the individual combats they saw or were part of; desperate little fights with no quarter asked or given as men shot, stabbed, clubbed and clawed each another in the gray dawn -- the last for many.

Butler's men and the left half of Wheeler's force were now heavily engaged around the Monroe house. Up to this point, with the exception of General Kilpatrick's narrow escape, the Confederate attack had gone about as planned. But on Wheeler's right, a swamp and some stubborn Unionists were about to change that. The two brigades under Harrison and Ashby were still struggling across the swamp in their front -- a body of water wider and deeper than originally thought. Moreover, the two commands were attempting to cross it mounted -- a nearly impossible feat under the circumstances if the force was to hit its target with speed and concentration.

Behind the swamp, an equally formidable waited: the 1st Alabama Union Cavalry. The Southern Unionists were the last of Spencer's mounted brigade to come into camp the night before and had filed past the other units and halted along the south bank of Nicholson Creek. Now they were alerted by the din of battle near the Monroe house, and were in position to give a hot welcome to the Confederates across the swamp.

The Alabama Federals, according to historian Mark Bradley, now "laid down a heavy fire into the swamp, forcing Harrison's and Ashby's troopers to dismount and seek cover.

"The men of the 1st Alabama Cavalry were fiercely independent Unionists from the hilly northern region of the state who refused to truckle to the secessionist cotton planters of the flatlands further south. In 1862 they formed their own regiment and joined the Union army.

For most of the war, these bluecoat Alabamians had served as scouts, raiders and railroad guards. At the moment, however, they were doing just what they had enlisted to do -- fight Rebels."

Fire from the Alabamians' Burnside, Spencer and Smith carbines poured into the swamp, forcing Harrison's and Ashby's men to give up their push and turn north to seek an easier route. As the Confederates across the creek pulled back, the 1st Alabama men turned their attention to the fighting near the Monroe house north of their camp. The 5th Kentucky had camped on the Alabamians' right, and now the two regiments combined forces to harry the Confederates and slow the pace of their attack.

As the 1st and 5th poured carbine fire into the Confederate attackers, First Lieutenant Ebenezer Stetson, commanding the brigade artillery section raced toward his two guns. The three-inch ordinance rifles had been posted on the only high ground in the vicinity -- a knoll so insignificant as to be almost invisible unless an observer carefully examined the contour of the immediate ground. Their crews had been shot down or driven off in the first assault and now the two guns stood silent, for all intents and purposes in the possession of hundreds of nearby Confederates who were pressing their advantage hard. Alone, Lt. Stetson managed to load a canister round into one of the two guns. He then raced to its rear where he single - handedly primed and fired the piece into the mass of struggling men. The round and its accompanying blast tore a terrible hole through the surprised Confederates. At such close range, men and horses were torn apart by flying iron or blown for dozens of feet. Those not hit were momentarily stunned by the sudden, unexpected discharge. Suddenly the momentum of the fight shifted to the blue troopers who until a moment before had been battling for their very lives.

Stetson continued to work his gun, grabbing another round and springing back to the loader's position at its muzzle. Here both Federal and Confederate accounts conflict as to exactly what happened. Some later recollections suggest that one of Stetson's sergeants and some of the surviving batterymen rushed to their lieutenant's aid and were later killed or wounded when the Confederates turned on the guns with renewed fury. Battery after-action reports don't confirm those accounts, however, listing one gun disabled, ten battery horses captured and no artillerymen killed.

By now the Confederates, recovering from the shock of Stetson's first round had turned their fire on the Federal cannoneers while forming for a counterattack to retake the guns. Lieutenant General Wheeler, working rapidly under fire, gathered several elements of the Confederate force into line and ordered a mounted charge against the Federal left. Wheeler knew that if he breached the line and took the guns on their tiny knoll, the blue troopers would have to abandon their camp. The Confederates came on with a rush, but the dismounted Federals, taking cover behind the many trees that covered the area and supported by the artillery, stopped Wheeler's men with a heavy toll. The Confederates pulled back toward the upper part of the camp where Hampton's men still had possession of the Monroe house and grounds.

As Wheeler's men fell back toward the Monroe house, he rallied them for a second charge and, within minutes, they surged again toward the Federal line. But the dis- mounted blue troopers and their breech loading carbines again devastated the Confederates Gray troopers and their horses were shot down wholesale, consumed by the Federal firestorm. On Wheeler's left Major General Butler was forming his men for still another charge, and they came on as Wheeler's men withdrew. The result was the same. Butler later reported:

"They [the Federals] had got to their artillery and, with their carbines, made it so hot for the handful of us we had to retire. In fact I lost sixty-two men there in five minutes' time."

Among the casualties was Lieutenant Colonel Barrington King, commanding Cobb's Georgia Legion, who was struck during the charge by a piece of shrapnel from one of Stetson's guns. He bled to death within minutes.

About this time, the brigade scout company under Captain Theo Northrop galloped up Blue's Resin Road from the swamp where he had wisely chosen to position his men. Along with him came a number of the Federals who'd been blown loose from their bivouac around the Monroe house by the initial Confederate charge. Apparently thinking that these might be reinforcements, rather than part of the force in front of them, the remaining Confederates withdrew slowly north toward the Morganton Road.

At this point Lieutenant Generals Wheeler and Hampton conferred and agreed that little could be gained by continuing the fight. They assumed, correctly as it turned out, that Federal infantry was on the way to support their opponents and, not wanting to be cut off and overwhelmed, they decided to withdraw. Posting a rearguard while they hurriedly retrieved as many of their dead and wounded as possible, the Confederates retired to the Morganton Road and moved off into the piney woods toward Fayetteville. For a time the rearguard remained, then -- with a few scattered shots to discourage pursuit -- they too withdrew.

Spencer's weary brigade remained in possession of the crossroads and its camps. Thanks to the stubborn Unionists of the 1st Alabama Cavalry, their comrades in the 5th Kentucky and, not least, Lt. Stetson and his guns, Kilpatrick's reputation and his major general's commission, were safe. But it was a chastened "Little Kil" who emerged from the fight at the Crossroads. Fearing that the Confederates might themselves return with infantry, he anxiously pushed his officers to finish tending the wounded and get the troops on the move. As soon as the last casualty was seen to, the brigade rejoined the 3rd Cavalry Division and left Monroe's Crossroads behind. But, as the saying goes, `once bit, twice shy.' As Kilpatrick moved south he no longer marched far out on the flanks of the army, staying much closer to the Federal infantry than had heretofore been his want.

Both sides claimed Monroe's Crossroads as a victory. Kilpatrick because his men regained their camps and inflicted heavy casualties on the Confederates, and Hampton because his men had captured over a hundred prisoners, freed all their own men held captive by the Federals, and opened the road to Fayetteville. In addition, the battle slowed Kilpatrick's advance and gave the Confederates additional time to evacuate the city and cross the Cape Fear River to safety.

Kilpatrick reported his casualties as 19 killed, 68 wounded and 103 captured. He further said of Confederate losses that his troopers buried "upward of 80 killed, including many officers," and captured 30 more. Confederate figures are imprecise and, not surprisingly, conflict with Federal reports. Lieutenant General Wheeler reported capturing 350 Union prisoners, and one of his biographers puts his losses at 12 killed, 60 wounded and 10 missing. There are no casualty figures for Butler's division, but it should be remembered that he later estimated his casualties at 62 in just the brief fight for the guns.

Kilpatrick's lack of vigilance while far out on the flank of the main Union army gave the Confederates a golden opportunity to inflict a stinging defeat on the Federal cavalry. The chance was lost because the swamp along Nicholson Creek stopped the right wing of the Confederate assault, and the fire of 1st Alabama and the 5th Kentucky drove it back. Their action bought the time the rest of the brigade needed to rally and drive out the attackers.

The following are reports from Major Sanford Tramel of the 1st Alabama Cavalry, USV and Major George H. Radar of the 5th Ohio Cavalry, USV about the battle:

HEADQUARTERS FIRST ALABAMA VOLUNTEER CAVALRY, Faison's Depot, N. C., March 28, 1865

At the sounding of reveille on the morning of the 10th instant, we were aroused from sleep by the whistling of bullets and the fiendish yelling of the enemy, who were charging into our camp. Then followed a most bloody hand-to-hand conflict, our men forming behind trees and stumps and the enemy endeavoring to charge us (mounted) with the saber.

S. TRAMEL, Major First Alabama Volunteer Cavalry, Comdg. Regiment.

HEADQUARTERS FIFTH OHIO CAVALRY VOLUNTEERS, THIRD BRIGADE, THIRD CAVALRY DIVISION, Faison's Station, N. C., March 31, 1865.

Simultaneous with the call of reveille on the morning of the 10th, and before my command had arisen from bed, my camp was overrun by a large force of the enemy. My command was taken completely by surprise, the enemy being in force in every part of my camp. The officers and men were completely bewildered for a short time, but through the almost superhuman efforts of some of the officers the men soon rallied and contested the ground inch by inch with the enemy, and finally, assisted by the men and officers of the First Alabama and Fifth Kentucky Cavalry, the enemy was forced to retire after one of the most terrific hand-to-hand encounters I ever witnessed, leaving the dead and wounded on the field.

Geo. H. Rader, Major, Commanding Fifth Ohio Volunteer Cavalry.

During their three years of service, the 1st Alabama Cavalry, USV traveled some 1800 miles by steamboat, 1000 miles by train, and several thousand miles in the saddle or walking. They fought in six states and traveled through some four or five more. The records show there were 2,678 white soldiers in the 1st Alabama Cavalry, USV, right in "The Heart of Dixie".

For those fortunate enough to see Monroe's Crossroads today, it's a rare chance to examine a battlefield practically unchanged by time. Terrain, vegetation, even weather, conditions are very, if not exactly, like those which existed in the day of battle. The Monroe house is gone but little has been added save a small monument. A soldier who fought there, could he return today, would find himself on completely familiar ground... ground for all practical purposes the same as it was on a wet March dawn 134 years ago.

A South Carolina soldier returning home at war's end visited the Monroe farm about a month after the battle. He arrived about dusk and never forgot the horrid scene. The house was still deserted, an empty shell. All around were rotting carcasses of some 300 horses and mules killed during the fight. Remains of some Union and Confederate dead were also visible, washed out of the graves or dug up by animals.

Local residents reburied the soldiers in mass graves. Many bodies of

197

Confederate soldiers were later transferred to Long Street Presbyterian Church Cemetery, a few miles east of the battlefield. Other remains were reinterred in Fayetteville, North Carolina. Some families from farther away retrieved their fallen relatives and took them home for burial, which was the case for Confederate Lieutenant Colonel Barrington S. King, killed in the last minutes of the battle. His brother had his remains returned to Georgia.

Beginning in 1921, the Army marked various Union graves, which reportedly contain the remains of 39 unknown Federal soldiers, graves pointed out by Neill S. Blue. When National Park Service archeologist Douglas Scott determined that a mass grave of 27 unknown Union soldiers was likely to contain unknown Confederate remains as well, the Army placed a Confederate marker at the gravesites. A monument was erected on the battlefield at Monroe's Crossroads by the Army and dedicated "To the American Soldier". (See picture in back of book of this monument and Cemetery at Monroe's Crossroads, NC where Confederate and Union soldiers killed in this battle were buried.)

Culmination of the Civil War

... Let perpetual light shine on them....

The loyal men who served in the 1st Alabama Cavalry, USA, had the strength to stand up and fight for what they believed was the right thing to do, which was to defend their country at all cost, and they paid a terribly high price for their loyalty and convictions. Even after the war, some were threatened, some murdered, and all were scorned by their southern neighbors. During the war the US Army had to escort many Union families, which totaled over 300, to Illinois for their safety because of the atrocities committed toward them by the CSA Home Guard and sympathizers. The McWhirters chose to remain in Marion County as did some of the Harpers. There is a strong possibility that two more of the Harper brothers might have been murdered by the Confederate Home Guard a year or so after the war ended.

At the culmination of the war, the exhausted, ragged soldiers of the 1st Alabama Cavalry, USV, had traveled about two-thousand miles by steamboat, over one-thousand miles by train and innumerable miles in the saddle and on foot. Many husbands, sons, and other loved ones would not return home to their loving families, leaving thousands of poor widows and orphans to suffer for years to come. The ones who were able to return home, returned to a life and land completely different from the one they had left behind.

After the war, prices in Alabama escalated excessively on groceries, horses, and most anything available for sale. Horses sold for from $1,500 - $2,000 each, Calico fabric sold for $15.00 per yard, bacon was over $4.00 per pound, Quinine was $150.00 per ounce, salt was $150.00 - $200.00 per sack, and a wagon and team would bring almost $3,000 for those in the market with the money.

For those unfortunate enough to need a place to stay, board was bringing $600.00 per month, meals $10.00 - $25.00 each, a cup of imitation coffee sold for $5.00, and a boiled egg brought $2.00.

Houses and crops had been burned, the Confederates had burned 97,000 bales of cotton to keep it out of the hands of the Union, mills and gins had been burned, and northwest Alabama was in shambles. Several men dressed as soldiers went to the Wilson home just outside of Florence, Alabama demanding Mr. Wilson give them his money and when he didn't say or do anything, they stripped him to his waist, tore pages from the Bible, set him on fire and burned him severely, although he survived. Wilson's grandson, not able to tell them anything, was shot, wounded and left for dead. His nephew was shot and killed when he told them he knew nothing about the money. The overseer came on the scene and was shot and killed as his wife begged for her husband's life to be spared. This went on for years after the war ended. This band of guerillas disguised as "Tories" were finally caught, tried and hung by the Union Army.

Sarah Harper McWhirter can indeed be proud of her husband, sons and brothers. She died a brokenhearted, lonesome woman and although she went on to have two more children, Nancy McWhirter, born in 1865 and Jasper Green McWhirter, born August 18, 1868.

Sarah Harper McWhirter's sad life ended December 28, 1883 and she was laid to rest in the O'Mary Cemetery in Marion County, Alabama.

As you can see, Sarah Harper McWhirter lived in a time of murder, torture, rape, theft, plunder, fear, etc. and the Union men who were supposedly "protecting the Union widows, and keeping them in salt and other needed supplies. These men also abused and molested some of these same widows. At times she probably had difficulty knowing who to trust. Grandma Sarah was a Godly woman who loved her husband, children, family and friends and she deserved a better life than the one she was forced to endure.

On September 6, 1871, Sarah was notified by the Bureau of Pensions in Washington, DC that she was eligible for a pension of $8 per month for herself and $2 per month for each of her three children. If she had married, that pension would have been stopped, and she certainly could not afford to lose that pension, especially after losing her farm immediately following the war.

(See Census Records on next page.)

The following are the 1870 & 1880 Marion County, Alabama Census Records for Sarah Harper McWhirter and her children:

1870 Marion County, Alabama Census, Eastern Subdivision, Thorn Hill Post Office

Name	Age	
Sarah Mcquirter	47	(Sarah McWhirter)
Hamilton Mcquirter	18	(William Hamilton McWhirter)
Mary Mcquirter	16	(Mary Caroline McWhirter)
John Mcquirter	14	(John Madison McWhirter)
Nancy Mcquirter	5	(Nancy Ann McWhirter)
Green Mcquirter	2	(Jasper Green McWhirter)

1880 Marion County, Alabama Census, Beat # 10. (This is the last census showing Sarah Harper McWhirter before her death in 1883, she was living between sons, John Madison McWhirter and William Hamilton McWhirter)

Marital Status: Widowed

Name	Age	
Sarah McWhirter	55	(Sarah Harper McWhirter)
Nancy McWhirter	14	(Nancy Ann McWhirter)
Jasper McWhirter	11	(Jasper Green McWhirter)

Pension Records

…As for me, I go on to my next adventure….

Sarah Harper McWhirter's Application for Pension (Sic)

(Some of these same records have purposefully been inserted in other appropriate areas of the book.)

On the 26th day of January, A.D. 1866, personally appeared before me, Judge of the Probate Court, in and for the County and State aforesaid, Sarah McWhirter, a resident of ___, in the County of Marion, and State of Alabama, aged 43 years, who being first duly sworn according to law, doth, on her oath, make the following declaration, in order to obtain the benefits of the provision made by the act of Congress approved July 14th, 1862, granting Pensions: That she is the widow of Andrew F. McWhirter, who was a Private in Company E, commanded by David D. Smith, in the Middle Regiment of Tennessee Cavalry, mustered into the service of the United States from the State of Alabama, in the war of 1861, and who died at Hospital No. 14, Nashville, Tennessee, with Rubiola whilst in the service, on the 23 day of October, 1862, as this deponent verily believes. She further declares that she was lawfully married to the said Andrew F. McWhirter, at Thomas Harper (home), in the State of Tennessee, by William Nubey, a Justice of the Peace, on the 7th day of June, 1841; that her husband, the aforesaid Andrew F. McWhirter, died on the day above mentioned. She further declares that she has remained a widow ever since the death of her said husband----as will more fully appear by reference to the proof hereto annexed. The personal description of the said Andrew F. McWhirter, her deceased husband, is as follows: Age, about 44 years; height, 5 feet 10 inches; grey eyes; fair complexion; black hair, occupation at time of enlistment, a Farmer. She further declares that she had, by said deceased husband, three children, now living, under the age of sixteen years, named, aged, and residing as follows: William H. McWhirter, age 13, Mary C. McWhirter, age 11, John M. McWhirter, age 7, and that she has not, in any manner, been engaged in or aided or abetted the rebellion in the United States, and that her maiden name was Sarah Harper, and that her Post Office address is Eldridge, County of Walker, and State of Alabama; and I hereby authorize C.D. Pennebaker, my lawful attorney, to procure for me the Pension mentioned in the above application, and to receive and receipt for any Certificate which may issue in my favor in connection with the same, hereby ratifying and confirming whatever my said attorney may do in the premises.

Signature of Claimant (her X mark) Sarah McWhirter.
(Sarah either made her mark a time or two or someone else did it for her because, later on she signed for herself.)

Also personally appeared Mary E. Tucker and Thos. Harper, residents of Marion County, of ____, and State of Alabama, persons whom I certify to be respectable and entitled to credit, and who, being by me duly sworn, say that they were present and saw Sarah McWhirter sign her name (or make her mark) to the foregoing declaration; and they further swear that they have known the parties above described to have lived together as husband and wife for twenty years previous to and up to the time of deceased going into the aforesaid service of the United States, and they have every reason to believe, from the appearance of the applicant, and their acquaintance with her, that she is the identical person she represents herself to be, and that they have no interest in the prosecution of this claim.
Witness (her mark) Mary E. Tucker
Witness (his mark) Thomas Harper

Sworn to and subscribed by both applicant and witnesses, before me, this 26th day of January, A.D. 1866; and I hereby certify that I have no interest, direct or indirect, in the prosecution of this claim--- (something about "said Probate Court")
Signed by John D. Terrell, Clerk & Judge of Probate Court

WIDOW'S APPLICATION FOR PENSION (sic)

State of Alabama
County of Marion
On the second day of June, 1871, personally appeared before me, a Judge of Probate, Court of Record in and for the County and State aforesaid, Sarah McWhirter, a resident of New River, in the County of Marion and State of Alabama, aged 48 years, who being duly sworn, makes the following declaration, in order to obtain the Pension provided by the Act of Congress approved July 14, 1862. That she is the widow of Andrew F. McWhirter, who was a Private in Company Commanded by David P. Smith, in the 1st Regiment of Tennessee Cavalry, in the war of 1862; that her maiden name was Sarah Harper and that she was married to said Andrew F. McWhirter on or about the 7th day of June, 1842, at Thomas

Harpers in the county of Warren and State of Tennessee by William Nubey, J.P., and she knows of no record of said marriage (clerk office of Warren County said to be burnt in time of the late war).

She further declares that said Andrew F. McWhirter her husband, died in the service of the United States as aforesaid, at Nashville, in the State of Tennessee, on or about the 23rd day of October 1862, of Measles, as she is advised. She also declares that she had remained a widow every since the death of said Andrew F. McWhirter and that she has not in any manner been engaged in, or aided or abetted the rebellion in the United States and she hereby appoints Samuel V. Niles, of Washington, D.C., as her lawful Attorney, with power of substitution, and authorizes him to present and prosecute this claim, and to receive her pension certificates. The following is the name, date of birth and place of residence of all the children of her deceased husband who were under sixteen years of age at the time of his death:

William H., born 19th July, 1852, living with mother
Mary C., born 17th May, 1855, living with mother
John M., born 15 February 1858, living with mother
My Post Office Address is Pikeville, Marion County, Ala.

STATE OF ALABAMA
MARION COUNTY   June A.D. 1871 (or 1877)

Personally appeared before me, John D. Terrell, Judge of the Probate Court in and for said county and state, the same being a court of records,   Mrs. Sarah McWhirter, (widow of Andrew F. McWhirter, Dcd. Who was a private in Co. E, 1st Regt. Of Tennessee Cavalry) who being duly sworn according to law, states on her said oath, that she was married to the Dcd. Andrew F. McWhirter, in Warren County, Tennessee on the 7th day of June 1842, that she has been informed and so believes that the Records of said marriage with the whole clerk's office of said Warren County, was during the late war, destroyed by fire, that she has applied for and can get no transcript of her said marriage and can make no proof by anyone who was present at her said marriage, her father and mother both being dead and no one in this country who was present and the next best evidence she makes is by her neighbors who have resided by her for the last twenty years and the said affiant states further that she has not again married, but is still now the widow of said Andrew F. McWhirter, Dcd.

Signed by (her mark) Sarah McWhirter
Attestants: John Lyons and Mariah Lyons

January 26, 1866, Thomas Harper signed a Widow's Application for Pension for his daughter, Sarah Harper McWhirter, before Judge John D. Terrell, Probate Clerk, Marion Co., AL

Mary Emoline Harper Tucker also signed on same date. Wife of James Richard Tucker.

Pension Record for Thomas Andrew McWhirter (Sic)

According to Thomas A. McWhirter's Pension Record, it states he was entitled to a pension at the rate of $18 per month from August 21, 1912; $24 per month from July 10, 1913; and $30 per month from July 10, 1918.

He was enrolled in the 1st Regiment Ala. Cav. Volunteers on July 24, 1862, at Huntsville for 3 years and is reported on Roll to October 31, 1862, present and so reported to June 30, 1863. However, Prisoner of War Records also show him captured at Rome, Georgia on May 3, 1863. He escaped from there and walked back home.

June 30, 1863 to October 31, 1863, (4 mo muster) Missing in Action at Vincent's Cross Roads October 26, 1863. Company was in action at that place and date. Dec 31, 1863, to February 29, 1864, name not borne. April 30, 1864 to December 31, 1864, present. From December 31, 1864 to April 30, 1865 at Annapolis, Maryland. Paroled Prisoner of war, wounded in battle. May and June 1865, present. Mustered out with company July 19, 1865 with remark "wounded in Skirmish near Richmond, North Carolina, April 1, 1865. Company was in action at Faison's Depot North Carolina March 30 & 31, 1865.

Prisoner of war Records show him captured at Rome, GA May 3, 1863 and confined at Richmond, VA. May 9, 1863, paroled at City Point, VA. May 15, 1863, reported at Camp Parole, Maryland May 16, 1863. Disposition not given. Reported at Camp Chase, Ohio May 22, 1863. No later record. No evidence of such_____?

Marion Co., AL, 13 November 1917 appeared John H. McWhirter, aged 40, resident of Glen Allen, Rt. 2, Marion Co., AL, makes the following declaration in order to obtain reimbursement from the accrued pension for expenses paid in the last sickness and burial of Thomas A. McWhirter who was a pensioner of the United States by Certificate No 1.006914 on account of the service of Thomas A.

McWhirter in Co. K 1st Regiment Alabama Calv. states Thomas A. McWhirter was married one time to Mary J. Hallmark and his wife did not survive him. Mary J. McWhirter died August 1902. Application stated Thomas had never been divorced and had no insurance or property.

W.J. McCrary and R. L. Hill, physicians from Winfield, AL tended to Thomas A. Harper. Also, R.H. Barnes of Glen Allen, AL saw him. John H. McWhirter & family nursed him during his sickness. Thomas A. McWhirter lived at the home of John H. McWhirter and also died there August 26, 1919.

Dr. R.H. Barnes, M.D. stated he held a claim against claimant, John H. McWhirter in the reimbursement claim to the amount of $55.00 for attending to Thomas A. McWhirter. Dr. Barnes stated that from Feb. till Thomas' death, he attended Thomas for Erysifilas, followed by Myoaarditis which brought about his death on Aug 26, 1917. He had no property at the time of his death.

Thomas A. McWhirter signed an affidavit for the Department of the Interior April 7, 1915 stating he was born in Walker Co., Ala. July the 10, 1843, and served in the 1st Regiment of Ala Cav. Co. K, and that his Post Office at enlistment was Eldridge, Walker Co., AL. His wife's full and maiden name was Mary J. McWhirter, her maiden name was Mary J. Hallmark and they married in Marion Co., Ala at her father's residence by S.V. John Lile (Lyle) and they had a family record. He stated he was never married but one time and she was never married previous to the time mentioned above.

His dates of birth of all his children, living or dead were: Sarah E. McWhirter, born December 18, 1866; Nancy M. McWhirter, April 16, 1872; Susan H. McWhirter, February. 10, 1874, John H. McWhirter, September 27, 1877; Manervy Ann McWhirter, Sept 18, 1879. (He didn't list all of his deceased children.)

Declaration for Pension dated May 20, 1912 states Thomas A. McWhirter was a resident of Glen Allen, Alabama, RFD #2 in Fayette Co. and he enrolled in the 1st AL Cav. 24 July 1862 in Huntsville, AL as a Private in Lt. J.H. Hornback's Co. K and was honorable discharged the July 19, 1865 at Nashville, Tenn.

He was 5' 7 1/4" tall, light complexion, hazel eyes, black hair and he was a farmer, born July 10, 1843 at Eldridge, Walker Co., Alabama. He was a pensioner under certificate No 1006914. John W. Baccus and John W. Grand were witnesses to this affidavit and it was signed by W.T. Hawkins.

L.G. Green and A.J. Ingle residing at Brilliant, Ala signed an affidavit stating they were present and saw Thomas A. McWhirter sign his name to the claim stating he had Rheumatism and Neuralgia of the bowels & rheumatism of the left leg and ankle. It was signed by E.S. Green, Justice of the Peace.

Calvin Miles signed an affidavit, date not shown, stating he was 64 years old, a resident of Marion County, Alabama and his address was Gold Mine, Ala and that he had been personally acquainted with Thos. A. McWhirter from the close of the war up to the present, living 12 1/2 miles distant from him from 1865 to 1870. He says he has frequently worked with him during said period and knows that he has been more or less troubled with piles and wound in the bowels. He further states that in his opinion that the said Thomas. A. McWhirter had not been during all of this time able to do at much more than 1/2 the labor of an able bodied man and according to the complaint made by him having personally examined his wound the attacks of piles being more severe at times he cannot locate the intervals he further states that is impossible to locate what his actual earnings has been during said period. He further states that it is impossible to locate the times he saw him each week he was very intimate with him during all of said period. He further states that his occupation is that of a farmer.

A.J. Ingle signed a General Affidavit stating he was 26 years old, his address was Gold Mine, Ala. and he had been very intimately acquainted with Thomas A. McWhirter for the last 20 years having frequently worked with and for hires working the entire year of 1883. He further states during the above named period the said McWhirter has been subject to severe attacks of his alleged disease to wit piles and derangement of the bowels which at said periods he was wholly unable for labor and was more or less disabled at all times. He further states that he cannot precisely locate the time he was not able to do the work of an able boded man. He further states that the said McWhirter done his work with and for his own family his exact earnings, he cannot precisely locate as a hired servant. Also personally appeared W.H. Ingle, aged 23 of said PO and often being duly sworn testifies to the above facts. He further states that he worked the entire year 1885 with the said McWhirter their occupation is that of farmers. They state they have no interest in said case. Signed A.J. Ingle and W. H. Ingle.

John M. Hallmark also signed an affidavit for Thomas A. McWhirter

Walter Bates signed a General Affidavit for Thomas A. McWhirter stating he had lived for the last eight years a near neighbor and further states that during said period he knows that McWhirter has been frequently attacked with piles and bowel disease which has during said time has given him much trouble, rendering him during those periods wholly unfit for service. He further states that according to his opinion, the said McWhirter is no more than half of his time fit for following his occupation which is farming. He further states that his occupation is that of a farmer. It was signed by Walter Bates and witnessed by A.J. Ingle and H.M. Lambert.

November 1, 1917, Pensioner Thomas A. McWhirter was dropped from the pension rolls because of death, August 26, 1917. He was last paid $24 to August 4, 1917.

Affidavit signed by Thomas A. McWhirter state Susan A. McWhirter Sexton was born Feb 10, 1876, rather than Feb 10, 1874.

According to the Pension Records Dept., the records furnished had no evidence of alleged disability. Regimental Hospl. records not on file. Co. Desc. Book shows him wounded in skirmish April 1, 1865 near Richland, NC. Nature and location not stated. Co. Mo???? Reports Jany 20, 1864, shows him returned from Missing in Action at Vincent's Cross Roads.

Pension Record states Thomas A. McWhirter died 25 July 1917. Just a few lines down it stated Thomas A. McWhirter died in the home of John H. McWhirter August 26, 1917.

McWhirter, Thomas A., Pvt., Co. K, age 19, EN & MI 7/24/62, Huntsville, AL, born Walker Co., AL, on courier post in Jan. & Feb. 1863, on detached duty at Vicksburg MS 1/24/64, served as orderly at regimental headquarters, wounded POW at the Battle of Vincent's Crossroads 10/26/63, escaped on or about 2/15/64 and walked back to Decatur, AL to find the regiment gone, again captured on or about 4/15/65 at Faun's Station, NC, paroled POW at Annapolis, MD, wounded in skirmish at Richland, NC 4/1/65.

The following was noted by record and Pension Office 2 March 1896 and in the file of William Dwyer.

Affidavit from Thomas A McWhirter dated 3 July 1865 stated "William Dwyer was taken POW by the enemy with him at Vincent's Crossroads, MS in action 10/26/1863 and taken to Cahaba Prison, AL. After remaining there for two months, they both escaped from the prison and started together for the Union lines at Camp Davies, MS.

After traveling six days, William Dwyer became exhausted and unable to travel any further when Thomas A McWhirter left him about 150 miles from their lines. (Thomas found a Unionist family who offered to take William Dwyer in and care for him until he was able to get back to camp.) There are several documents on file that state how William tried to get back to his regiment. Due to weather conditions and his illness, he was not able to return until January 5, 1864, when he reported to Major Shurtleff who was the only officer left. The rest of the regiment had gone with Major General W.T. Sherman." (At some point, Thomas A. McWhirter was able to catch up with the regiment as he was on the march to the sea and wounded and captured in North Carolina on the way back. By the time they reached Goldsboro, North Carolina, over 4,000 soldiers were barefoot. They were also out of rations and out of clothing. It was terrible!)

Pension Records for Andrew Jackson McWhirter

Andrew Jackson McWhirter was barely 15 years old when he enlisted in the 1st AL Cav. USV. The only muster roll found was dated March 1864 and stated he was in Co. K, which was the same company his father and brothers were in, and he was released from Adams USA Hospital to return to duty. His father and two brothers, George Washington and Thomas Andrew McWhirter had already enlisted. It is not known if he enlisted before or after his father and brother died but according to the length of time he served and when he was mustered out, it must have been right after they died. George W. McWhirter died October 8, 1862 in US Hospital #14 in Nashville, Davidson County, Tennessee just 15 days before his father died in the same hospital. Andrew Ferrier and Sarah Harper McWhirter's son, Thomas A. McWhirter served his time in the war, although he was captured three times, and lived to return home to Marion County, Alabama and raise a large family.

After Jackson died, his widow applied for a pension and Andrew D. Mitchell gave the following statement: "When I became a member of Company L 1st Alabama Calvary, Andrew J. McWhirter, was then

209

a member of Company K 1st Alabama Calvary. Captain Hornback was the Captain and Andrew J. McWhirter was with his Company and Regiment in Tennessee, Alabama and Georgia, I was with this Regiment one year, eight months and five days, Andrew J. McWhirter was with this Regiment all the time I was with it, Andrew J. McWhirter just prior to the close of the war went to Ohio and did not return until the Company was disbanded, I know this of my own personal knowledge." Other affidavits state he served in Co. K of the 1st AL for almost two years and was present and served as an artilleryman during the Battle of Monroe's Crossroads in North Carolina. The request for a pension was denied stating Andrew Jackson McWhirter was a Servant, which was a Civilian position and was not a pensionable classification. George W. Whitehead gave the following statement trying to help Nancy Jane draw a pension from her husband's service in the 1st AL Cav. US. "I know of my own personal knowledge that Andrew J. McWhirter was an Orderly under Captain Hornback United States Army, I know that Andrew J. McWhirter served more than eighteen months in Tennessee, Alabama and Georgia. He fought with the Artillery in the battle of Monroe's Cross Roads, North Carolina, March 10, 1865, in this battle Captain Hornback was wounded, a day or two after this battle Andrew J. McWhirter got on a boat with Captain Hornback at Fayetteville, North Carolina, and went home with Captain Hornback some place in Ohio, where he remained until late in the summer of 1865 when he returned to Alabama. During the absence of Andrew J. McWhirter, Company K 1st Alabama Cavalry was disbanded, I was a member of Company K 1st Alabama Cavalry and was discharged and returned home, I know this of my own personal knowledge." Signed George W. Whitehead on October 11, 1928, J.T. Curtis, Notary Public. There was another note in the file stating A.J. McWhirter had escorted Hornback home to Ohio because he was worried about him being wounded and afraid he might not make it by himself.

Robert/Mary Harper's Application for Pension

On January 26, 1866, Nancy Jane Lane Harper signed an Application for Widow's Army Pension stating Robert Harper died of measles March 7, 1863 at Corinth, Mississippi while still in service. She stated they were lawfully married by John Gamble, a Minister of the Gospel on November 31, 1851, and that she had remained a widow since her husband's death. She gave the following description for Robert Harper: He was 5', 4" tall, had yellow eyes, fair complexion and black hair and was a farmer at time of enlistment. She stated she had six children by Robert Harper: Rubin J. Harper, born January 24, 1853; Wm. A. Harper, born September 26, 1854; Sarah E. Harper, August 29, 1856; Robert A. Harper, April 7, 1858; Mary J. Harper, January 11, 1860; and Martha S. Harper, March 29, 1863. Sarah McWhirter, Matilda Tidwell and Delila Tucker stated they were aware of the births and dates of these children.

On December 27, 1869, Drewry C. Whitehead and James T. Morton signed an affidavit stating they knew of Robert Harper's death on March 8, 1863, from measles contracted while in service of the United States.

James R. Tucker and Thaddius M. Walker, residents of Eldridge, County of Walker, State of Alabama, signed an affidavit stating they knew Nancy Harper and that she was the true Nancy Harper, widow of Robert.

There were different dates of birth for some of Nancy and Robert's children but this was straightened out in the following affidavit:
Sarah McWhirter & Matilda Tidwell signed an affidavit stating the following dates are the true dates that Robert and Nancy Jane Lane Harper's children were born:
Reuben J. – January 24, 1853
William A. - September 26, 1854
Sarah E. - August 29, 1856
Robert A. - April 7, 1858
Mary Jane - January 11, 1860
Martha S. - March 28, 1863
Martha Taylor and Sarah Walker also signed an affidavit as sisters of the mother of above children and they knew these dates of birth to be correct.

Martha Taylor & Nelson Walker signed an affidavit stating they were present at the marriage of Robert Harper and Nancy Lane and saw the marriage take place at Eldridge, Walker Co., AL on or about November 30, 1851 and that John Gamble Minster of the Gospel administered the oath of marriage.

Robert has a tombstone in Jackson Cemetery in Wayne Co., TN but he is not buried there according to Louise Hanson.

Robert served in the First Alabama Cavalry, USA and his wife's Pension Application was signed by some of the same names as Sarah

211

Harper McWhirter's were: Sarah Harper McWhirter, A.J. Ingle, J.R. Tucker (Mary Emoline Harper's spouse), Delila Tucker (William Tucker's spouse, also, their son Kimber Foster married Martha Ann Harper.) They signed on the same day that Thomas Harper and Mary Emoline Tucker signed for Sarah Harper McWhirter to get her pension, on January 26, 1866.

Thomas Wade Harper's Widow Files for Pension

Thomas Harper's widow, Mary Elizabeth Lane Harper filed an Application for Pension and it stated (sic):
"State of Alabama - Walker County
On this the 7th day of January 1863, personally appeared before me J.C. Myers, a Justice of the Peace in and for the County aforesaid. Mary E. Harper, who after being duly sworn according to law, deposes and that she is the widow of Thomas W. Harper deceased who was a Private of Captain W. H. Lawrence Company H, 43 Regiment of Alabama Volunteers - Commanded by Colonel ------- in the service of the Confederate States in the present and with the United States that the said Thomas W. Harper Entered the service at Tuscaloosa in Tuscaloosa County and state of on or about the 7th day of May 1862 and died at Knoxville Tennessee the 15th Day of Sept. 1862 leaving her a widow and no children that she makes this deposition for the purpose of obtaining from the Government of the Confederate States whatever may have been due the said Thomas W. Harper at the time of his death for pay Bounty on/an after allowences for his services as Volunteer afforesaid.
Sworn to and Subscribed before me the 7th Day of Jan 1863. J. C. Myers, Justice of the Peace.
Signed Mary E. Harper (There was a little "x" between the E. and Harper so she may have made her Mark rather than signing her name.)

James Richard Tucker's Application for Pension

James Richard Tucker first married Mary Emmaline Harper, daughter of Thomas A. and Mary R. Harper. Emmaline died in an untimely death in 1867 and he married Didena Tucker. This is her request for his pension from the 4th Alabama Cavalry, CSA

Analysis of Pension Record of Didema Webb Tucker - Transcription of Nov. 12, 1914, document from Pension Record File for Didena Tucker.

212

Member of Co. K, 4th AL Cav., My husband had his parole and was careful with it. I have seen it many times but could not read it, but he and kin read it. The Parole was burnt up when our house burned 35 years ago.

She submits this on her answers to said citation and if the same is not full and sufficient will try to furnish such other evidence as may be required. Her husband lived in Marion Co. Ala. when he enlisted and it would be necessary for her to go there to get up any further evidence. Respectfully submitted Didema (her X mark) Tucker Sworn to & subscribed before me this the 12th day of November, 1914. J.C. Shunpe Judge of Prob.

Discussion of the Pension Record Data -
The widow's given name differed in spelling on some documents-- "D.M., Didena, Didema," but it must be remembered that she could not read or write (census data). She gave differing birth dates for herself, Sept. 4, 1836, and Sept. 15, 1832 and September 15, 1834 (birth dates are said to have not been of great importance to illiterate "country people").
She gave differing death dates for her husband as she got older: Nov. 15 1895 (in 1899), Nov. 1898 (in 1921) and Oct. 1898 (in 1923). Note that she was described in 1914 as being "very old and feeble." However, to be eligible for the widow's pension, her husband's death had to have been before April, 1898, the date of her first application. The most reasonable date was the date she listed in 1899, Nov. 15, 1895 (his gravestone shows Nov. 28, 1894--refer to research notes). Even then (in 1899) his death date could have been approximated by her with the help of the reviewer. People often are unsure about exact family birth and death dates when called upon to give such data from memory.

In 1921 she said that J.R. Tucker was in the Chickamauga battle and not wounded, then in 1923 she said he was wounded in the Selma battle, captured and imprisoned. It is odd that she signed with "X" until 1923 when she wrote her signature in what appears to be her own hand.

Nov 17, 1914, Lawrence Co., AL - Mrs. Tucker appeared Nov. 11, 1914, to restate her affidavit. Husband's name is given as James Richard Tucker.
July 29, 1915, Lawrence Co., AL, Pension #36444; Didena Tucker states that she was born at or near Winfield, Marion Co., AL on Sept. 4, 1836, being 88 years of age.

213

July 14, 1921, Lawrence Co., AL, Widows Blank for Reclassification (condensed in this analysis):
Didena Tucker of Moulton, AL, living with H.H. Tucker (son).
Born Sept. 15, 1832 in Winfield, Marion Co., AL. Her father was Thomas Webb; deceased.
Husband was James R. Tucker, married in 1866 in Marion Co., AL and he died in 1898, in Franklin Co.
He enlisted in Walker Co. & enlisted at first of war
Service Branch: Inf., Rank: Private, Colonel's name: Wines - Captain's name: Kelley
Wounded in Chickamauga battle in leg and in neck at same battle.
Captured: No - Imprisoned: No, When/Where did he quit the service of the Confederate States: at end of war. Paroled? Yes, No personal property.

August 10, 1921, Lawrence Co., AL
Tax Assessor's Certificate - Nothing
August 10, 1921, Lawrence Co., AL - Tax Assessor's Certificate - None
April 14, 1923, Lawrence Co., AL, Widows Blank for Reclassification, Number on Pension roll: 25742, Living with Mr. Joe Tucker, her son
She was born: Winfield, Marion Co., AL, Sept 15, 1834 to Thomas Webb; he died in Marion Co., AL
She married J.R. Tucker in Winfield, AL; He died in Franklin Co., AL Oct. 1898
Said she lived in Franklin Co. 1900, Lawrence Co. in 1910
Gave same data about husband's service, except:
He was wounded at Selma and was captured at Selma in 1865
Imprisoned at Selma in 1865
Discharged from prison "from April to May 1865"
"He was a Prison of War and was payroll at end of the war" (sic)
He was paroled; Parole was burned
She signed April 14, 1923, Didena Tucker -- looks like someone may have guided her hand-- no X.

John Lyons Southern Claim about Josiah Houston Harper (Sic)

In John Lyons Southern Claim, he stated the following about Josiah Harper. The witness testifies that some prominent Union men in the area were George S. Tucker, John P. Lyle and Samuel Roberts.
"I don't know whether or not they could testify to claimants loyality." The witness states that the claimant knew she was

adherent to the Union cause, "he knew it by my talk, and my acts and deeds, and by my husband being in the Union army."

Witness testifies that "the Confederate cavalry came to the house of Claimant and cursed and abused his daughters and said that they would take claimant in out of the wet and put him where the dogs wouldn't bite him, and called him a damned old Tory traitor and everything else that was mean. My husband, Josiah Harper, went into the Union army. Served out his time and came home. Claimant after my husband came home, saw him several times. My husband was at Claimants house. Claimant and him were on the best of terms up to his death. The Confederates caught him and hanged him. Claimant and his family help look for him until he was found. Claimant took his wagon and stears (and) hauled him to the grave yard and help bury him."

If Nancy Jane Berryhill Harper had stated this in her Pension Application, it would not have been proved and I'm sure she needed the money. Instead, she talked about him contracting measles and diarrhea in the service and stated he died from that, which he very well may have if he had not died such a tragic death.

When Nancy Jane Berryhill Harper applied for pension she stated he died of chronic diarrhea contracted while in service. If she had put he was killed by home guards after the war, she probably wouldn't have drawn a pension. She stated he was discharged Jan 24, 1864 and died April 22, 1864, so that's probably when they caught up with him and hung him.

Mary Miles filled out an affidavit for Nancy Jane to get a pension. Some of these affidavits say Mary E. Harper when listing their children and some of them say Mary C. Mary Miles says "Mary C.", T.W., and B.J. and gives a birth date for B.J. as 1861, where as I have 1862. She states she was present at the birth of all of them. I'm assuming that was Thomas' wife, Mary.

W.H. McWhirter (William Hamilton) signed an affidavit for Nancy Jane stating Josiah Harper came home in Feb 1864, and was sick with the measles when he came home and taken the sore eyes and was blind with the sore eyes until his death. He stated the reason he knew was because they waited on him at their mother's house and stayed there while he was sick until his death. This affidavit was signed by William H. McWhirter and Mary C. Harbin. I suppose this was Mary Caroline McWhirter Harbin.

Mary Miles and George H. Tucker signed a General Purpose Affidavit stating Josiah's health was fine when he entered service and he was very much changed when he came home, with measles, bad eyes and diarrhea. (In 1889, Mary Miles stated she was 60 years old.) They say he was disabled from the time he returned home until he died as the result of measles and diarrhea and seemed to waste away.

Harry Brown, could be Hardy, stated he had known Josiah Harper since a little boy and he was always stout until he came home from the army and when he died, he was blind from measles. Adaline Brown, probably Harry's wife, stated the same thing.

A strange statement from Nancy Jane Harper stated in a Claimant's Testimony that she was unable to furnish the testimony of the physician who attended her husband in his last illness for the reason that the said physician, Dr. Sarah McWhirter, who attended him, is dead. She died in 1886. (Sarah actually died December 28, 1883, but the form was completed in 1889, so it would have been easy for Nancy Jane not to remember Sarah's correct date of death.)

On October 23, 1916, she submitted a request for an increase in her pension 333182 from Childress Co., TX. I have Nancy Jane's death date as March 1916, so apparently that is incorrect. At the time she requested the increase she was drawing $12 per month.

James L. Lee and Mary I. or J. Lee stated they had known both Josiah and Mary Jane since 1851. It was also signed by W.A. Lee and George W. Harbin. It was completed in Marion Co., AL stating the Lees lived in Fayette Co., AL.

A Ben D. Kelley and Betsy J. Kelley signed a General Purpose Affidavit stating they had seen the family Bible of Mrs. Nancy J. Harper that contained a record of her children's birth.

Nancy's pension was dropped from the pension roll because of death March 15, 1917, so apparently that was indeed the date she died. There was a note from the Bureau of Pensions stating her voucher was returned because of her death, same as above, and she had been living with her grandson, W.W. Dodson.

I think probably Josiah did have chronic diarrhea and measles, but if they had said he was killed by the home guard after he was discharged, she probably wouldn't have drawn a pension, so they

216

used the diseases in order to obtain it. I'm sure the poor thing needed every dollar she drew.

Josiah was born in the Village of Texas, Marion Co., AL and died in Village of Texas, Marion Co., AL. Nancy Jane was dropped from the pension roll May 21, 1917, the last payment being $20.00 on February 4, 1917.

Josiah H. Harper enlisted in the First Alabama Cavalry, Co. B, USA. On a return visit to his home, he was captured and killed by the Confederate Home Guards. He left a wife and four children (source: Southern Claims Commission, John Lyons, Case No. 20850, Marion Co., AL).

Nancy Jane Berryhill Harper signed the following document in 1874 for a claim from the Southern Claims Commission, for John Lyons. (SIC)

Nancy J. Harper, 43 years of age and a resident of Fayette County, Alabama for one year testified, Before that, I lived in Marion County from my childhood. I am no kin to the claimant and am not interested in the success of his claim. I have been living a close neighbor to him 18 years and have known him intimately all that time. I lived after the year 1862 in 1/4 mile of him. Before that time, I lived about in 4 miles of him. I saw him after the year 1862 most every day during the war, that he passed by my house in going to his fields. I conversed with the claimant and heard him converse about the war frequently, its causes, its progress and results. He and my husband talked together frequently. They both voted against seccession, done all they could against it. After the war came up, I heard claimant tell my husband that he was here and had to stay here, that we must hold our peace and do the best we could.

I know that claimant done all he could and dare to do during the war for women and children whose husbands was in the Union army. He went to the salt works and got salt and let the Union women have it. He done everything he could to keep the Confederate cavalry off of them and saved their property all he could. My husband was in the Union army. He treated me as above stated and as far as I know, he treated other Union men's wives the same way. I have heard nothing more than above stated except similar things and favors for Union women and their families by claimant for the Union Cause. I have heard or know nothing he has ever done for the Confederate cause.

217

I can't say that I know his public reputation. He was reported to the Cavalry as a Union man. James Tucker, George S. Tucker, John P. Lyle and Thaddeus Walker are his neighbors and was during the war. They perhaps can testify to his public reputation.

"The witness testifies that some prominent Union men in the area were George S. Tucker, John P. Lyle and Samuel Roberts.
"I don't know whether or not they could testify to claimants loyality." The witness states that the claimant knew she was adherent to the Union cause, "he knew it by my talk, and my acts and deeds, and by my husband being in the Union army."
Witness testifies that "the Confederate cavalry came to the house of Claimant and cursed and abused his daughters and said that they would take claimant in out of the wet and put him where the dogs wouldn't bite him, and called him a damned old Tory traitor and everything else that was mean. My husband, Josiah Harper, went into the Union army. Served out his time and came home. Claimant after my husband came home, saw him several times. My husband was at Claimants house. Claimant and him were on the best of terms up to his death. The Confederates caught him and hanged him. Claimant and his family help look for him until he was found. Claimant took his wagon and stears (and) hauled him to the grave yard and help bury him." Nancy J. Harper (Her mark), John C. Moore, Special Commissioner

John Lyons, Marion Co., Alabama 1874, Southern Claim # 20850

This claim, totaling $458, is for one bay horse, 7 or 8 years old, valued at $100, 150 bushels of corn valued at $300, 200 pounds of bacon valued at $50 and 800 pounds of fodder valued at $8. This property was taken by Union forces commanded by General Wilson on or about March 26, 1865.

The claimant called as witnesses George S. and Martha Tucker of Fayette County, John P. Lyle of Walker County, Nancy J. Harper and Harvey and Adaline Brown of Fayette County, and H.W. Farris and Sarah McWhirter of Marion County.
Testimony was taken by Special Commission John C. Moore at the home of John Lyons on October 22 and 23 and on November 14, 1874. The claimant states that he is 66 years old and was born in Augusta County, Virginia. Claimant is a farmer and a resident of Marion County for 30 years. "I did not change my occupation or residency from the beginning of the war to the end. I was on the side of the Union at the beginning and was so to the end, though I had to

218

act different and talk different before some. I never did do anything or say anything willingly against the Union cause. After the war started, living where I did, I had obliged to talk to suit the ground that I was on."

"40 out of 80 men in my beat went to the Union army. I aided their wives and family all I could. I cut and hauled wood for them. I went to the salt works and got salt for them. This was done during the war. Joseph Harper, a Union soldier, went to the war, served out his time and came home. While here I protected him from being caught by the Confederates all I could without being found out at it. They at last caught him and hanged him. Myself and family looked for him after he was hanged until fund. I hauled him to the graveyard and help bury him, and other like favors I done for the Union cause and its defenders.

The claimant states that he "lived in a section of the country where I dare not contribute anything to the Union cause and let it be found out on me. I worked against secession and opposed it with all my mind, heart and strength." Claimant testifies that because of his Unionist stance that, "The Union raiders would always pass my house without pestering or taking anything I had or mistreating me or my family in any way." Some of the leading and best known Unionists in claimants area were T.P. Harper, George Hallmark, Joseph Harper, Doc Smith, Aron Bolin (?), William Miles and many others. They are all dead, most all died in the Union lines."
Claimant states, "I have never taken any oath to the so-called Southern Confederacy." Because of his views he was, "Threatened and abused by talk and the taking of my corn and threatened to be hanged and called a damned old Union man because I was protecting and assisting Union men and their wives and children."

John Lyons, Marion Co., Alabama – 1874, Union Claim (sic)

Harvey Brown, 58 years of age and a resident of Fayette County, Alabama testifys, "I have lived here all my life. I am a farmer. I am here in favor of the claimant. I have known him thirty years intimately. I lived in three miles of him. I met him frequently, sometimes 2 or 3 times a week. I did not hear the claimant say anything as to how he voted before the war came up, he and I talked about it, and I heard him talk about it to other people, he always talked against the war, and was opposed to it, talked in favor of the Union."

Josiah Harper was a Union man went to the Union army. He, claimant, cut wood and hauled it for his wife while her husband was in the Union army. The Confederate soldiers caught said Harper and hanged him. Claimant and his family hunted for said Harper until he was found. The claimant always told me he was a Union man but he had to ly low and keep the thing dark, he was severely treated by the Confederate Cavalry, and strongly suspicioned by them of being a Union man. I have heard him speak against the Confederate cause....his public reputation was that he was loyal to the United States." Those who could testify to his public reputation are, "George S. Tucker, William Tucker and Joseph Roberts." Prominent Union men in the area were, T.P. Harper, A.J. McWhirter, George M.D. and Josiah Harper, James Mills and Peyton Burnett."

"I know the Confederate cavalry threatened him heavy and talked about killing him, said he was carrying news to the Union people. His property was taken as was said by the Confederate calvary."
Harvey Brown
(His mark)
John C. Moore, Special Commissioner

My Grandma's Hands

...O shed a tear or two, if you must, for our time now ended,
for dreams unrealized and hopes unfulfilled.
In memory of me, live to the fullest....

"I sit here staring at my hands and think about how they have served me well throughout the years. These hands, though wrinkled, shriveled and weak have been the tools I have used all my life to reach out and grab and embrace life. They braced and caught my fall when as a toddler I crashed upon the floor. They put food in my mouth and clothes on my back. As a child my mother taught me to fold them in prayer. They tied my shoes and pulled on my boots.

They held my husband and wiped my tears when he and our three sons went off to war. They have been dirty, scraped and raw, swollen and bent.

They were uneasy and clumsy when I tried to hold my newborn son. Decorated with my wedding band they showed the world that I was married and loved someone special.

They wrote my letters to my sons and husband while they were off fighting for this country. They trembled and shook as my husband, parents, sons and brothers died or were brutally murdered, one by one. They have held my children and grandchildren, consoled neighbors going through their own hardships, and shook in fists of anger when I didn't understand anything about the war. They have covered my face, wiped my tears combed my hair, and washed and cleansed the rest of my body.

They have been sticky and wet, bent and broken, dried and raw. They also held my Bible as I searched for comfort from God. And to this day when not much of anything else of me works real well these hands hold me up, lay me down, and again continue to fold in prayer. Yes, I still believe in God and talk to him daily, even after he has taken all of these loved ones from me because I know He had his reasons and he felt that they could do more for him in Heaven than they could for me on earth. He gave me the grace and strength He knew I needed to survive each death and assured me I would reunite with my loving family, one day.

These hands are the mark of where I've been and the ruggedness of my life, they held the plow while I was making the gardens and

221

tending the crops after my husband and three sons went off to war, so my children and I could eat while they were gone. But more importantly it will be these hands that God will reach out and take when he leads me home. And with my hands He will lift me to His side and there I will use these hands to once again embrace my loved ones and touch the face of God."

During Sarah's lifetime, she not only outlived her mother, father and two (2) step-mothers, but she lost her husband, two (2) sons, eight (8) brothers and sisters between 1862 and 1870, and eight (8) grandchildren, including a set of twins, between 1868-1880.

She had a heart of gold and a constitution of steel! We only know a fraction of what this wonderful lady endured during and after the Civil War. I would venture to say that most people in this day and age would probably not be tenacious enough to endure the adverse forces exerted upon, not only Sarah Harper McWhirter, but of many of the other citizens of northwest Alabama. She was a wonderful Christian lady and I'm sure her faith in God is what carried her through the frightfully shocking, terrifying and revolting savagery of a Civil War in northwest Alabama where neighbors were fighting against neighbors and brothers were fighting against their own brothers, fathers and sons. Sarah did what she had to do in order to survive, not only the destruction of the country side, but the grotesque physical and mental harm inflicted by the wickedness of men who had a different view than the Southern Unionists. She was determined to feed and care for her young children who were left fatherless, and she did an excellent job, raising five (5) wonderful, God-loving children, as shown below in the article, *A Remarkable Family*.

A REMARKABLE FAMILY

...And so, despite the emptiness, honor the void, in tribute to what once was....

This article was published in the *Marion County Herald* on May 30, 1889.

"Marion County has one of the most remarkable families within her borders, probably, that exists within the limits of the State. It is the family of Andrew F. McWhirter.

Some 50 years ago Mr. McWhirter moved to Marion County, from Tennessee, and settled near Goldmine, where he lived to the date of his death which occurred during the war. At the time of his death he had 5 children, 4 boys and 1 girl. The daughter married Mr. Harbin and lives near the old homestead. The boys are all temperate men, two of them never even drank a cup of coffee and not one of them use tobacco. The combined weight of the four men is over 800 pounds. The four have 22 living children and 7 dead. Three of them are farmers and one a preacher. The oldest, T.A. (Thomas Andrew) is a farmer and is 47 years of age; W.H. is a farmer and 35 years old; and A.J. (Andrew Jackson), who is the baby, is 30 years old and weighs 211 pounds. He also is a farmer (and preacher) and holds the office of county commissioner, and by the way he is one of the best commissioners in the State. They are highly respected, and gentlemen of moral worth, and men of which any county might well be proud."

Sarah Harper McWhirter can indeed be proud of her husband, sons and brothers but she died a lonesome, broken-hearted woman although two more children were born to her after the war.

As you can see, Sarah Harper McWhirter lived in a time of murder, torture, rape, theft, plunder, fear, etc. and the Union men who were supposedly protecting the Union widows, and providing them salt and other needed supplies, also abused and molested some of these same widows. It came to the place where they probably didn't know who to trust. As stated before, Grandma Sarah was a Godly woman who loved her husband, children, family and friends and she deserved a better life than the violence and torture inflicted upon her. She drew a measly $8.00 per month pension and if she had

223

married someone who could have helped with the farm and children, her pension would have been stopped, so she couldn't afford to take that chance since it was the entirety of her income.

After the war, Sarah, along with others in the area, lost their homes and almost everything they had. The money they had was worthless and she was broke. Here she was with three young children, no husband, home, or much of anything. Grandma Sarah was lonely and trying to raise her children as both mother and father, as were so many other widows of the war.

As one can imagine, after losing her loved ones during the war and suffering as she did at the hands of the abominable enemy, Sarah was vulnerable, as were many of the widows of the war. She felt worn and torn and the thought of making a garden each spring, harvesting the fruits of her labor and tending the children all alone, was bearing on her mind. She turned to a neighbor who befriended and helped her on the farm. He was also wiped out after the war's end. If Sarah had remarried, her measly pension would have stopped and she would have had absolutely nothing. Her first priority was her children and she did what she had to do to keep them fed and alive.

The 1870 Thornhill, Marion County, Alabama Census shows Sarah Harper McWhirter living next door to her son, Andrew Jackson McWhirter, and shows her with the following children, Hamilton, (William Hamilton McWhirter) age 18; Mary, (Mary Caroline McWhirter) age 16, John, Madison McWhirter), 14, Nancy, (Nancy Ann) McWhirter, age 5, and Green McWhirter, (Jasper Green McWhirter) age 2 years. Nancy Ann McWhirter was born about 1865, married George Washington Miles in Marion County, Alabama on January 05, 1888. George was born February 22, 1857, and died November 2, 1954 in Marion County, Alabama. Nancy McWhirter Miles died in 1892 giving birth to an infant daughter, and the child died, also.

Jasper Green McWhirter was born August 18, 1868. He married Mary Silvania Tucker on January 5, 1888, and was killed by a train about 1903 in Winnsboro, Wood County, Texas. Mary Silvania was born March 19, 1870, and died about 1901 in Quitman, Wood County, Texas

Jasper Green McWhirter followed the share crop work and went

224

more or less where Kimbril Foster Tucker and Martha Ann Harper went. He and Mary Silvania left Marion and Fayette Counties in Alabama with their relatives, George Washington Harbin and his wife, Mary Caroline McWhirter, daughter of Andrew Ferrier and

and Sarah Harper McWhirter, and Kimber Foster Tucker and his wife, Martha Ann Harper, to Texas in the last decade of the 1800's. Jasper followed his father-in-law and mother-in-law wherever they could find work. The fields were larger and more productive in Oklahoma and Texas.

They moved to Wichita Falls, Texas, then to Hunt County, Texas. They later moved to Atoke, Oklahoma. By 1910, they were living in Hunt County, Texas again. Kimber Foster and Martha Ann moved to LaFlore Co., OK where Kimber Foster died in 1922. In 1900 Jasper and Mary were in Hunt Co., Texas, where both of them died.

After Jasper Green McWhirter was killed, Mary Caroline McWhirter Harbin, daughter of Sarah Harper and Andrew Ferrier McWhirter, applied for guardianship of his children, in Wood County Texas. Jasper Green's wife, Rebecca, had died just a few days before he did.

1910 Census showed LaFayette, Andrew and Laura McWhirter, children of Jasper Green McWhirter, in the home of George W. Harbin and Mary Caroline McWhirter Harbin in Wood County, Texas. It also showed Edgar was with Alonzo A. and wife Mazie in Wood County, Texas

Andrew Jackson McWhirter and his brother, Thomas Andrew McWhirter, were both fortunate enough to survive the war and return to northwest Alabama to their sainted mother. Thomas married in Marion County, Alabama in 1866, and Andrew Jackson married there in 1867. Andrew also lived close to his mother after he married.

O'Mary Cemetery

...that simple faith to save our soul, that perfect love to make us whole....

The grave where Sarah Harper McWhirter is buried in the O'Mary Cemetery in Marion County, Alabama is an unusual grave, which is how they used to bury people. The grave was first covered with stones to keep the animals from digging up the bodies, because they didn't bury them as deep in 1883 as they do in modern day times. Then the two large stones were leaned over coming together at the top, like a tent. These type graves were called tent graves. Some people even built little house-type buildings over the graves to protect them, and they were called "grave houses"

After the burial of the casket, part of the removed dirt was placed back in the hole but due to the volume the coffin had displaced, some of the earth did not fit in the grave, so the earth is piled on top of the ground in a mound. However, after a while, the mound would sometimes totally disappear due to the rain or freezing and thawing, leaving a shallow depression, over the grave therefore, they would place two simple slabs of native stone or concrete over the graves in a pyramid form. They would also have a tombstone on one end and another stone at the other end to cover the holes the pyramid stones left.

Sarah Harper McWhirter's granddaughter, Susan A. "Susie" McWhirter, died three years before Grandma Sarah did and she is also buried in a Tent Grave in the O'Mary Cemetery close to her grandmother.

(See pictures of these graves in back of book.)

Each trip we made to Marion County, Alabama, I would ask someone where the O'Mary Cemetery was and they would laugh and say I would have to have a four-wheel drive vehicle to get there and a guide to show me where it was. Finally, after a few years, a cousin from Jackson, Mississippi called one day in November and said he had someone lined up who had a Jeep, knew where the O'Mary Cemetery was and was willing to take us up there if we would meet them in Winfield, Alabama at 9:00 AM the next Saturday. We met my cousin and his wife at Hardee's in Winfield and all drove out to where we were supposed to meet the "guide" to take us to the cemetery. At 2:30 PM he showed up in his topless Jeep.

We drove for several miles, went through an extremely tall chain-link gate into a coal company, and drove for some time until he slammed on his brakes, backed up looking to the left and said he thought that was the old road. I looked and didn't see anything that looked like a road, but he was supposedly the one who knew the way to the cemetery, and I had no idea where I was. He started up a mountain, through the briars and weeds, around felled trees, to the top and then we started down the other side of the mountain, drove through a pond backed up by beavers, and water came rushing up through the floorboard, but I still had confidence in the gentleman, especially since he was the first hope I had had in years to get to my great, great grandmother's place of burial. We kept dodging trees and driving until we reached the top of another mountain and there was the beautiful old secluded cemetery with three wooden crosses constructed from landscape timbers, hovering over the entrance to the cemetery.

I stood at Sarah Harper McWhirter's grave which had the appearance of such a sacred place. I felt almost as though I could reach up and touch the hand of God. There was such a quiet peace surrounding the old cemetery with absolutely nothing else around this lonely, peaceful cemetery up here on this mountain where the remains of my great, great grandmother's body lay buried a few feet under the ground.

Epilogue

...the flag for which they died....

Behind the facade of a neat secluded home surrounded by dogwood, redbud, and magnolia trees hovering over the well-kept yard, it appeared as though an average happy family dwelled behind the closed doors. The lawn was splotched with bare spots indicating the play of happy children. It was dispersed with peonies, buttercups, iris and other flowers, along with a well kept garden off to the side that kept Sarah and her children alive, not only during the Civil War, but until she died. However, looks are deceiving and instead of the happy family, there was a very lonely, heartbroken widow scratching out a life for herself and her young children. What is so very important about this is the fact this lady was only one of thousands of women across northwest Alabama, east Tennessee and other areas where a bitter vengeance over the Civil War, continued for many years. However, it was apparently much worse in northwest Alabama than anywhere else in the country.

Many of the Union soldiers had moved Westward after the war because of the continued bitterness and attacks from the opposing side. Most of the families the Union Army had escorted to Illinois in 1863 for their protection had continued to live, work, and were buried there. Sarah decided to remain where she was since it was all she had left of her husband and her sons, Thomas and Jackson, certainly did not want to move off and leave her.

A crackling fire danced in the fireplace as the gathering August storm clouds fittingly descended and the rains bore down on the Alabama hills. The turgid Buttahatchie River rushed on through its swollen banks, and little was left showing of the ravages of the unspeakable Civil War. Life went on and the area began to grow. Sarah continued to grieve over the loss of her loved ones and especially the husband she had loved and cherished.

Sarah lay languidly beneath the quilts clutching the covers to her wrinkled bosom. Her two youngest children, Nancy Ann and Jasper Green, were the only two children left at home and they had summoned Jackson and Thomas to Sarah's bedside. She was aware of their presence but the only thing she was focused on was how the firelight from the hearth was illuminating her beloved Andrew's suit and hat she had left hanging on the wall directly across from their

228

bed. It had continuously hung in that same place since he rode off to war with their three sons. Knowing he was with God made it easy for her to want to go home.

On December 28, 1883, God reached out and took Grandma Sarah and led her home with Him, beyond a life in the world as she had known it. As I researched her life and put this book together, I had a beautiful sense of Sarah Harper McWhirter's presence, like music remembered by heart, and it continues to linger. She has a wonderful home in a new world that only faith can divulge, and she no longer has to worry about the tragedies and torment that plagued her sad life during and after the Civil War.

My life has been touched by Sarah Harper McWhirter's presence on this earth and she has indeed been the wind beneath my wings in this endeavor, but there remains a sadness that I continue to feel for her, because of the tragic times in which she lived and the brutality she suffered at the hands of the roaming outlaws during a war in which her family wanted no part, a war that killed hundreds of thousands of fathers, brothers, sons, cousins and uncles, leaving many grieving and heartbroken widows and orphans destitute.

The area in which she lived was ravaged and torn apart by the worst sort of warfare, a vicious guerilla struggle between relatives, former friends, and neighbors, with atrocities such as murder, butcheries and mutilations committed that have not been told to this day. All we have is what has been left us in the way of documents; diaries and letters which do not scratch the surface of all that happened. This was the kind of fight where no one wins anything and everyone loses something.

Let me reiterate, the Confederacy did not have a monopoly on the abuse, torture and murder in northwest Alabama, there was enough blame to go around.

When my hands are hurt or sore or when I stroke the face of one of my grandchildren, I think of Grandma Sarah Harper McWhirter. I know she has been held by the hands of God and touched His face with her smooth hands no longer calloused from her life of hard work. With God's help I, too, will be held by Him and feel not only His hands upon my face, but hers as well. I want to be with this Godly woman who endured the pain of the abuse she suffered and the heartbreak of losing her loving husband, son, brothers, friends and neighbors that she watched, with a sad heart and trembling

229

hands, as they rode off to war. One by one, they went to fight on opposite sides in a war that should never have been fought. Even with her faith in God, during and after the war there was never a moment in her life that went by unburdened with worry for her family and friends. Sarah only lived fifty-eight years and six months, but what we need to remember are the hardships and terror she encountered during those years

I am certain there were days such as when Grandma Sarah lost her loved ones, or when she was being abused, molested and tormented by the men calling themselves the "Home Guard"; she thought she could not go on living, but she never succumbed to fear or despair. Out of utter desperation and love, she continued raising her children the best she knew how, planted a garden each year and canned and preserved the fruits of her labor, sewed, knitted and cooked for them, all the while instilling in them the love of God, as her father had instilled in her.

Grandma Sarah died with a broken heart, and never remarried. None of the Harper widows, who lost their husbands in the tragic war, were ever found to have remarried. Sarah Harper McWhirter was laid to rest in the O'Mary Cemetery in Marion County, Alabama and one of her descendants loved her enough to place a beautiful tombstone at her grave.

Each day for almost two years, as I began to write about Grandma Sarah's life, I asked God to guide my fingers and give me the words needed to tell the world about the life my sainted great, great grandmother, Sarah Harper McWhirter, who was forced to live during those unimaginable abhorrent times. I hope, with God's help, I have been able to describe the consequences borne by the loyal Americans in northwest Alabama due to their determination to fight for the country they loved.

Grandma Sarah, go placidly among the Heavens embracing your creator, and submitting your most humble, troubled life to Him. May you be at peace with God and finally have the rest you have needed for so many years. Your labors and aspirations, in this noisy confusion of life, have not gone unnoticed, and I am sure God looked at you and said, "Job well done, my child". Many fears are born of fatigue, loneliness and war, and you certainly suffered more than your share, never letting it blind you to what good there was in life. You continue to be an inspiration to all of your endearing descendants. While it is evident you died with a broken heart, my heart also breaks when I think of how you were forced to endure not only the unnecessary deaths of your loved ones but the violence and abuse forced upon you during and after the war. Your children were forced to grow up in hurry and you and the other Civil War widows grew old in a hurry. You learned how strong you could really be when forced to do so. You endured violence, vengeance, poverty, war, disease, and wicked men preying on vulnerable women and children. You craved a life that was not oriented to fear where your children could grow up thinking violence was not a way of life. You wanted some type of order to emerge out of all the chaos so your children could have a more humane existence.

Sarah's fighting spirit and love of God are still alive in my mind.

Rest in peace, Grandma Sarah, I love you!

The Author

APPENDIX

...I see the weary look upon your face....

Harper Family Traced Back To Early 1500'S
(Information from Quinnie Harper)

The first known Harper in this family was a John Harper of Noke, Oxfordshire, England. John married a lady by the name of Margerie or Marjory, but her last name has not been discovered as yet. John and his wife both died in Noke in 1584.

Children of John and Margerie, however birth dates are not known:
John Harper, died about 1575
John Harper (probably born after his brother, John, died.
Christian Harper
Katherine Harper
Margaret Harper, married a Nash
Elizabeth Harper, married a Tommis or Tomes
Jane or Joane Harper, married a Roberts or Roberte
John Harper, again, (This is John and Margerie Harper's child who was our ancestor)

JOHN HARPER (2)

John Harper (2), son of John and Margerie, was probably the youngest of the three sons named John. He was born about 1575-1576, and died August 22, 1617. John (2) was buried in a vault beside the door of St. Giles Church at Noke, Oxfordshire, England. He made a will August 17, 1617. He married Bryget Greene November 26, 1595. John described himself as "husbandman of Noke in ye countie of Oxon." At sometime before his death, John entered suit in chancery court against Joan Bradshaw, who resided at the manor house with her grandson, Benedict Winchcombe. In this suit John recited that his father had been seized in fee of certain freehold land in Noke, and of "customary land held of the Manor of Noke,"which Henry Bradshaw and Joan, his wife, had agreed to purchase and make him a grant of copyhold. It is evident that the Harpers were a family of very considerable property in the parish.

Children of John Harper (2) and Bryget Green Harper:
Margery Harper, Christened July 24, 1596, and married John Day. She was living in 1667.

<u>Alse or Alice Harper</u>, Christened July 9, 1598, and married February 1, 1619 to Richard Cox.

<u>Bryget Harper</u>, Christened August 24, 1600, and married Thomas Smith

<u>John Harper</u>, Christened October 20, 1602. He apparently either took or was given the name of "George" later to distinguish him from his younger brother who was christened John. He moved to Beckley in the same parish in Oxfordshire.

<u>John Harper (3)</u>, Christened November 18, 1604. (This is our line)

JOHN HARPER (3)

John Harper (3), son of John and Bryget Green Harper (2), was born at Noke, Oxfordshire, England. He was Christened there November 18, 1604 and died the last week of November 1667. John (3) was buried December 1, in the family vault in the St. Giles Churchyard at Noke beside the remains of his father. His will probated December 21, 1667, described himself as "of Noke in ye countie of Oxon, yeoman". He married Charatie whose surname has not been found. She was buried at Noke February 7, 1641.

Children of John Harper (3) and Charatie Harper:

<u>Bridget Aston Harper</u>, Christened January 1, 1629. (This is the latest reference to the Harper family in the Village of Noke.)

<u>Joan Harper</u>, Christened November 3, 1633 and married a Mr. Trudy. They had a son, John.

<u>John Harper (4)</u>, Christened March 5, 1634, (This is our line)

<u>Ralph Harper</u>, christened November 7, 1636

<u>Josias Harper</u>, Christened October 14, 1638

<u>Charatie Harper</u>, Christened April 26, 1640

JOHN HARPER (4)

<u>John Harper (4)</u>, immigrant ancestor, son of John Harper (3) and Charatie Harper, was born in Noke, Oxfordshire, England and Christened there March 5, 1634 by the rector of the parish, Robert Warland. John married Ann Butcher April 6, 1667, and when they immigrated to America he changed the spelling of his surname from Harpar to Harper. John (4) died in Pennsylvania April 29, 1716. His will was dated February 26, 1714, and proved May 4, 1716. He and his wife were buried side by side in the Churchyard of Trinity Oxford Episcopal Church Cemetery in Oxford Township, Philadelphia County, Pennsylvania. Ann was born in King Sultland, North Hampshire, England in 1646. Her father was Charles Butcher

and mother Ann, last name unknown. The inscriptions on their markers are as follows:

John Harper
Son of John Harper
Of Noke, in Oxfordshire in Old England
Arrived in Pennsylvania 2d of August 1682
Who died ye 29th day of April 1716
aged 83 years

In Memory of
Ann Butcher
Widow of John Harper
And
Daughter of Charles Butcher
Of King Sutton, in North Hamptonshire
In Old England
Who died ye 4th of March 1723/24
aged 77 years

John joined the Quakers at a meeting in Barton, England on February 3, 1682. The Quakers were not accepted by the monarchy. Many of them were imprisoned. John and Ann brought their children to America on one of William Penn's fleet, "Welcome", arriving in Philadelphia, Pennsylvania on August 2, 1682.

Children of John Harper (4) and Ann Butcher Harper:
(1) Josiah Harper, born about 1669 in Bichester, Oxfordshire, England, died 1733 in Oxford Township in Philadelphia County, Pennsylvania. He married Lydia Swanson, III about 1700. Lydia was born in 1680, to Ollie Svenson, born 1640 at sea and Lydia Ashmen, born about 1645 in Philadelphia, Pennsylvania.

Children of Josiah and Lydia Harper: John Harper, married Cathrine Brown January 17, 1733 in Christ Church in Philadelphia, Pennsylvania, and died 1763. He and Cathrine had three known children: Isaiah, born November 1735, Ebenezer, born May 1738, and Rebecca, born about 1721 and died between 1772 and 1785.

(2) Charles Alfred Harper, born November 30, 1671 in Chesteron, Oxon, England, and died about 1748 in Philadelphia, Pennsylvania, married Mary, last name unknown. Children: John, born before 1730, Hannah, Sarah, Thomas, born about 1730, Ann, Mary, and

234

Rebecca. Charles Alfred's will was dated June 7, 1748, and proved July 27, 1748. They lived in Oxford, Pennsylvania.

(3) John Harper, born 1677 in Oxfordshire, England, died 1714 in Philadelphia, Pennsylvania. He married Deborah Paver or Parver on May 31, 1711 in Christ Church, Philadelphia, Pennsylvania. Deborah died in 1716. Children of John and Deborah were John, born June 25, 1712, and Deborah, born in 1714.

(4) Elizabeth Harper, born November 28, 1684 in Oxford Township, Philadelphia, Pennsylvania and died June 16, 1761. Elizabeth married Joseph Griffin or Griffeth.

(5) Ralph Harper, born November 2, 1687 in Oxford Township, Philadelphia, Pennsylvania, died June 16, 1761, married 1st Sara, last name unknown, about 1724. Sarah died February 1, 1738/39. Married 2nd, Mary Gregory, born September 12, 1742 in Christ Church, Philadelphia, Pennsylvania. Mary died February 21, 1778/79. Children by Sarah were Sarah, born 1725 and Mary, born 1727. Children by Mary were Catherine, born 1743, Elizabeth, born 1746 and Gregory, born 1747.

(6) Mary Harper, born about 1681 in Oxfordshire, England, died 1755, married John Mills of Oxford Township in Philadelphia, Pennsylvania.

(7) Joseph Harper, born November 30, 1674 in Chesterton, Oxon, died 1746 in Philadelphia, Pennsylvania, married Sarah Moore Jackson. (This is our line)

(8) Bridget Harper, born in Noke 1669, appears to have remained in England.
Will of John Harper (4)

JOSEPH HARPER (5)

Joseph Harper (5) was the son of John Harper (4) and Ann Butcher Harper. He was born November 30, 1674 in Chesterton, Oxon, England and died 1746 in Philadelphia, Pennsylvania. He married Sarah Moore Jackson in 1708. Joseph was a joiner and cabinet maker.

Children of Joseph and Sarah Jackson Harper:

Joseph Harper, born June 12, 1714, died 1752, married Elizabeth Russell, who was born 1718 in New Castle, Delaware and died 1805. Joseph and Elizabeth Russell Harper married before 1748.

Sarah Harper, born June 12, 1717 in Oxbridge Township, Philadelphia, Pennsylvania, and died in 1786. She married Matthias Keen about 1740 and they had the following children: Matthias, born June 1736; John, born June 1745; Joseph, born Oct 1747; Jonas, born February 1749; Robert, born April 1752; and Josiah, born February 1754.

Robert R. Harper, born 1718 in Oxbridge Township in Philadelphia, Pennsylvania and died October 2, 1782. He is buried at Ivy Hill Cemetery, which is the Harper Family Cemetery, in Berkley County, West Virginia, and was the Harper of Harper's Ferry in West Virginia. He married Rachel Griffin in 1738. Robert and Rachel did not have any children but had many collateral descendants. Robert was baptized by the Rev. John Talbot on November 27, 1718. (See information on Harper's Ferry, West Virginia at end of Harper History)

John Harper was born August 18, 1720 in Oxbridge Township in Philadelphia, Pennsylvania and died in 1793 in Berkley County, West Virginia. His first wife is unknown, but he married 2nd to Margery Robinson who was born in 1738.

Ann Harper, born in 1712, died in 1747 and married Moses Wells in 1749. Ann was buried at Trinity Episcopal Church in Oxford Township in Philadelphia, Pennsylvania.

Josiah Harper, (Author's line) was born after 1725 and died March 16, 1768 in Frederick County, Maryland. He married Rachel Owings.

JOSIAH HARPER (6)

Josiah Harper (6), was the son of Joseph Harper (5) and Sarah Moore Jackson Harper. He was born about 1725 and died in 1768 in Frederick County, Maryland. His brother, Robert, was the executor of his estate. Josiah married Rachel Owings, whose father was Robert Owings and mother, Rachel Hook. Josiah owned Prospect Plantation in Frederick County, Maryland.

Children of Josiah and Rachel Owings Harper:

Josiah Harper, (Author's line) Josiah was born in 1762 and died in 1838 in Smith County, Tennessee. He married Sarah Parrott December 27, 1787 in Franklin County, Virginia.

Robert Harper, was born about 1765 and died 1841 in Tuscaloosa County, Alabama. He married Marjory Payne December 21, 1787, in Bedford, Virginia. Her father was John Payne and mother was

Mary, last name unknown. Child of Robert and Marjory was John Payne Harper, born March 22, 1790 in Virginia and died June 30, 1863 in Scottsboro, Jackson County, Alabama. He married Martha Patsy Phillips March 12, 1813 in Madison, Mississippi Territory. She was born January 22, 1796 in Kentucky, and died after 1870 in Van County, Texas. They had ten children.

Sary Harper, Name spelled this way in will. Birth and death dates unknown.

Rachel Harper, born about 1788, death date is unknown. She married James Duncan about 1821 and had the following children: Joseph, born 1822, Thomas, born 1824 and Jefferson, born 1826.

JOSIAH HARPER (7)

Josiah Harper (7) was the son of Josiah Harper (6) and Rachel Owings Harper. He was born in 1762 and died 1838 in Smith County, Tennessee. Josiah married Sarah, "Sallie" Parrott December 27, 1787 in Franklin County, Virginia by Thomas Douglas, Minister. Sarah was born in 1761 and died in 1839. They are both buried in Smith County, Tennessee in the Rock City Community. Sarah's father was Joseph Parrott and he had married Winea, last name unknown.

Children of Josiah and Sarah Parrott Harper:

John Harper, was born 1788 in Franklin County, Virginia and died October 7, 1846, in Smith County, Tennessee, Rock City Community. He was converted in Hogan's Creek Baptist Church in July 1827. He married 1st to a Miss Hodges, and 2nd to Jane Fleming Skelton. John and Jane are buried in the Harper/Sampson Cemetery in Smith County, Tennessee. John established a church in New Middleton and Plunkett's Creek Baptist Church. (Quinnie Harper, purveyor of this Harper Family Research, stated he visited this area in 2002.

Josiah Harper, Jr., was born in 1794 in Virginia and died September 28, 1859 in Fayette County, Texas. He married Elizabeth, last name unknown, about 1802 in Kentucky. Josiah was a Primitive Baptist Church Elder in Fayette County, Texas. Children of Josiah, Jr. and Elizabeth were: Thomas, born 1823, died after 1874; Robert Hamilton, born 1833, in Alabama; Benjamine Franklin, born 1836 in Arkansas, and Rebecca Jane, born 1841.

Thomas Harper, born about 1802 in Virginia and died between 1866 and 1870 in Marion County, Alabama. Thomas' daughter, Sarah Harper McWhirter, is the subject of this book and their family information can be found elsewhere in this book.

237

Rachel Harper, born 1803 in Virginia. Her death date is unknown. She married an unknown McGuffie, and in 1850 she was living in Lebanon, Wilson County, Tennessee as head of household with the following children: Edmond, Nancy A., Mary, Elizabeth and Jessee McGuffie.

Robert Harper, was born in 1805 in Tennessee, and died in 1879 in Mississippi County, Missouri. He married Nancy Williams in 1832. (Quinnie Harper's Line)

Rebecca Harper, born 1805 in Tennessee, married Nevel Hamilton Smith and moved to Benton County, Tennessee in 1840. They raised a large family.

Benjamin Franklin Harper, birth and death dates unknown.

Will of Josiah Harper, Sr. (sic)

Smith Co., TN Will Book 6, pg. 197, FHL Microfilm 9319,179, Will of Josiah Harper, Sr.

"I Joseph Harper of Smith County and state of Tennessee do make and publish this my last will and testament ...working and making void all other wills by me at any time heretofor made. First I direct that my body be decently enterd in a manner suitable to my condition in life and as to such worldly estate.... hath pleased God to entrust me with. I disclose the same as following. First I direct that all my debts and funeral expenses be paid as soon after my death as possible out of any monies that I may... .. of ... or may first commit to the hands of my executor from any portion of my Estate real or personal. Second it is my wish that my beloved wife Sally Harper be decently supported out of the rest of my farm during her natural life and also any live stock that I may give her. 3rd, I give to my wife one cow & calf the cow known by the name of White Face also my bed & furniture. I also give to my wife in Rom Maro (Mare) all the above described property at the death of my wife to go back to my children to be equally divided amongst them. 4th it is my will and wish that all the balance of my property both personal and real be sold in twelve months ... to the highest bidder and then divided equally amongst all my children to wit, John Harper, Sally Blue, Josiah Harper, Jr., Thomas Harper, Rachel McGuffie, Robert Harper, Rebecca Smith and Benjamin Harper. It is expresily understood that my farm is to be sold as the balance of my property at the death of my wife. I also give to my son, Josiah Harper, Junior twenty dollars more than any of the rest of children as I consider I owe him that amount. I do hereby make ordain and append my sons John Harper and Benjamin Harper executors of this my last will and testament. In

witness whereof I Josiah Harper. The said testator hav. to this my will written on one sheet of paper set my hand and seal this 9th day of September the year of our Lord One Thousand Eight Hundred Thirty Six.
Signed Sealed & published in the presence of the Testator of each other.
Josiah Harper Seal
Attest James McDonnald, his mark.

State of Tennessee Smith County, November Term ... . 1838. This the last will and Testament of Josiah Harper was produced in open court for probate and was ... proven in open court of the oath of Lin?"
(If any of the readers decide to obtain a copy of Josiah Harper, Sr.'s will, you need to order it from the National Archives because when FHL copied it they omitted one complete sentence which mentioned some of the children, including Thomas.)

THOMAS HARPER

Thomas Harper, son of Josiah Harper, Sr. and Sarah "Sally" Parrott, was born between 1798 and 1802 in Virginia, most likely Franklin County, Virginia. He died between 1866 and 1870 in Marion County, Alabama. Although his place of burial has not been proven, he is most likely buried in an unmarked grave in the Hopewell Cemetery in Fayette County, Alabama where so many of his children and other relatives are buried. He was a delegate to the Hopewell Primitive Baptist Church Convention from 1850 to 1855. His first wife is unknown but died young. After her death, Thomas married Mary E., possibly Mary Elizabeth, last name unknown, about 1817. She died after 1850 in Alabama. This Mary was only eight years older than his first daughter, Sarah. After Mary's death, he married Mary Jane Griggs, who was born 1829 in Alabama and was the daughter of Jesse Griggs and Rebecca Tucker. Mary Jane was the widow of William Miles.

Children of Thomas Harper and Unknown Wife

1. Sarah Harper b. June 24, 1825, in Smith County, Tennessee, married June 7, 1842, in Warren County, Tennessee to Andrew Ferrier McWhirter, born, Nov 9, 1824, died October 23, 1862, Nashville, Davidson County, Tennessee. Sarah died December 28, 1883, in Marion County, Alabama and is buried in the

O'Mary Cemetery, which is in Marion County, Alabama on the border of Winston County.

2. Robert Harper, born about 1826, in Smith County, Tennessee, married November 20, 1851, in Walker County, Alabama, to Nancy Jane Lane, born about 1828, Alabama. She was the daughter of Alfred G. Lane and Mariah Pate. Robert died March 7, 1863, Corinth, Mississippi while serving in the 1st Alabama Cavalry,USV.
3. James W. Harper, born about 1829 in Smith County, Tennessee, and was married about 1848, in Alabama to Sarah Drucilla Byars. Sarah was born, about 1834, in Alabama. James died October 4.
Mary Emmoline Harper was born about 1832 in Smith County, Tennessee and married James R. Tucker about 1852 in Alabama. James R. Tucker was born May 26, 1826, Alabama and was the son of George Tucker, Jr. and Milla Roberts. Mary died before 1867, probably Marion County, Alabama.
5. Josiah Houston Harper was born March 12, 1833 and married Nancy Jane Berryhill, who was born about 1857 in Alabama. Josiah died July 22, 1864, and is buried in the Hopewell Cemetery, Fayette County, Alabama.
6. Rebecca Jane Harper was born about 1836 in Smith County, Tennessee. She married Daniel Webster Tucker, who was born May 26, 1825, in Alabama and died December 15, 1901, in Union Parish, Louisiana. Rebecca died February 1, 1902, in Union Parish, Louisiana and is buried in Zion Hill Cemetery.
7. Thomas Wade Harper was born about 1839, in Smith County, Tennessee and married Mary Elizabeth Lane who was the daughter of John Lane and Phoebe Walden. Thomas died September 15, 1862, Knoxville, Tennessee while serving in the 43rd Alabama Infantry, CSA. He is buried in the Bethel Cemetery in Knoxville where there is a monument to both the Union and Confederate soldiers who lost their lives in Knoxville during the Civil War. His name is on this marker on the Confederate side.

Children of Thomas Harper by unknown wife or Mary E., last name Unknown
8. Elisha Denton "Dent" Harper was born about 1841 in Smith County, Tennessee and married Lucinda Ann Lyle about 1862. Lucinda was born about 1840 in Georgia and was the daughter of John P. Lyle and Elizabeth Noland. "Dent" died between 1866 and 1870 in Alabama.
9. Tennessee Polk Harper was born about 1843 in Walker County, Alabama, and died December 9, 1862, in Nashville, Davidson

County, Tennessee. He is buried in the Nashville National Cemetery, Nashville in Grave #7159.

10. <u>George M.D. Harper</u> was born in July 1847 in Marion County, Alabama, and married Martha E. Morton in 1865. Martha was the daughter of James F. and Mary E. Morton, both born in Alabama. Children of George and Martha were Mary, born about 1868; Rosa E., born 1870; Nancy, born 1872; Thomas, born November 1877; Martin Emmett, born December 25, 1885, and died October 15, 1966; and Charley E. Harper, born May 1888. George was listed as George W. Harper on a couple of census records and E.W. on the 1870 Sanford County, Alabama Census. The 1900 Lamar County, Alabama Census was the last census on which George was found, indicating he must have died between 1900 and 1910.

<u>Children of Thomas Harper and Mary E. Harper</u>

11. Jasper Green Harper b. June 1850, Marion County, Alabama and married Mary Elizabeth Hyder December 17, 1874. Mary Elizabeth was born about 1855 in Alabama and died 1898, and is buried in the Hyder Cemetery in Fayette County, Alabama. His second wife was Mattie Gilreath and they married November 4, 1899. Mary Elizabeth died in 1903. Jasper "Green" Harper died in 1925 and is buried in the New River Cemetery in an unmarked grave.

<u>Children of Thomas Harper and Mary Jane Griggs</u>

12. Martha Ann Harper was born September 14, 1854 in Marion County, Alabama and married Kimber Foster Tucker, born July 14, 1847 in Alabama. He died June 30 1922 in Oklahoma. Martha Ann died September 13, 1914 in Oklahoma and is buried in the Talahina Cemetery in Leflore County, Oklahoma

13. Nancy Harper was born in 1855, in Alabama and died before 1870, in Alabama.

14. Malyssa "Melissa" A. Harper was born in June 1887 in Marion County, Alabama and married E. J. "Lige" White on June 28, 1888 in Alabama. He was born July 1855 in Alabama. Melissa died in Arkansas.

15. Jesse Harper was born in 1860 in Marion County, Alabama and married Sarah "Sallie" Whitehead September 3, 1882 in Fayette County, Alabama. "Sallie" Whitehead was born in 1862 in Fayette County, Alabama and died in 1959. Jesse died in 1942 in Alabama and is buried in the Griggs Cemetery in Marion County, Alabama.

241

ROBERT HARPER (8)

Robert Harper (8) was the son of Josiah Harper (7) and Sarah "Sallie" Parrott. Robert was born in Smith County, Tennessee in 1805 and died in 1879 in the Long Prairie Township of Mississippi County, Missouri in 1879. He married Nancy Williams in 1832. Nancy was born in 1812 in Smith County, Tennessee and died in 1879 in Mississippi County, Missouri. She and Robert moved to Mississippi County, Missouri in 1873. Nancy's father was Giles Williams and mother Agnis, last name unknown. Robert and Nancy are buried at Oak Grove Cemetery between Bertrand and Charleston, Missouri.

Children of Robert and Nancy Harper:

James Harper, born 1834 and died about 1864 during the Civil War. He had two children, James B. and John H. Harper who were born in Benton County, Tennessee.

Robert Harper was born 1837 in Tennessee and died about 1864 during the Civil War. He was buried in his father's orchard in Benton County, Tennessee. He had two children, William F. and Robert H. Harper.

Sarah Elizabeth Harper, born 1839 and died in Bertrand, Missouri. She married 1st to a Mr. Williams, and 2nd to William Love. Children by William were Spencer and Ella.

Maria Frances Harper, born 1841, and died 1915. She married 1st to Caleb Macken and 2nd to Samuel Walters.

John Bell Harper, born December 25, 1844, and died January 8, 1928, in Nashville, Tennessee. He married 1st to Laura Ann Yarbrough and 2nd to Rebecca Frances Harrison.

Josiah S. Harper, born 1847 in Henry County, Tennessee, death date is unknown. He served in the Civil War and lived in Tecumseh, Oklahoma, in Indian Territory. He married Belle, last name unknown, and had three children: Will, Cora, and Ophilia Harper.

Thomas Jefferson Harper, born December 22, 1848 in Benton County, Tennessee and died March 16, 1922 in Greenwood, Arkansas. He married Elizabeth Susan Weeks in Carroll County, Tennessee in 1870. Elizabeth died October 30, 1905 in Greenwood, Arkansas.

David H. Harper, born July 23, 1851 in Henry County, Tennessee and died in 1948 in Liberty, Missouri. He lived in St. Louis in 1922. David married 1st Mabel Dodge in 1876 and 2nd Lucinda Dodge in 1884. Mabel died in 1882.

William L. Harper, born November 18, 1855 in Henry County, Tennessee and died 1922 in Webster Groves, Missouri. He married

Fannie Ostner, who was born in 1856 and died January 30, 1913. Children, Ferd, Joe and Eunice Harper.

Green H. Harper, born 1855 in Henry County, Tennessee and died in Nutbush, Tennessee, near Tibbs. In 1922, he was living in Brownsville, Tennessee. Green married Allie B. Love.

WILL OF ROBERT HARPER (8) (sic)

In the name of God Amen I Robert Harper of Berkeley County in the Commonwealth of Virginia being sick and weak in Body but sound in memory and judgment calling to mind the frailty and vicisitudes of this life and succeeding eternity do hereby make constitute ordain and appoint this my last Will and Testament revoking disallowing and recinding all other wills or testaments by me heretofore made, in manner and form as follows viz: I leave my body to the earth to be buried in a decent manner at the discretion of my Executor after mentioned & recommend my Soul to the hands of that God who gave it in hopes of a glorious resurection thro the atone merits and attonement of our Lord and Saviour Jesus Christ and for what worldly estate it hath pleased God to bestow on me I give leave and bequeath as follows, after my Just Debts Death Bed and funeral expenses are paid off, Viz IMPRIMIS
I give leave and bequeath to my Nephew Robert Griffith one moiety or half of my Ferry Survey to form a straight direct line to run along the two fences on the east side on that side next to the ferry the one fence lying on the north and the other on the south side of the road leading from the ferry to Winchester the sides of the above mentioned fences to be a director or to shew where each end of the division line shall terminate. The end of the line leading to Potomak to terminate as soon as it strikes that river the end leading to Shannadoah to keep a straight till it likewise strikes said river and to contain and include the Island opposite where the said line strikes, then to run in my line joining Samples line to continue with said line and to include Ninety Acres of a new survey thence to continue its course till where the division line shall strike Potomac River including therewith my Saw Mill and Grist Mill with all the utensills belonging to both mills likewise I do leave unto my said Nephew all my moveable estate whatsoever except my Negro Wench Beck.
2ndly I give leave and bequeath to my neice Sarah Harper daughter of my brother Joseph Harper joiner & Cabinet Maker late of Philadelphia or her heirs, my Ferry and ferry house on Potomack

River and all the remainder of my Ferry Survey not before devised to Robert Griffith together with all my estate right and title to the Maryland Shore of the said Ferry and also all my Estate Right Title to and for Ten Acres upon what is called the big Island up Potomack River adjoining the Ferry aforesaid. But it is my will that neather nam-neice or her husband if a live shall enjoy the said Ferry and lands hereby demised and bequeathed longer than their natural life or lives and it is likewise my will that my said neice Sarah or her husband shall and may have full power & authority to leave and bequeath the said Ferry and lands to them demised as above to either of their sons whom they shall judge most deserving thereof and in case of failure of male issue to leave and give the premises aforesaid to either of their Daughters as may appear to them or the survivor of them the most suitable. It is likewise my will that my debts all and sundry shall be paid out of the rents of my Ferry by my Executors after mentioned who are hereby empowered to retain the same till all just claims and demands against my estate are paid and discharged thereby. It is my will in consideration of what is above devised and made over to my said neice Sarah that she or her assigns shall be obliged to Ferry over at the Ferry above mentioned passaged free every person or persons who shall bring with them grist of any kind to the mills on the lands now belonging to me adjoining the same.

FOURTHLY I hereby give leave and bequeath unto my Nephew Joseph Keen a tract of land containing three hundred Acres of Land lying at the mouth of Indian Run Sleepy Creek in Berkeley County being the same as was purchased by me from Aaron Rice.

FIFTHLY I hereby give leave and bequeath unto my Nephews Robert Harper, Josiah Harper, Jonas Keen, Hezekiah Keen and Israel Keen the whole amount of what my Negro Wench Beck shall bring to be equally divided and shared amongst them and for that purpose it is my will that my Executors shall as soon as convenient after my deceased cause the said Negro Wench Beck to be sold, and for the more sure carrying this my Last Will and Testament to be put into due execution I do hereby ordain nominate constitute and appoint and by these present have ordained nominated constituted and appointed my well beloved friends Edward Lucas John Ryon of Berkeley County and Robert Griffith of Bedford County in the Commonwealth of Virginia to be my only true and lawful Exors. for the purposes before mentioned hereby ratifying and confirming all and whatsoever my said attornies shall lawfully do with regard to the premises and they either of them shall not be liable to any neglect or omissions respecting the same

244

IN WITNESS WHEREOF I have hereunto set my hand and seal unto this my last Will and Testament this Twenty Sixth Day of September in the year of our Lord One Thousand Seven Hundred and Eighty two.
Robert Harper
Robert Harper (L.S.)

Signed Sealed published pronounced and declared by the said Robert Harper to be his last Will and Testament in presence of us Ro. McKnight, T. Hamilton, John Duncan, William Duncan, William Darke Be it known to all men by these presents that I Robert Harper of the County of Berkeley and Commonwealth of Virginia have made and declared my last Will and Testament in writing bearing date the first day of October One Thousand Seven hundred and Eighty Two I Robert Harper by this present Codicil do ratify and confirm my said last Will and Testament and it is further my last Will that four Acres of land most convenient round my grave yard shall be laid of by my Executors and be entirely appropriated to the use of a grave yard and all my debts due by bond note or book debt and all rents now due from my ferry be by my Executors be disposed of in the best manner towards erecting a grave yard and building a church on said four acres of land and having a head and foot stone for my wifes grave and likewise for my own, and my will and meaning is that this Codicil be adjudged to be a part and parcel of my last Will and Testament and that all things contained therein be faithfully and truly performed and as fully and amply in every respect as if the same had been declared and set down in my last Will and Testament as witnessed my hand this first day of October One Thousand Seven Hundred and Eighty two.
Robert R. Harper (L.S.) his mark

Signed in the presence of us Ro McKnight Wm. Darke James Claypool at a court held for Berkeley County the 15th day of October 1782 This last Will and Testament together with the Codicil thereto annexed of Robert Harper Deceased was presented in Court by John Ryon Edward Lucas and Robert Griffith the Executor therein named who made oath therto according to law and the same being proved by the oaths of Robert McKnight, William Darke and William Duncan witnesses thereto and ordered to be recorded and on the motion of the said Executors who entered into bond with William Darke and John Briscoe joins their securities in the penalty of five hundred pounds conditioned for their true and faithful administration of the said estate certificates granted them for obtaining a Probate thereof in due form of law.

245

Examined Teste Will Drew Clk
State of West Virginia
County of Berkeley To Wit:
I Harold O. Keedy, Clerk of the County Court of Berkeley County, a
Court of record in and for said County and State, do certify that the
foregoing is a true, accurate and complete copy of The Will of
Robert Harper as the same appears of record in the office of the said
Clerk of the County Court in Will Book No. 1, Page 291.

John Bell Harper

John Bell Harper (9) was the son of Robert Harper (8) and Nancy
Williams Harper. He was born December 25, 1844 in Smith County,
Tennessee and died in Nashville, Davidson County, Tennessee
January 8, 1928. John married his first wife, Laura Ann Yarbrough
in 1869 in Nashville, Tennessee. Laura was born 1851 and died May
6, 1898 in Nashville, Tennessee. Her parents were Isaac S.
Yarbrough and Mary Ann Burton. John's 2nd wife was Frances
Rebecca Harrison, who was born in 1858, death unknown. John and
Rebecca were married in Davidson County, Tennessee in 1916. John
is buried in the Confederate Circle in Mt. Olivet Cemetery in
Nashville, Tennessee. Funeral services were held at Belmont Baptist
Church in Nashville.

John worked with his father, Robert, and siblings on a 160 acre farm
in Camden, Tennessee which is in Benton County. Their house was
made of logs and planks and had ten rooms.

While living in Benton County, Tennessee, he enlisted in Captain
William A. Jones' Battalion, Company A. Confederate Army which
later became the 55th Tennessee Infantry Regiment. He fought under
General Joe Jackson and was wounded June 1, 1864 at New Hope
Church by a Minnie ball passing through his right lung, which
disabled him for life. John returned to Benton County and taught
school for several years while also studying medicine. Later John
moved to Bertrand, Missouri which is in Mississippi County, where
he worked as a shipper of watermelons, making many trips to
Nashville, Tennessee with the melons. John went in the medical field
as a pharmacist. He and his family moved to Nashville in 1916,
where he worked at the Capitol as Commissioner in the Land Office
Department until his death in 1928.
Children of John and Laura Yarbrough Harper:

246

Blanch Harper, born 1872 and died 1918 in Chicago, Illinois. She married John Bailey Bruce on August 28, 1893, and had one son, Bailey Harper Bruce, who was born October 16, 1894, and died November 15, 1969. John was born 1866 and died August 28, 1924.

Fannie Harper, born 1873 and died in June 1918 in Nashville, Tennessee. She married William Frank Burton in March 1867, and had two children: Ivo and William Burton.

Loula Belle Harper, born January 6, 1882 in Bertrand, Missouri and died September 13, 1970 in St. Louis, Missouri. She married Charles Fred Jacobsmeyer May 3, 1905. Charles was born in 1831 and died April 15, 1964. They had two children, Robert and John Jacobsmeyer. "Fred" and Loula are buried in St. Louis at Oak Grove Cemetery. He and Loula were members of Bethal Lutheran Church at University City, St. Louis, Missouri.

Quinnie Bush Harper, Sr., born January 4, 1884, and died July 1, 1966 in Hendersonville, Tennessee. Quinnie married Edna Cathryn Waltemate.

INTERESTING FACTS ABOUT JOHN BELL HARPER

1861 – Volunteered in Company A, Jones Battalion, Confederate Army, which afterwards became the 55th Tennessee Infantry.

1864 – Wounded at Now Hope Church June 1, 1864 by a Minnie ball passing through his right lung.

1880 – Lived in Bertrand, Missouri with Laura A. Yarbrough, his first wife. John was thirty-six (36) and Laura was twenty-nine (29), and children: Fannie, eight (8), and Blanch seven (7). He worked as a druggist and shipper of melons from Bertrand, Missouri to Nashville, Tennessee.

1891/92 – Lived at 417 Cedar Avenue, Nashville, Davidson County, Tennessee

1893 – Insurance Agency while living at 119 Belmont Boulevard in Nashville, Tennessee.

1894 – Solicitor, Noel Block Buildings, 125 McLemore, Nashville, Tennessee

1895/96 – Sold life insurance.

1897 – Lived at 125 McLemore Street and worked at 136 South Market Street.

1898 – Salesman

1899 – Insurance Salesman, Canvasser r. 6 & 7 Twin Building.

1901 – Capitalist

1902 – Collector

1916/1828 – Lived at 1006 Gilmore Street, Nashville, Tennessee, Commissioner of the State Land Office. He also worked as a Travel Agent during this time.

1922 – Made picture at the Confederate Convention in Memphis, Tennessee with his siblings: Thomas Jefferson, David, John Bell, Maria, Sarah, Josiah, and Green H. Harper.

1928 – Died at 1006 Gilmore Street of the infirmities of his advanced age. Funeral services were held at Belmont Baptist Church in Nashville, Tennessee at 2:30 on a Tuesday Afternoon.

INTERESTING FACTS ABOUT BLANCH AND FANNIE HARPER

Blanch at age eighteen (18) began working at Tennessee Manufacturing Company which was located at 108 Wheless near Filmore Street in Nashville, Tennessee. She worked there from 1890 to 1894.

Qunnie Bush Harper, Sr. (10)

1.   Quinnie Bush Harper, Sr. (10) was the son of John Bell Harper (9) and Laura Yarbrough Harper. Quinnie was born in Bertrand, Missouri January 4, 1884, and died in Hendersonville, Tennessee July 1, 1966. He married Edna Cathryn Waltemate September 10, 1905 in Columbus, Kentucky. Edna was born March 15, 1887 in Columbus, Kentucky and died February 4, 1960. Quinnie and Edna are buried in Mt. Olivet Cemetery in Nashville, Davidson County, Tennessee (This is the line of Quinnie Harper of Portland, Tennessee who supplied the Harper Family information.)

Children of Quinnie and Edna

1.   Frances Lee, born May 5, 1907, Nashville, Tennessee, died April 11, 1977, in Madison, Tennessee, married Henry Laux and they had four children: Barbara Ann, born September 14, 1927, died March 14, 1985; Nancy Cathrine, born September 1, 1928; John "Bub" Henry, III, born October 5, 1930, died July 12, 1998; James Harper Laux, born July 31, 1933, died May 11, 2001.

2.   Quinnie Bush Harper, Jr., born October 19, 1913, in Nashville, Davidson County, Tennessee, died June 3, 1974, married Virginia Claire Cox, March 23, 1938. Virginia was born February 19, 1921, in Nashville, Tennessee, and died November 18, 2000, in Madison, Tennessee. (This is the line of Quinnie Harper in Portland, Tennessee who supplied the Harper Family information.)

248

3.   John Bell Harper, born September 9, 1919, in Hendersonville, died July 19, 1989 in Donelson Tennessee, married Mary Ann Peden September 2, 1949. Children: Julie Ann, born August 14, 1950; Edna Cathryn, born July 21, 1954; John Bell, born December 31, 1955.
4.   Edna Cathryne Harper, born February 11, 1921, in Hendersonville, Tennessee, died January 1999, in Louisville, Kentucky. Buried in Mt. Olivet Cemetery in Nashville, Tennessee, Section 27, Lot 138.
5.   Brandon Neville Harper, born February 21, 1923, in Hendersonville, Tennessee, died May 17, 1993, in Louisville, Kentucky. Buried in Mt. Olivet Cemetery in Nashville, Tennessee, Section 28, Lot 99.
6.   Betty Sue Harper, born June 6, 1927, in Nashville, Tennessee, died November 23, 2000. Buried in Mt. Olivet Cemetery in Nashville, Tennessee, Section 27, Lot 138.

Quinnie and Edna Cathryne Harper were affectionately called by many as "Daddy Harper and Mama Harper.

Qunnie Bush Harper, Jr. (11)

Quinnie Bush Harper, Jr. (11) was the son of Quinnie Bush Harper, Sr. (10) and Edna Cathryne Waltemate Harper. Quinnie was born October 19, 1913, in Nashville, Davidson County, Tennessee, and died June 3, 1974, in Madison, Tennessee. He married Virginia Claire Cox March 23, 1938, in Franklin, Kentucky. Virginia was born February 19, 1921 in Nashville, Tennessee and died November 18, 2000 in Madison, Tennessee.

Children of Quinnie and Virginia:
1Quinnie Bush Harper, III, married Betty Malone Farley February 11, 1967, at Gallatin Road Baptist Church in Nashville, Tennessee by Reverend W. W. Harrison. (This is the line of Quinnie Harper in Portland, Tennessee who supplied the Harper Family information.)
2.   Richard Dale Harper, married Suzanne Driver at Gallatin Road Baptist Church in Madison, Tennessee September 21, 1968.

Children of Dale and Susanne:
1.   Emily Suzanne Harper, married Chad Travis Mack Eads,I
2.   Children: Carson Williams Harper, and Carley Suzanne

249

Richard Dale Harper, born December 3, 1975 in Nashville, Tennessee, married Suzanne Driver at Gallatin Road Baptist Church in Madison, Tennessee September 21, 1968.

1.	Richard Reid Harper, married Breanna Melynda Dean, April 2003.They had one child, Davis Jason Harper
2.	Wallace Drew

Qunnie Bush Harper, III (12)

Quinnie Bush Harper, III is the son of Quinnie Bush Harper, Jr. (11), and Virginia Claire Cox. Quinnie married Betty Malone Farley of Nashville, Tennessee on February 11, 1967. Betty was born March 15, 1945, in Nashville, Tennessee and is the daughter of Glen Malone Farley, born December 4, 1914, and Mary Ann Garner Farley, born December 31, 1919.

Children of Quinnie and Betty

1.	Elizabeth "Beth" Anne Harper McReynolds, married Randy Quentin McReynolds November 16, 1990 at Southside Baptist Church in Gallatin, Tennessee.
Children of Randy and Beth:
2.	Alexander Quentin
3.	Charis Elizabeth
4.	Kendal Elise
5.	Camden Asher

2. Amanda "Mandi" Margaret

For those of you who descend from the Robert Harper, born 1718 in Oxbridge Township in Philadelphia, Pennsylvania, and lived in Harper's Ferry, West Virginia, below is some history of the area.

Harper's Ferry, West Virginia

Harpers Ferry is a historic town in Jefferson County, West Virginia. In many books the town is called "Harper's Ferry" with an apostrophe. It is situated at the confluence of the Potomac and Shenandoah rivers where the U.S. states of Maryland, Virginia and West Virginia meet. The town is located on a low-lying flood plain created by the two rivers and surrounded by higher ground. Historically, Harpers Ferry is best known for John Brown's raid on the Armory in 1859 and its role in the American Civil War. As of the 2000 census, the town had a population of 307.

The lower part of Harpers Ferry is located within Harpers Ferry National Historical Park. Most of the remainder, which includes the higher more populated area, is included in the separate Harpers Ferry Historic District. Two other National Register of Historic Places properties adjoin the town: the B & O Railroad Potomac River Crossing and St. Peter's Roman Catholic Church.

The Appalachian Trail Conservancy (ATC) headquarters is located in Harpers Ferry and the town is one of only a few that the Appalachian Trail passes directly through.

Thomas Jefferson wrote in *Notes on the State of Virginia*, published in 1785, that "The passage of the 'Patowmac' through the Blue Ridge is perhaps one of the most stupendous scenes in Nature."

Early Years

In 1750 Robert Harper was given a patent on 125 acres (0.5 km²) at the present location of the town. In 1761 Harper established a ferry across the Potomac, making the town a starting point for settlers moving into the Shenandoah Valley and further west. In 1763 the Virginia General Assembly established the town of "Shenandoah Falls at Mr. Harper's Ferry."

On October 25, 1783, Thomas Jefferson visited Harpers Ferry. He viewed "the passage of the Potomac though the Blue Ridge" from a rock which is now named for him. Jefferson was actually on his way to Philadelphia and passed through Harpers Ferry with his daughter Patsy. Jefferson called the site "perhaps one of the most stupendous scenes in nature."

George Washington, as president of the Patowmack Company (which was formed to complete river improvements on the Potomac and its tributaries), traveled to Harpers Ferry during the summer of 1785 to determine the need for bypass canals. In 1794 Washington's familiarity with the area led him to propose the site for a new United States armory and arsenal. Some of Washington's family moved to the area; his great-great nephew, Colonel Lewis Washington, was held hostage during John Brown's raid in 1859.

In 1796 the federal government purchased a 125-acre (0.5 km²) parcel of land from the heirs of Robert Harper. In 1799 construction began on the United States Armory and Arsenal at Harpers Ferry.

This was one of only two such facilities in the U.S., the other being Springfield, Massachusetts, and between them they produced most of the small arms for the U.S. Army. The town was transformed into an industrial center; between 1801 and its destruction in 1861, to prevent its capture during the Civil War, the armory produced more than 600,000 muskets, rifles and pistols. Inventor Captain John H. Hall pioneered the use of interchangeable parts in firearms manufactured at his rifle works at the armory between 1820 and 1840; his M1819 Hall rifle was the first breech-loading weapon adopted by the U.S. Army.

This industrialization continued in 1833 when the Chesapeake & Ohio Canal reached Harpers Ferry linking it with Washington, D.C. One year later the Baltimore & Ohio Railroad began train service through the town.

John Brown's Raid on Harper's Ferry

On October 16, 1859, the radical abolitionist John Brown led a group of 21 men in a raid on the arsenal. Five of the men were black: three free blacks, one a freed slave and one a fugitive slave. During this time assisting fugitive slaves was illegal under the Dred Scott decision. Brown attacked and captured several buildings; he hoped to use the captured weapons to initiate a slave uprising throughout the South. The first shot mortally wounded Hayward Shepherd. Shepherd was a free black man who was a night baggage porter for the B&O Railroad that ran through Harpers Ferry near the armory. The noise from that shot roused Dr. John Starry from his sleep shortly after 1:00 am. He walked from his nearby home to investigate the shooting and was confronted by Brown's men. Starry stated that he was a doctor but could do nothing more for Shepherd, and Brown's men allowed him to leave. Instead of going home Starry went to the livery and rode to neighboring towns and villages, alerting residents to the raid.

When he reached nearby Charles Town, they rang the church bells and aroused the citizens from their sleep. John Brown's men were quickly pinned down by local citizens and militia, and forced to take refuge in the engine house adjacent to the armory.

The secretary of war asked for the assistance of the Navy Department for a unit of United States Marines, the nearest troops. Lieutenant Israel Greene was ordered to take a force of 86 Marines to the town. In need of an officer to lead the expedition, U.S. Army Lieutenant Colonel Robert E. Lee was found on leave nearby and was assigned as commander along with Lt. J. E. B. Stuart as his aide de camp. The whole contingent arrived by train on October 18, and after negotiation failed they stormed the fire house and captured most of the raiders, killing a few and suffering a single casualty themselves. Brown was tried for treason against the State of Virginia convicted and hanged in nearby Charles Town. Starry's testimony was integral to his conviction. Following the prosecution (by Andrew Hunter), "John Brown captured the attention of the nation like no other abolitionist or slave owner before or since." The Marines returned to their barracks and Col. Lee returned to finish his leave. The raid was a catalyst for the Civil War.

Civil War in Harpers Ferry

The Civil War was disastrous for Harpers Ferry, which changed hands eight times between 1861 and 1865. When Virginia seceded in April 1861 the U.S. garrison attempted to burn the arsenal and destroy the machinery. Locals saved the equipment, which was later transferred to a more secure location in Richmond. Arms production never returned to Harpers Ferry.

Because of the town's strategic location on the railroad and at the northern end of the Shenandoah Valley, both Union and Confederate troops moved through Harpers Ferry frequently. The town's garrison of 14,000 Federal troops played a key role in the Confederate invasion of Maryland in September 1862. Gen. Robert E. Lee did not want to continue on to Pennsylvania without capturing the town, which was on his supply line and would control one of his possible routes of retreat if the invasion did not go well. Dividing his army of approximately 40,000 into four sections, he used the cover of the mountains to sent three columns under Stonewall Jackson to surround and capture the town.

The Battle of Harpers Ferry started with light fighting September 13 to capture the Maryland Heights to the northeast while John Walker moved back over the Potomac to capture Loudoun Heights south of town. After an artillery bombardment on September 14 and 15, the Federal garrison surrendered. Lee, because of the delay in capturing Harpers Ferry and the movement of Federal forces west, was forced to regroup at the town of Sharpsburg, leading two days later to the Battle of Antietam, the bloodiest single day in American military history.

253

On the 4th of July 1864, Gen. Franz Sigel, who was then in command withdrew his troops to Maryland Heights. From there he resisted early attempt to enter the town and to drive the Federal garrison from Maryland Heights.

Shortly after the end of the Civil War, Harpers Ferry, along with all of both Berkeley and Jefferson counties, was separated from Virginia and incorporated into West Virginia. The inhabitants of the counties, as well as the Virginia legislature protested, but the federal government went ahead anyway, forming the West Virginia "panhandle" of today.

Controversy over Arsenal Firehouse (John Brown Fort) Bell

During a Union Army occupation of Harpers Ferry, a contingent of soldiers from Marlborough, Massachusetts, removed a bell hanging in the Harpers Ferry arsenal firehouse. The Harpers Ferry firehouse had served as John Brown's Fort. Several of those from Marlborough were in the fire department in Marlborough, called the "'Torrent' Fire/Engine Company", according to the city of Marlborough website. They took the bell back to Marlborough where it has remained ever since. Harpers Ferry has made some attempts over the years to retrieve the bell, none of them successful.

On December 15, 2009, the residents of Marlborough, Massachusetts challenged Harpers Ferry to reclaim the John Brown Bell. It is unclear whether or not the residents of Harpers Ferry will attempt to reclaim the bell for themselves, but it is believed the majority of the 35,000 residents of Marlborough are ready to defend the bell.

New Light on the 'Old England' Connection:

The Harpers of Harper's Ferry, Virtinis
By Tony Johnson, Oxford, UK

Recent research in a tiny village deep in the English countryside is throwing new light on the early roots of the Pennsylvania connection with England. The village is called Noke in Oxfordshire. This small community, which lies five miles north of the famous University City of Oxford and has a population of only one hundred, can justly lay claim to being the original home of the Harpers, one of the early settlers.

John Harper (the grandfather of Robert Harper, who set up the original ferry at Harpers Ferry), was a Quaker who would have been 48 years old when he left England with his wife and five children. In 1682 they set sail for America aboard the *Welcome*, one of the ships in William Penn's fleet, arriving some months before Penn himself. They purchased 500 acres of land in the new colony of Pennsylvania, and settled close to Philadelphia, the township to which the Harpers gave the name of Oxford. John Harper and his wife Ann are buried there. His interesting and historic tombstone commemorates his roots:

John, son of John Harper, of Noke in Oxford Shire in Old England, arrived in Pennsylvania the 2d of August, 1682, who died ye 29th of April 1716, aged 83 years

So it was well before 1700 that the Harpers were firmly established in America, together with seven of their eight children: John, Joseph, Josiah, Mary, Charles, Elizabeth and Ralph, the youngest two having been born in the New World (their eldest daughter Bridget did not accompany them to America). Robert Harper, the founder of Harpers Ferry, was descended from their second son, Joseph.

Back in Noke in Oxfordshire in Old England, exciting new research in the churchyard has identified what is probably the tomb of John's father (died 1667) and grandfather (died 1617), which makes him a contemporary of William Shakespeare (Shakespeare would no doubt have often passed by Noke, as the village lies within half a mile of the old London-to-Worcester road, the shortest route to Stratford at that time). The Harpers (or Harpurs) appear in the earliest of the parish registers (1575), and probably lived in the village for generations. They were leading landowners and farmers.

Unfortunately, by 1870 the Harper tomb in Noke had become so dilapidated that it was dismantled. The churchwarden made a note in the parish register that states, "This day took down and removed fifteen or sixteen inches nearer the S. wall of the Church, the Altar Tomb of the Harpers, father & son, the Tomb having become insecure by age—the stones bearing inscriptions are laid beneath the top slab of the Tomb." By then there were no Harpers remaining in the village, John's eldest daughter being the last recorded family member entered in the Noke baptism register in 1669.

255

Although we are told what was supposedly inscribed on the old Harper tomb, the two inscriptions today lie buried beneath the capstone of the monument and are no longer visible, although a large stone overgrown with grass close to the church porch may give a clue to its location. An old etching has been found, drawn in 1822 (50 years before the tomb was reduced to ground level) showing a tomb in this position, which seems to be the one to which the note refers. It is hoped some time in the future to investigate these stones, confirm the discovery, and then rebuild the Harper tomb.

This small English village has become increasingly concerned about the maintenance of its 800-year-old church, and has formed a group called the "Friends of St. Giles, Noke" to assist with the funding of the repairs to the fabric, history and American connections for future generations. For those interested in this intriguing story and supporting the friends of the church, you can visit the English website, with a full list of families dating from 1574 and other interesting information. Here you can check your own family name against the village records.

St. Giles Church

St. Giles Church is an attractive 12th-century parish church just north of the city center of Oxford. It was consecrated by St. Hugh of Lincoln at a time when this area was outside of the main town center. Now it provides an oasis of calm in a busy area of the city.

History

Oxford's St. Giles Church is first mentioned in the Domesday Survey of 1086, which recorded that the owner of the land north of the city intended to build a Romanesque-style church on it. The church was finished in 1120, but not consecrated until 1200. In 1138, the Empress Matilda and her son Henry Plantagenet (the future Henry II) granted the church and all its property to the newly created Godstow Priory.

At the time of its founding, the St. Giles Church stood in the midst of fields and there were no buildings between it and the city walls, which was marked by the Church of St Michael at the North Gate. The city had a population of about 1,000, all crowded inside the walls. Over the centuries, houses and other buildings began to gather around the church and today it lies between two busy streets.

It was St. Hugh of Lincoln, the great Carthusian monk and bishop, who consecrated St Giles Church in 1200 AD. A cross of interlaced circles incised on the western column of the tower is said to commemorate this act. And it was also in commemoration of this consecration that the St Giles' Fair was founded. The fair still takes place today, on the Monday and Tuesday after the Sunday following St. Giles' Day (September 1). St. Hugh also expanded the nearby Church of St. Mary Magdalene in 1194.

Upon the Dissolution of the Monasteries in 1535, St Giles Church and its lands were given to Dr George Owen of Godstow, a physician of Henry VIII. His son conveyed it in 1573 to Sir Thomas White, Lord Mayor of London, who in 1555 had refounded the Cistercian House of St Bernard as St. John's College. White settled the church on his newly established College, which has presented vicars to the church ever since. (See pictures of St. Giles Church in back of book.)

257

SHADES OF BLUE

I see the weary look upon your face
As you rock by the glowing fire,
In your little cabin of hand hewn logs
You helped build with love and grace.

You thought your life was most complete
With your loving family and friends all around,
In the greatest country on this earth,
Where freedom and love abound.

Then whispers of war began to spread
Through the hills of your Southland,
The unthinkable was about to happen
And your family was forced to take a stand.

If they followed the South, they would have to fire
On "Old Glory", the Flag they so admired,
The flag their grandfathers fought to preserve,
The flag for which they died.

They stood up and fought for what they believed,
Their country, flag and honor,
But, oh, what a price your family paid
Even long after the war was over.

Your second born son would be the first to die,
Your husband's death would come two weeks later,
But your oldest son's fate would be the worst of all
In the prisons of hell and torture.

Thomas marched from Alabama to Atlanta
From Atlanta to the sea,
Through the icy swamps of the Carolinas
Before being captured by the enemy.

He lived on hardtack and marshy water,
In the overcrowded prison camps,
Where disease and torment ravaged
In the glow of the clouded moon lamp.

258

Then one by one your brothers fell
On the battlefields stained in red,

First Thomas, Robert, Josiah and Tennessee Polk
Lay among the fields of the dead.

Although Josiah survived the gruesome war,
His southern neighbors refused to agree
That he fought on the side of freedom
And they tortured him as they hung him from a tree.

How sad and lonely, you, the widowed mother
As you received the messages one by one,
About the dreadful fate of your loved ones
And the damage the war had done.

You had already buried your young son, Robert
Even before the war began
Then you buried your sister Nancy,
Long before the end of her life span.

What would you do, how would you live,
how could you possibly survive this alone,
Tending the fields and raising four young children,
Left in your care in your mournful home.

As you picked up the plow and continued your plight
You had solace in the reason for their fall,
And it brought back many memories of...
The Flag of Freedom, freedom for us all!

Written for my beloved great, great-grandmother, Sarah Harper
McWhirter. If only I had half of her perseverance. May she truly
rest in peace.

Glenda McWhirter Todd

JUST A COMMON SOLDIER
(A Soldier Died Today)
By A. Lawrence Vaincourt
Used with permission of R.C. Vaincourt

He was getting old and paunchy and his hair was falling fast,
And he sat around the Legion, telling stories of the past.
Of a war that he had fought in and the deeds that he had done,
In his exploits with his buddies; they were heroes, every one.

And tho' sometimes, to his neighbors, his tales became a joke,
All his Legion buddies listened, for they knew whereof he spoke.
But we'll hear his tales no longer for old Bill has passed away,
And the world's a little poorer, for a soldier died today.

He will not be mourned by many, just his children and his wife,
For he lived an ordinary and quite uneventful life.
Held a job and raised a family, quietly going his own way,
And the world won't note his passing, though a soldier died today.

When politicians leave this earth, their bodies lie in state,
While thousands note their passing and proclaim that they were
great.
Papers tell their whole life stories, from the time that they were
young,
But the passing of a soldier goes unnoticed and unsung.

Is the greatest contribution to the welfare of our land
A guy who breaks his promises and cons his fellow man?
Or the ordinary fellow who, in times of war and strife,
Goes off to serve his Country and offers up his life?

A politician's stipend and the style in which he lives
Are sometimes disproportionate to the service that he gives.
While the ordinary soldier, who offered up his all,
Is paid off with a medal and perhaps, a pension small.

It's so easy to forget them for it was so long ago,
That the old Bills of our Country went to battle, but we know
It was not the politicians, with their compromise and ploys,
Who won for us the freedom that our Country now enjoys.

Should you find yourself in danger, with your enemies at hand,
Would you want a politician with his ever-shifting stand?
Or would you prefer a soldier, who has sworn to defend
His home, his kin and Country and would fight until the end?

He was just a common soldier and his ranks are growing thin,
But his presence should remind us we may need his like again.
For when countries are in conflict, then we find the soldier's part
Is to clean up all the troubles that the politicians start.

If we cannot do him honor while he's here to hear the praise,
Then at least let's give him homage at the ending of his days.
Perhaps just a simple headline in a paper that would say,
Our Country is in mourning, for a soldier died today.

The Soul Cries Out

By Joseph R. Veneroso, M.M.
(Used with his gracious permission)

Between wordless sobs the soul cries out,
Grant them eternal rest, O Lord,
And prays despite a haunting doubt,
Let perpetual light shine on them.

Yet for us, the living, who remain
to mourn the loss, to feel the pain,
to bear the shock, to question why
in God's great plan they had to die,
there is no peace, no rest, no light
nothing but an endless night.

When we, defeated by the truth,
surrender to death's other face,
robbed of innocence and youth,
no power on earth can e'er replace,
only in this, our darkest hour,
can we truly hope to find
among our tears
God's healing power,
among our fears
true peace of mind,
that simple faith to save our soul,
that perfect love to make us whole.

Against the sadness and the sorrow
With every ounce of faith confessing
Hope for a better life tomorrow
In our mourning we find blessing.

Only an open heart can break
only an empty heart can take
all the love God has to give
all the love we need to live
In a world of sorrow and pain
To lose ourselves, ourselves to gain.

Honoring the Void

By Joseph R. Veneroso, MM
(Used with his gracious permission)

O shed a tear or two, if you must, for our time now ended,
for dreams unrealized and hopes unfulfilled.
Yet know the love and life we shared remain.
Even as do you. For a time.

In memory of me, live to the fullest,
for one minute of mindfulness
echoes more than a decade
of mindless busyness.
As for me, I go on to my next adventure.

Confident the smallest atom in the farthest galaxy obeys God's
command,
how can we, made of billions of atoms, ever be forgotten?
The One who fashioned us from stardust and seashells
and breathed in us a living spirit,
creates, comforts and calls u still
to rise higher and become more.

And so, despite the emptiness, honor the void
in tribute to what once was;
Bless the pain, as proof it was real and
Light a candle of prayer in the quiet chapel of your soul
to dispel this hour's darkness

And only when you are ready, let go of even this.
Do not be afraid. I shall live on in your heart as you do in mine
and as we do in God's.

Seek me in the sunrise or in the pounding surf.
See me in the autumn leaves or
hear me howling in the wintry storm.
Then you will know, as I now do,
how yesterday's death
gives birth to eternal tomorrow.

"The Story Tellers"

(We Are The Chosen)

My feelings are in each family we are called to find the
ancestors.
To put flesh on their bones and make them live again,
To tell the family story and to feel that somehow they
know and approve.

To me, doing genealogy is not a cold gathering of facts
but, instead,
Breathing life into all who have gone before.
We are the story tellers of the tribe.
We have been called as it were by our genes.
Those who have gone before cry out to us:
Tell our story.
So we do.

In finding them, we somehow find ourselves.
How many graves have I stood before now and cried.
I have lost count.
How many times have I told the ancestors you have a
wonderful family, you would be proud of us.
How many times have I walked up to a grave and felt
somehow there was love there for me.
I cannot say.

It goes beyond just documenting facts.
It goes to who I am and why I do the things I do.

It goes to seeing a cemetery about to be lost forever to
weeds and indifference and saying I can't let this
happen.
The bones here are bones of my bone and flesh of my
flesh.

It goes to doing something about it.

It goes to pride in what our ancestors were able to accomplish.
How they contributed to what we are today.

It goes to respecting their hardships and losses,
their never giving in or giving up.
Their resoluteness to go on and build a life for their family.

It goes to deep pride that they fought to make and keep us a Nation.
It goes to a deep and immense understanding that they were doing it for us

That we might be born who we are.
That we might remember them.
So we do.

With love and caring and scribing each fact of their existence,
Because we are them and they are us.

So, as scribe called, I tell the story of my family.
It is up to that one called in the next generation,
To answer the call and take their place in the long line of family storytellers.

That is why I do my family genealogy,
And that is what calls those young and old to step up and put flesh on the bones.

~ By Della M. Cummings Wright and re-written by her grand daughter,
Della JoAnn McGinnis Johnson~

Bibliography

Pictures of Conestoga Wagons – Landis Valley Museum Website and Conestoga Area Genealogical Society Website

Joint Committee on Reconstruction, Brevet Brigadier General George E. Spencer, "I raised the Only Regiment of Alabama Federal Cavalry"

The Southern Loyalists, by Robert E. Hurst

Story of the 1st Alabama Cavalry, USV" by Dean Barber

Report of Major Sanford Tramel, First Alabama Cavalry, of operations, January 28 – March 24

Pension Records of different 1st Alabama soldiers obtained from the National Archives and Records Administration in Washington, DC.

Best Little Stories of the Blue and the Gray, by C. Brian Kelly.

"God Rest Ye Merry Soldiers", by James McIvor

Civil War Recipes Website at:
http://civilwarinteractive.com/cooking/

Home of the American Civil War Website at:
http://www.civilwarhome.com/

God Rest Ye Merry Soldiers: A True Civil War Christmas Story by James McIvor

National Park Service Website at:
http://www.nps.gov/seac/fierydawn/fd-index.htm
(This is a terrific website and has a good account of the Battle of Monroe's Crossroads)

Cahaba Prison and the Sultana Disaster by William O. Bryant

God Rest Ye Merry Soldiers: A True Civil War Christmas Story by James McIvor

The March to the Sea and Beyond, by Joseph T. Glatthaar

266

Gettysburg National Military Park Website

Friends of the Battle of Mansfield, Texas, April 8, 1864

Civil War and Reconstruction in Alabama by Walter Lynwood Fleming

Conestoga Wagon Tavern Sign, The Conestoga Area Historical Society Website

Picture of Conestoga Wagon in use in 1935 from PA State Archives

Digging the Wells of Revival by Lou Engle

Hard Times, The Civil War in Huntsville and North Alabama by Charles Rice

The Lightening Mule Brigade, Abel Streight's 1863 Raid into Alabama by Robert L. Willett, Author of "One Day of the Civil War"

Picture of Corn Crib – Michael R. Allen, Architectural Historian http://ecoabsence.blogspot.com/2008/08/monroe-county-corn-crib-still-in-use.html

Religion in History: Conflict, Conversion and Coexistence by John Wolffe

Story of Drury Henry Cox Whitehead, who was a brother to my ancestor, Archibald Whitehead.

Wikipedia - History of Harper's Ferry, West Virginia

The Southern Loyalists by Robert Hurst

Civil War Journal of Lt. George C. Jenkins, 1st Alabama Cavalry, USV

Civil War Diary of Lt. Francis Wayland Dunn

Civil War Diary of Thomas A. McWhirter

Official Records, Series I, Vol. XXIII

New Light on the Old England Connection: The Harpers of Harper's Ferry
Baltimore Chronicle, February 6, 2002,
home.btconnect.com/stgiles_noke, used with permission

Quinnie Harper's References for Harper Research

The Friends of St. Giles, Noke, Oxfordshire, England, Dr. Anne Johnson

Frances Harper, Charleston, Missouri

Mississippi County, Missouri Abstract & Loan, Charleston, Missouri, Mrs. Hazel Williams

The Enterprise Courier, Charleston, Missouri

Death Notices from Mississippi County, Missouri Newspapers 1858-1899, Compiled by Joan Tinsley Feezor

Mississippi County Loose Probate Papers, 1845-1899, Dorothy Renaud

Trinity Episcopal (Oxford) Church Records, Oxford Township, Philadelphia, Pennsylvania

Colonial and Revolutionary Families of Pennsylvania, Genealogical and Personal Memoirs, Editor Wilfred Jordan, 1942

The First Harper Line, Indiana State Library, Call No. G9 929.11 A512c. v. 17, pp.323-326

Tennesseans in the Civil War. A Military History of Confederate and Union Units with Available Rosters of Personnel, Published by the Civil War Centennial Commission, Nashville, Tennessee, 1964

Marriages of Mississippi County, Missouri 1888-1902, Vol. 2

Tennessee Land Grants, Volume 1 A-K

Encyclopedia of American Quaker Genealogy, Volume 11

Charleston Missouri Sesquicentennial 1837-1987, Lineage Book, pp. 369-371

Tennessee Confederate Widows and Their Families, Abstracts of 11,190 Confederate Widows Pension Applications, Edna Wiefering, Charles A. Sherrill, 1992

Genealogical Abstracts of Revolutionary War Pension Files, Volume 11, F-M
Abstracted by Virgil D. White

Marriage Bonds of Franklin County, Virginia 1786-1858, by Marshall Wingfield

The 1787 Census of Virginia, Volume 1, Compiled by Netti Schreiner-Yantis & Louis Manarine, State Archivist

Colonial and Revolutionary Lineages of America, The American Historical Company, Inc., New York 1953

Mississippi County Library, 105 E Marshall Street, Charleston, Missouri

Smith County Library, Carthage, Tennessee

Sumner County Archives

Tennessee State Library and Archives

Elmer Hinton Library, Portland, Tennessee

Jefferson County Virginia Historical Society

John Harper (1) "Berks and Oxon Wills and Administrations," Series I, Vol. VIII, p. 434, Vol. X, p. 212; Somerset House, London, England. Records from the research of Mame Ellison Wood, genealogist for the family.

John Harper (2) "Berks an Oxon Wills and Administrations," Series I, Vol. VIII P. 434; Vol. X, p. 212; Somerset House London, England. Copy of Original Register of the Parish Church at Noke, Oxfordshire, England, now in possession of the Rector of the Church of Islip. John Dunkin: "History and Antiquities of Oxfordshire," Vol. I, p. 85. Records of Parish Church of Noke County, Oxford, England. "Oxfordshire Wills and Administrations C," Series II, Vol

II, p. 368, Somerset House, London England. Records from the research of Mame Ellison Wood, genealogist for the family.

John Harper (3) "Records of Parish Church of Noke, Oxon, England," "Oxfordshire Wills and Administrations," Original Will "C", December 21, 1667, Somerset House, London, England. Records from the research of Mame Ellison Wood, genealogist for the family.

John Harper (4) Research of Mame Ellison Wood, genealogist for the family. "Philadelphia Will Book H," p. 199. "Records Trinity Oxford Church", p. 1. "Pennsylvania Magazine of History and Biography," Vol. III, p. 341.

Index

A

B

C

D

E

F

G

Gamble, John	84, 88
Gann, Mr.	24
Gibson	99
Gipson, Al	57, 60, 65
Gilreath, Martha M.	95
Grant, Gen. Drewry	144
Grant, Gen. Ulysses S.	53, 154
Green, Jasper	121, 122, 175
Green, Samuel	121
Grigg, Jess	141
Grigg, Rebecca	141
Guess	145
Guess, William Mack	143
Gulick, Cecela Amanda	102

H

Hagan, Col. James	191
Halleck, Gen. Henry	132
Hallmark, George	44, 48, 58, 64, 65, 120, 123, 128, 141, 158
Hallmark, James W.	48
Hallmark, John	141
Hallmark, John Madison	48
Hallmark, Mary	141
Hallmark, Mary Jane	64, 123, 124, 125, 141, 182, 185, 186
Hallmark, Nancy Mahaley	123
Hallmark, Phoebe	141
Hallmark, Sarah	141
Hallmark, Sarah "Sally"	43, 65
Hallmark, Sarah Elizabeth	123
Hallmark, Sarah Jane	128
Hallmark, Susan Angeline	123
Hallmark, Thomas Frank	48, 141
Hallmark, Washington	141
Hampton, Gen. Wade	135, 188, 189, 190, 191, 195, 196
Harbin, Alonzo A.	129
Harbin, George W.	129
Harbin, Ida Mae	129
Harbin, Jasper Green	129
Harbin, Jessie J.	129
Harbin, Nancy Alice	129

I

<u>N</u>

V

W

Glenda McWhirter Todd at grave of Sarah Harper McWhirter

Sarah Harper McWhirter's Tombstone, buried in
The O'Mary Cemetery in Marion County, Alabama

Side View of Sarah Harper McWhirter's "Tent-Grave"

**"Tent-Grave" and Tombstone of Sarah Harper McWhirter's
Granddaughter, Susan A. McWhirter, daughter of
John Madison McWhirter**

Old Log House in Smith County, Tennessee. Photo Courtesy of Friends John & Retta Waggoner

This picture of a corn-crib in East Tennessee will give you an idea of how they were made

This is more like the corn-crib Andrew built

Old Smoke House in Smith Co., TN

Old Smoke House

Different cuts of meat hanging from leather straps in smoke house

Butter paddle and Lid with Lower Half of the Crock Butter Churn

Old Crock Butter Churn

Old Fashioned Pancheon used for milk or Bread Making

This is a picture of a Conestoga Wagon, usually pulled by a team of six horses

This is a Conestoga Wagon modified to use on the farm

Conestoga Wagon Tavern Sign on old Roads to let
People who, could not read, know it was a Tavern

Sugar Cane Growing

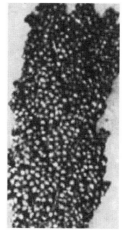

Sugar Cane Seed Saved From Previous Year

Mule turning sorghum Mill to squeeze juice from Sugar Cane

Conestoga Wagon with Lazy Seat on Side where Driver sat

Wagon Train Parked in a Circle at End of Day

Kind of Dutch Oven Sarah's Parents used

The Birthing Tree in McMinnville, Warren County, Tennessee

Chamber Pot kept under or by the side of the bed to be used at night and emptied the next morning in the outhouse.

Picture of typical old Outhouse

Seat in old Outhouse

Cave on Winston and Marion County, Alabama Line called the "Rock House

Quilting Bee

CSA Marker at Bethel Cemetery in Knoxville, TN
With Thomas Wade Harper's name as among the dead buried
there. There are no individual tombstones for the soldiers,
Union or Confederate.

Thomas Wade Harper's name as it appears on above
Marker.

Monument at Bethel Cemetery in Knoxville, TN dedicated to Union and Confederate Soldiers who died there during the Civil War.

Execution of Alex J. Johnson in Corinth, Mississippi

Picture of Dead Union Soldiers in Field
I kept seeing this picture in my mind, even in my dreams.

Nashville National Cemetery Entrance

Nashville National Cemetery

Andrew Ferrier McWhirter's Tombstone
Buried in Nashville National Cemetery

George Washington McWhirter's Tombstone
Buried in Nashville National Cemetery

Flag of the 1ˢᵗ Alabama Cavalry, CSA

Civil War Scout as They Dressed

Josiah Houston Harper's Tombstone in HopewellCemetery

Daniel & Rebecca Harper Tucker's Old Log House in Louisiana

43rd Alabama Infantry, CSA Regimental Flag

**Tennessee Polk Harper's Tombstone
In Nashville National Cemetery in
Nashville, Davidson County, Tennessee**

**This is how the author pictured Sarah as she
rocked her dying sister, Nancy Harper**

Sarah "Sallie" Whitehead & Jesse Harper on their 50th
Wedding Anniversary.
Their cake looks like it is about to slide off his lap

Joseph Hornback

Thomas Andrew McWhirter

**Thomas A. McWhirter's Tombstone, Buried in the
Old Poplar Springs Primitive Baptist Church Cemetery in
Rock City, Marion County, Alabama**

Eagleville Primitive Baptist Church where Andrew Jackson
McWhirter used to preach. The Women used to go in one Door
And the Men would go in the other.

Sign on Eagleville Primitive Baptist Church showing it was
Organized September 14, 1889

Andrew Jackson McWhirter and Nancy Jane Whitehead
This is a portrait painted by an artist in the French Quarter in
New Orleans, LA from two black & white pictures of them.

Jasper Green McWhirter

**This is a picture of the way my husband and I found
Andrew Jackson McWhirter's Tombstone**

**Andrew Jackson McWhirter's Tombstone .He is buried on
His farm just out of Eagleville, Tennessee**

Old Popular Springs Primitive Baptist Church in Rock City,
Marion County, Alabama Where Andrew Jackson McWhirter
used to preach. It has been demolished.

William Hamilton McWhirter, in center front with hat, and his
family.

Family portrait taken at the McWhirter homeplace in Wood County. Those pictured are, (back row, left to right) Andrew McWhirter, George Washington Harbin and his wife, Molly Mary Harbin, Nancy Ida Harbin and her husband, Robert Andrew Harbin, Alice Harbin Wood, Jessie Jackson Harbin, Walter Foster Harbin and Fet McWhirter. (Front row, left to right) Ida Harbin Malone, Laura McWhirter, Emmie Harbin Cochran, Rosa Harbin Harris, Etta Harbin Cooley, James Washington (Jim) Harbin, Claude McWhirter and Floyd Wood. (Photo courtesy of Bud Harbin)

Mary Caroline McWhirter & George Washington Harbin Family

Raymond Blanchard McWhirter, Father of author, ca 1930

George Washington and Mary Caroline McWhirter Harbin

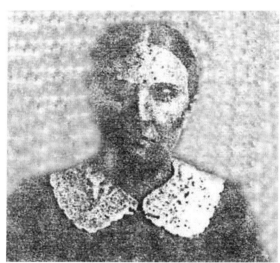

Nancy Ann McWhirter
This is a very poor quality picture of Nancy Ann McWhirter
But the only one I was able to locate

Jasper "Green" McWhirter

Cemetery & Monument at Monroe's Crossroads, NC

Andrew Jackson McWhirter

Mary Caroline McWhirter and George Washington Harbin

**Hospital #14 in Nashville, Davidson County, Tennessee
Where Andrew Ferrier & George W. McWhirter Died
Formerly the Nashville Female Academy and Taken Over
By the Union to use as a Hospital during the Civil War**

Execution of Alex J. Johnson in Corinth, Mississippi

Front Row:(Left to Right) Allen Kinslow(Baby Homer Kinslow)- Jennie Harper Smith- Mrs. Mary Harper- Minnie White- Daniel White- Georgia White

Second Row: Lucy Harper Kinslow- Tom Harper- Eva McKinney Harper- Flora Harper Wilson- Billy Wilson- Annie Harper White

Third Row: Hamilton Harper- Joe Ed Harper- Sam Alfred Harper

Josiah H. Harper Family. This Josiah was the son of Josiah Harper, Sr.

Harper and White Family

Back Row-William Lee, Thomas Jefferson, & David H. Harper
Front Row- John Bell, Maria, Green, Sarah E. & Josiah Harper

L-R Front: Fannie Harper Burton and Quinnie Bush Harper, Sr.
L-R Back: Blanch Harper Bruce, Loula Belle Harper and
John Bell Harper

St. Giles Church in Oxford, England

Modern Picture of St. Giles Church in Oxford, England

George Ferrier McWhirter, son of George Marlin McWhirter
He was Mayor of McWhirtersville, just out of Nashville, TN,
For several terms, and was a Mason.

6814096R0

Made in the USA
Charleston, SC
11 December 2010